CobX130

TUNING AND MAINTENANCE
OF MG CARS

TUNING AND MAINTENANCE
OF MG CARS

Overhead-camshaft engines, 1929—1936
Pushrod engines (T series), 1936—1954

PHILIP H. SMITH, F.I.Mech.E., M.S.A.E.
Member of the Guild of Motoring Writers

ISBN 0 85429 098 2

First Edition .	.	*1952*
Reprinted	. .	*1953*
Revised	. .	*1954*
Reprinted	. .	*1955*
Revised	. .	*1956*
Reprinted	. .	*1969*
Reprinted	. .	*1971*
Reprinted	. .	*1978*

© Philip H. Smith, 1952, 1954 & 1956

a FOULIS Motoring book

Published by
Haynes Publishing Group
Sparkford, Yeovil, Somerset BA22 7JJ, England

Distributed in North America by
Haynes Publications Inc
861 Lawrence Drive, Newbury Park, California 91320

Acknowledgements

The author would like to express his appreciation of the assistance given, in providing photographs and technical data, by the Nuffield Organization (Service Technical Publications); Shorrock Superchargers Ltd.; Wade Engineering Ltd.; Renold Chains Ltd.; Joseph Cockshoot & Co. Ltd.; the publishers of *Autosport*, London, and last, but by no means least, to Gregor Grant, Editor, *Autosport*.

CONTENTS

Page

Introduction 7

PART I. OVERHEAD-CAMSHAFT ENGINES

Chapter 1. O.H.C. Types and Characteristics 9
2. Dismantling the P-type Engine 12
3. Examination and Renovation 18
4. The Overhead-valve Mechanism 23
5. The Lubrication System 30
6. The Ignition System 35
7. Reassembly of Major Items 38
8. Replacement in the Chassis 43
9. Starting Up the Engine 50
10. The P-type Chassis 55

PART II. PUSH-ROD O.H.V. ENGINES

Chapter 11. Push-rod Engine Types and Characteristics 60
12. Dismantling the TA Engine 65
13. Examination and Renovation 71
14. The TA Overhead-valve Mechanism 74
15. The Lubrication and Ignition Systems 78
16. Reassembly of the TA Engine 84
17. Engine Replacement and Starting-up 91
18. Dismantling the TC and Allied Engines 98
19. Examination and Renovation 101
20. The TC Overhead-valve Mechanism 105
21. The Lubrication System and Miscellaneous Items 108
22. Reassembly of the TC Engine 110
23. Engine Replacement and Starting-up 116
24. The T-type Chassis 120
25. TD/TF Engines 122
26. TD/TF Gearbox and Chassis 123

PART III. SPECIALIZED ATTENTION

Chapter 27. Cylinder Bore Renovation 132
28. Overhaul and Tuning of S.U. Carburetters 136
29. Supercharger Installations 143
30. Super-tuning the T-type Engine 148

PART IV. CHARTS AND DIAGRAMS

Wiring Diagram, Series TC, 1945/8 (home) 158
,, ,, Series TC, 1945/6, RHD & LHD (export) 159
,, ,, Series TC, 1948, RHD & LHD (export) 160
,, ,, Series TC, 1948/9 (home) 161
,, ,, Series TC, 1948/9, U.S.A. (export) 162
,, ,, Series TD 163
,, ,, Series TF 164
,, ,, Key to recommended Lubricants, Series TC 165

	Page
Lubrication Chart, Series TC	166–7
„ „ Series TD/TF	168–9
Key to recommended Lubricants, Series TD/TF	170
Sectional drawing of the TD engine	171
Transverse sectional drawing of the TD engine prior to engine No. 14224 ...	172
Transverse sectional drawing of the TD engine, No. 14224 onwards ...	173
Sectional drawing of the TF engine	174
Transverse sectional drawing of the TF engine	175
Sectional drawing of the gearbox and clutch, TD/TF	176
Sectional drawing of the front suspension, TD/TF	177
TD/TF engine mountings	178
Index	179

ILLUSTRATIONS

	Facing page
The P-type M.G.	16
The P-type engine, nearside	17
The P-type engine, offside	17
The TA-type engine, nearside	32
The TA-type engine, offside	32
The TA crankshaft and bearings	33
The TA cork-insert clutch dismantled	33
The TA crankcase, with oil-pump, distributor, camshaft and tappet block dismounted	64
The TA cylinder head and valve mechanism	64
TA camshaft drive, showing " timing " links in correct position on marked teeth	65
The TA gearbox dismantled	65
The TC-type engine, nearside	80
The TC-type engine, offside	80
The TC crankshaft and bearings	81
The TC clutch dismantled	81
The TC crankcase, with oil-pump, distributor, camshaft and tappets removed	96
TC camshaft drive, showing " timing " links in correct position on marked teeth	96
The TC gearbox dismantled	97
1,250-c.c. M.G. TD-type engine, offside	112
„ „ „ „ nearside	112
Laystall alloy cylinder head for TB/TF engines...	113
A TD engine ready for removal...	128
The rear end of a TD engine ready for removal	128
A jig for holding the gearbox when dismantling, threaded into the drain plug hole	129
Withdrawing the TD mainshaft assembly through the top of the box ...	129
An alloy rocker-box design by the author	129
Exploded view of a Wade blower	144
The Wade supercharger installation fitted to a type TC engine ...	144
The Shorrock installation on a TD engine	145
View showing internal arrangement of Shorrock supercharger... ...	145

INTRODUCTION

This book has been written for the " Private Owner " M.G. enthusiast with the object of providing him with comprehensive information which will assist him not only in keeping a good car in first-class trim, but also in restoring a much-used model to its original condition.

The whole of the chapters devoted to overhaul of the various types of engines and other components are based on the Author's experience in carrying out the work in his private workshop. The problems which have cropped up during some of the operations are typical of those which any enthusiast will be called upon to solve when undertaking similar work.

It will be noted that the book has been sub-divided to deal with various engine types. Whilst in general each section concerning a particular engine is self-contained, there may be many occasions where reference to a page not dealing specifically with the type under consideration, will prove useful, since all engines have, of course, certain common features.

It is naturally assumed that the enthusiast who is desirous of overhauling or modifying one of these engines is familiar with the normal routine of such work, and is possessed of adequate skill in the handling of tools, and reasonable workshop facilities. This does not imply that a machine-shop is essential, but simply the use of a serviceable bench, plenty of good hand tools, and room to work.

Where more complicated machining or special fitting jobs are concerned, there are plenty of competent specialists to be entrusted with such work. There are also plenty not so competent—so pick and choose carefully.

Apart from a comprehensive assortment of hand tools, further essential items of equipment will comprise an outsize metal container, large enough to take the engine crankcase, which will help to keep the cleansing fluid within bounds. For actual cleaning, paraffin is adequate, along with several stiff paint brushes of various sizes. If a few wooden slats are put across the bottom of the container before any parts are put therein, the dislodged sludge will fall clear of the components which will rest on the slats. A paraffin squirt (a Wesco oil can does admirably) will be useful for clearing oilways and other small-bore passages.

In view of the title of the book, it might be as well to mention, thus early, that it does not contain any of those mysterious "secrets of tune" which sometimes come up in conversations between enthusiasts. It has always seemed to the Author that this magic word is much abused. Literally, it is suggested that it implies only that all the components are operating, in tune, to the maximum advantage. In actual fact, there are surprisingly few vehicles on the road to which this condition applies. Therefore, if all items are dealt with in a fit and proper manner, and assembled with due regard to cleanliness and correct fitting, the results will not disappoint.

Author's Note

Before the war, the M.G. Car Company produced, in addition to their " real " sports cars, larger vehicles which, while capable of an exhilarating performance were, generally speaking, used by a different class of driver from that generally accepted as the typical M.G. enthusiast. Recently, the Company has introduced a model having a similar appeal.

In detailing relatively ambitious overhauling operations, it is considered advisable to concentrate on the types of car which are most likely to be the subject of owner-attention of this kind. This book is therefore confined in its scope to the small o.h.c. pre-war models and to the T-series cars. Interested owners of other types will nevertheless find many points of similarity in their engines, this applying particularly to the Y-series saloon, and incidentally, to the Wolseley 4/44 power unit, both of which have a strong family connection with the TD.

PART I

CHAPTER 1

O.H.C. Types and Characteristics

RELIABLE POWER.   ENGINE BASED ON MORRIS MINOR.

Between 1929 and 1936 the M.G. Car Company produced types of sports cars fitted with fundamentally the same design of o.h.c. engine, in capacities ranging from 0.75 to 1.29 litres. The adaptability of these vehicles for all classes of sporting events from rough-stuff trials to road racing, and the responsiveness of the power units to intensive tuning and modifications without affecting reliability, resulted in almost legendary fame for the type. Although the company ceased manufacture of the o.h.c. design in mid-1936, there are still thousands giving excellent service and many no doubt undergoing rebuilding and overhauling operations. As a preliminary it might be useful to give brief details of the range of M.G. o.h.c. engines of the type with which we are concerned. The following list has been compiled from what is described as an " official source," with the exception of the figures given for cubic capacity. These have been calculated on the stated bore and stroke to avoid anomalous comparisons.

In addition to the above, which covers cars supplied in some quantity, there were one or two other types, for example the R-type supercharged racing cars of 1935, which never reached the public in any number. The family resemblance between the whole of the range tabulated is quite apparent. For example, the cylinder bore is identical throughout with the single exception of the PB Midget.

Engine Based on Morris Minor

It is common knowledge that the original M-type Midgets used a practically standard Morris Minor power unit, produced for installation in an economical and reliable small family car which, while having a good performance did not make any claim to outstanding liveliness. It can be said that the potentialities inherent in the engine design were brought to the fore almost by accident, as a result of its installation in the very light M-type M.G. chassis. Actually, the basic soundness of the design is due to a comparatively small number of factors which were " right " from the start. The unit is compact and very rigid, with minimum distance between bearings and ample bearing area. The cylinder head design gives a very easy gas flow and an excellent degree of turbulence. Finally, the overhead camshaft, driven by two sets of bevel gears via the vertically mounted dynamo armature-shaft, provides a degree of accuracy in the valve-timing that is unsurpassed

9

Year	Makers' Model	Mark	Makers' h.p.	Cyls.	Bore	Stroke	c.c.	Wh'lbase ft. in.	Size of Std. tyres
1929/31	Midget	M	8/33	4	57	83	847	6 6	4 × 27
1932	Midget (short)	M	8/33	4	57	83	847	6 6	4 × 27
1932	Midget (long)	D	8/33	4	57	83	847	7 0	4 × 27
1932	Montlhéry Midget	C	12/95	4	57	73	745	6 9	4 × 27
1932	Magna	F	12/70	6	57	83	1271	7 10	4 × 27
1933	Midget	J1/J2	8	4	57	83	847	7 2	4 × 19
1933	Midget	J3	8	4	57	73	745	7 2	4 × 19
1933	Midget (s/c)	J4	8	4	57	73	745	7 2	4 × 19
1933	Magna	F2/F3	12	6	57	83	1271	7 10	4 × 19
1933	Magnette	K1	12	6	57	71	1087	9 0	4.75 × 19
1933	Magnette	K2	12	6	57	71	1087	9 10	4.75 × 19
1933	Magnette (s/c)	K3	12	6	57	71	1087	7 10	4.75 × 19
1933	Magna	L1/L2	12	6	57	71	1087	7 10	4.50 × 19
1934	Midget	J2	8	4	57	83	847	7 2	4 × 19
1934	Midget (s/c)	J4	8	4	57	73	745	7 2	4.50 × 19
1934	Magna	L1/L2	12	6	57	71	1087	9 0	4.50 × 19
1934	Magnette	K1	12	6	57	71	1087	9 10	4.75 × 19
1934	Magnette	K2	12	6	57	71	1087	7 10	4.75 × 19
1934	Magnette (s/c)	K3	12	6	57	71	1087	7 10	4.75 × 19
1934	Midget	P	8	4	57	83	847	8 0	4 × 19
1934	Magnette	N	12	6	57	84	1286	7 3.5	4.75 × 18
1935	Midget	P	8	4	57	83	847	7 3.5	4 × 19
1935	Midget (s/c)	Q	8	4	57	73	745	7 10	4.75 × 18
1935	Magna	L1	12	6	57	71	1087	8 0	4.50 × 19
1935	Magnette	NA	12	6	57	84	1286	9 0	4.75 × 18
1935	Magnette	KN	12	6	57	84	1286	7 10	4.75 × 19
1935	Magnette (s/c)	K3	12	6	57	71	1087	7 3.5	4.75 × 19
1936	Midget	PA	8	4	57	83	847	7 3.5	4 × 19
1936	Midget	PB	8	4	60	83	939	7 3.5	4 × 19
1936	Magnette	N	12	6	57	84	1286	8 0	4.75 × 18

and quite possibly not equalled, by any other method. Much of the o.h.c. M.G.'s capacity for maintaining its power at very high r.p.m. can be put to the credit of its valve-gear layout. In this connection it is instructive to note that Lt.-Col. Gardner's M.G. which in 1939 took 1,100 and 1,500 c.c. records at over 200 m.p.h. and which up to a few years ago appeared in various other capacity classes with equal success (with, of course, the engine suitably modified) used this original type of valve gear and camshaft drive.

So much for the general design of the engines. For our purpose it is proposed to deal with typical modern examples of the type—the PA and PB four-cylinder engines of 847 and 939 c.c. respectively. Where useful tips can be given regarding the other models, this will be done.

CHAPTER 2

Dismantling the P-Type Engine

THE PRELIMINARIES.   CYLINDER HEAD REMOVAL.
LUBRICATION SYSTEM DISMANTLING.   CONNECTING RODS AND PISTONS.
WITHDRAWING THE CRANKSHAFT.   STRIPPING THE CYLINDER HEAD.

When carrying out the normal top overhaul of the P-type and similar engines it is not necessary to remove the radiator. Since, however, it is intended to remove the engine from the chassis for complete dismantling, the radiator will have to come off, and this operation will be described first.

The water cooling system is drained by means of taps at the bottom of the radiator and on the cylinder block and the hose connections should be removed. If the latter are stuck, do not use brute force, as damage to the radiator may be caused. Remove the

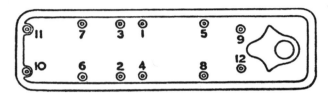

Order of attack—correct sequence of tightening cylinder head holding down nuts on the P type

hose clips completely, and insert a thin knife blade between the hose and the pipe stub, gently freeing the hose and separating it from the pipe. Application of a squirt of petrol at the point where the hose has been separated will result in it coming off without any further difficulty. Before tackling the main radiator supports uncouple the two tie-rods which run from the bulkhead to the back of the radiator, and also the nuts and bolts holding the headlamp brackets. Judicious pressure on the mudguards will enable the headlamp brackets to be freed from the supporting lugs on the radiator shell, but the brackets will remain firmly attached to the mudguards. The bottom of the radiator is attached to the front engine nose-piece platform by two studs, rubber washers being interposed between the bottom of the radiator and the platform which is integral with the nose-piece. Either wired nuts or ordinary nuts with locknuts will be found below the platform, which ensure a firm attachment. These can be removed with a box spanner, but as there is quite a lot of road filth in this region, a dose of penetrating oil may be necessary before commencing operations, and will undoubtedly facilitate removal of the nuts.

Having disposed of the lower fixing, the top attachment can be tackled. This comprises a mild steel plate between the cylinder head, which has a machined facing to receive it, and the back of the radiator shell. The plate is secured to the cylinder head by two nuts, and to the radiator by four ditto. After removal of these, the plate can be lifted off, the holes being slotted for this purpose. The radiator may now be lifted clear of the car, taking care to retrieve any rubber or metal washers which might fall off the bottom studs.

The aluminium rocker-box can next be removed, together with its packing washer, after disconnecting the tachometer drive at the rear; this pulls out after undoing the union nut. The aluminium top water pipe and exhaust manifold should present no difficulty. The carburetters must be taken off the induction manifold, it being impossible to remove the induction arrangements complete because the manifold is secured by two nuts inside it. These are accessible only through the carburetter ports, and are removed by a box spanner after taking off the carburetters. Control attachments will, of course, have been dealt with, and there should be no further snags to induction removal.

CYLINDER HEAD REMOVAL

The oil pipe connections to the head comprise one small diameter feed pipe located at the front near-side, and three large diameter drain pipes from head to sump. These are positioned one at the extreme rear of the head, and the other two at the off-side front. The method of removing these pipes will be self-evident. They should be removed completely, and no attempt made to save time by leaving the lower end attached, even if only a top overhaul is contemplated.

It will be found that in the oil feed hole to the head there is inserted a pressure-restricting pin. This may be seen protruding when the pipe is removed, and should be pulled out with pliers. If it is by any chance firmly jammed, leave it in position until the head is on the bench.

The camshaft drive is taken from the top of the dynamo at the commutator end, through a flexible coupling of the steel disc type. The coupling can be parted by removing two of the diametrically opposite nuts and bolts. The ignition distributor should be taken out as a complete unit, after disconnecting the cables, and put on one side for further attention. Spark plugs should be left in place for the moment.

The cylinder head nuts can next be tackled. There are twelve of these on the P-type engine, and there is not much room to spare for getting around them. The correct spanner, giving twelve angles of attack is essential and is obtainable from M.G.s. Equally important is the order in which the nuts are undone. Attention is invariably given to this point when tightening up the head on reassembly, but for some reason or other it is not always appreciated that quite serious stresses can be set up by haphazard slackening off. The diagram gives the correct order both for dismantling and reassembly.

The P-type cylinder head is a hefty and weighty casting, and makes an unusually large-area joint with the block. Consequently, it is apt to become well and truly stuck. The standard gasket has notches cut therein, provided for the insertion of a screwdriver to facilitate levering as a means of inducing the joint to part. Unguarded, and sometimes even careful, attempts at this may cause damage to the gasket, and a safer way is to crank the engine, with the starting handle, with the plugs in position. (If care is taken to ensure that the camshaft coupling dogs are in contact, there will be no danger of damaging the coupling as a consequence of removing the coupling nuts and bolts.) It will be found that a few quick turns of the handle will invariably lift the head. If unsuccessful, first make sure that all the nuts have been removed! Having got the joint free, the head can be lifted clear. During this operation it must be kept absolutely level, as the holding-down studs are a close fit in their holes, and will bind therein if the head is on the skew. After the head has been removed and put on the bench, the gasket should be lifted off the block.

Lubrication System Dismantling

The cylinder head having been removed it can be left as a unit for the time being, and attention given to the further dismantling of the engine in order to facilitate its removal from the chassis. Having drained the oil-sump, the large-diameter suction pipe running from the front of the sump to the oil-pump should be detached at its unions. The sump can then be dropped after removing all the nuts from the studs which run through the sump casting, and the set-screws on the front and rear flanges. When pushing down the sump, keep it parallel, otherwise it may jam on the long studs, which are easily bent. It will facilitate handling if the studs in question are unscrewed from the crankcase, and this is a simple operation.

A suction filter will be found in the sump, comprising a long gauze cylinder built on to a tube, the front end of which terminates in a union for receiving the suction pipe. The filter can be removed from the front by unscrewing its large hexagon.

The oil-pump is attached to the crankcase by five bolts, and can be withdrawn after taking these out. The pump spindle is castellated, and engages the distributor drive spindle which carries its driving pinion. The spindle and pinion may readily be pulled off the pump-shaft. The dynamo is lifted clear after removing the four nuts securing the lower flange. Make a note of the number of shims interposed between the flange and the housing. The shims should, of course, be taken off at the same time. Do not worry about timing markings on the dynamo gears, as there is no real difficulty in arriving at the correct timing on these engines.

A water-pump was not normally fitted to this type of engine, but was available for special purposes such as trials work or use in tropical climates. If fitted, it will be found on the near-side just above the oil-pump, its spindle having its own skew gear engaging the same crankshaft gear as is used for driving the oil-pump and distributor. The water-pump unit is held by two nuts and studs.

The oil filter is an aluminium casting, flange-fitted to the side of the crankcase. It has three external pipe connections, one receiving the delivery from the pump, the second (at rear) the oil-gauge connection, and the third taking the pipe feeding the front main bearing and o.h.v. gear. Method of removal of the filter is obvious on examination. The same remark applies to the starter motor. This completes removal of the more obvious bits and pieces, and a start can now be made on removing the unit from the chassis.

The first thing to do is to block up underneath the crankcase with some form of support which will take the weight of the engine. With the unit satisfactorily supported, the bracket securing the engine nose-piece to the front cross-member can be removed complete with its rubber bush. The nose-piece, together with the integral radiator platform, should then be taken off the front engine housing by removal of the four studs. This will allow plenty of room for withdrawing the unit forwards. The bolts securing the clutch housing flange can then be withdrawn, when it should be possible to pull the unit away from the clutch housing on the gearbox.

If difficulty is experienced, do not imagine snags that are not there. The only handicap to easy removal is the fact that the end of the clutch-shaft may be a pretty tight fit in the flywheel spigot bearing (ball-race). If such is the case, do not force things. Make sure that the engine is dead level, and then, very gently, lever the clutch housing flanges apart by equal effort on both sides with a couple of tyre levers.

Do not on any account use undue force, otherwise there is danger of distorting or even cracking the housing. If judicious persuading and patience are employed it will be found that the shaft can be withdrawn without damage. The prior removal of the front engine mounting will have left plenty of room for sliding the unit forward, and no difficulty will be experienced in lifting it clear and on to the bench.

CONNECTING RODS AND PISTONS

The connecting rod big-end bearings are each held by two split-pinned nuts. After removal of the caps, each rod should be pushed upwards as far as it will go until the big-end fouls the cylinder bore. It will be found that the piston has emerged from the top of the bore sufficiently far to allow the floating gudgeon pin to be pushed out; the piston is then pulled clear from the top, and the rod withdrawn from below. Should a gudgeon pin prove unduly tight, apply penetrating oil and then use a pin extractor comprising a band encircling the piston, provided with a jacking screw for pressing out the pin. Means must be employed, when using such a tool, to prevent damage to the gudgeon-pin end-pads.

The crankshaft runs in three main bearings on P-type engines. Earlier models have two bearings only, whilst six-cylinder units have four. In all cases the construction is generally similar. The fore and aft bearings comprise white-metal lined sleeve bushes carried in the respective end-housings, the intermediate bearing being a white-metalled split steel housing which is a snug fit in a circular register, the latter being large enough to allow the crank webs to pass through it when withdrawing the shaft. The spilt housing is located in the crank-case by means of long bolts locked by tab washers. When these bolts have been removed, the bearing housing complete can be withdrawn along with the shaft, and remains in position on the shaft.

WITHDRAWING THE CRANKSHAFT

Before withdrawing the crankshaft it is, of course, necessary to remove the flywheel. Dismantling the clutch is quite a straightforward operation, it being necessary only to take out the eight nuts and bolts securing the pressure-plate cover to the flywheel rim. When these clutch parts have been taken off, the nuts holding the flywheel to its crankshaft flange will be exposed. These nuts also secure the housing for the clutch-shaft spigot bearing, which will come away after the nuts have been removed. This gives access to the large crankshaft nut, for which an outsize in substantial box spanners is necessary. Avoidance of damage at this point is most important, and after removal of this nut, the services of a proper puller must be obtained to draw the flywheel crankshaft flange off its taper. When this has been done the starting handle dogs should be unscrewed from the front end of the shaft, and the fan pulley, dynamo bevel pinion and oil-pump distributor skew gear drawn off the shaft in that order. The front and rear housings can then be removed and the shaft withdrawn, the centre bearing housing being then split and removed from the shaft.

STRIPPING THE CYLINDER HEAD

Having described the dismantling of the main engine block, it will be logical to complete the sequence by indicating the operations involved in stripping the overhead-valve gear from the cylinder head, and these will now be described.

The camshaft is supported on three split bearing housings carrying white-metal liners. The front one also has an integral shroud covering the camshaft bevel gear, a thrust washer being interposed between this bearing and the bevel to keep the gears properly in mesh and reduce noise. The camshaft is readily removed after taking off the three bearing caps. The latter should be marked together with their respective mating halves so that the caps are subsequently replaced correctly. Use paint for marking, don't file notches in important components.

The rocker-shafts will come away without trouble as the majority of the supports will already have been freed due to removal of the cylinder head nuts which secure them. They should be pulled out of their locations in the front camshaft bearing housing, after which the various items on the rocker-shafts—cam followers, spacing bushes and spring washers—can be slid off the shafts. Make a note of the order of removal of these components. If the engine has been " messed about " the order may not be correct anyway, but this point will be clarified when describing reassembly. The valves are removed in the normal manner; there should be two springs on each valve (or possibly three if the engine has been modified for high-speed work), and they are held by the usual top cap with split collets. The valves may be found to be numbered, with a corresponding number on the head face,

The P-type M.G.

The P-type engine, nearside.

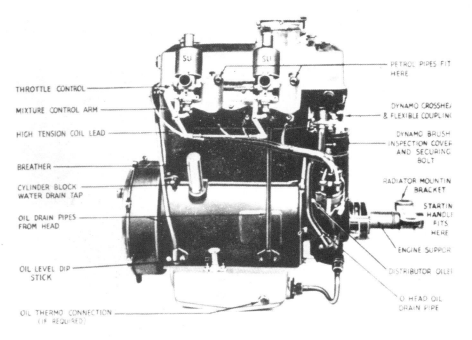

PETROL PIPES FIT
HERE

THROTTLE CONTROL

MIXTURE CONTROL ARM

HIGH TENSION COIL LEAD

DYNAMO CROSSHEA
& FLEXIBLE COUPLIN

DYNAMO BRUSH
INSPECTION COVER
AND SECURING
BOLT

BREATHER

CYLINDER BLOCK
WATER DRAIN TAP

RADIATOR MOUNTIN
BRACKET

STARTIN
HANDLE
FITS
HERE

OIL DRAIN PIPES
FROM HEAD

ENGINE SUPPOR

OIL LEVEL DIP
STICK

DISTRIBUTOR OILER

O HEAD OIL
DRAIN PIPE

OIL THERMO CONNECTION
(IF REQUIRED)

The P-type engine, offside.

but if this identification is by any chance obliterated, means must be taken to ensure that the valves are replaced in their original positions, assuming, of course, that the valves and seatings are not in such bad shape that a major operation is necessary.

The vertical camshaft drive assembly which transmits the power from the dynamo coupling is a self-contained unit in a housing which is held to the underside of the cylinder head by four studs and nuts. Correct meshing of the bevels is arrived at by the use of shims between the housing and the cylinder head facing, which naturally alters the height of the bevel as required in relation to the camshaft. Note how many shims are removed. After taking out the complete assembly, the half-coupling, which is held by a nut and key, can be drawn off the bevel-shaft, allowing the latter to be withdrawn, exposing the two Hyatt roller bearings, thrust washer and oil thrower.

There is just one final point regarding the head dismantling, that is, the restrictor pin in the main oil-feed hole. As previously mentioned, it is possible through neglect for this to become firmly seized in its hole. It is unlikely that such drastic measures as drilling it out will have to be resorted to, but it is quite possible that unavoidable damage to the pin may be caused by the use of pliers or other aids to grip. If this happens, a new restrictor will be necessary, and the dimensions of this easily made item will be given later on.

CHAPTER 3

Examination and Renovation

EXAMINATION AND RENOVATION.
THE CRANKSHAFT AND BEARINGS. CYLINDER BORE CONDITION.
VALVES AND VALVE GUIDES. PORT AND MANIFOLD ALIGNMENT.
COMPRESSION RATIO MODIFICATIONS.

We have now completed the dismantling of the major items of the engine, and are ready to get to work on a preliminary inspection. First of all, we have to get everything to a really adequate state of cleanliness. For this purpose the aids mentioned in the opening chapter should be called upon. Every scrap of internal and external filth must be dealt with. As regards the more inaccessible " internals," the type of engine under consideration is, of course, relatively free from internal oilways compared with some others, and there are no long galleries to worry about, but such internal passages as do exist must be thoroughly cleaned. A paraffin squirt (a Wesco oilcan does admirably) aided by a length of Bowden inner cable if necessary, will ensure that all ways are cleared and freed from gritty particles which will do a lot of harm if allowed to remain.

The Crankshaft and Bearings

Having arrived at a satisfactory state of cleanliness for all parts with which we are immediately concerned, a start can be made with an examination of the crankshaft, main bearings and connecting rods. As far as the crankshaft and mains are concerned, there is little that the average enthusiast can tackle himself. If the shaft surfaces show signs of scoring (and they invariably will, unless renovation has been recent) the shaft and bearing housings should be handed to an M.G. specialist for renovation. This will involve grinding the shaft-bearing surfaces slightly under size and remetalling the bearing bushes to fit. It is absolutely vital that the correct diametral clearance is maintained in all M.G. bearings, so that the work must only be entrusted to a competent source.

The same procedure applies to the connecting rod big-ends, which have the bearing surfaces metalled direct on the rods. No attempt must be made to " take-up " these bearings by machining the faces of the cap and rod at the bolts, in the time-honoured manner of vintage jobs. The crankpins should be ground at the same time as the mains, and connecting rods to fit obtained on an exchange-service basis which is available from authorized M.G. repairers.

The connecting rod small-end bearings are extremely long-lived, and should not require renewal unless the engine has been grossly neglected. If the gudgeon pins are a free push fit when dry, but without side shake, all is well. In any case, however, renewal of these bushes is a simple operation; the bushes are readily obtainable, and should be reamered to fit after insertion. Removal and refitting of small-end bushes is done without difficulty by the usual method of a long draw-bolt having a washer of a diameter slightly smaller than the outside diameter of the bush. This is placed through the bush with the washer against the bush end. A distance tube of a diameter slightly larger than the bush outside, is then put over the other end of the bolt, bearing up against the rod eye. If a large washer and nut are now threaded on to the bolt, and the nut screwed on with a spanner, the bush will be withdrawn. The operation " in reverse " can be used to insert the new bush.

The importance of having main and big-end bearings attended to by a competent M.G. specialist has already been stressed. For this reason, it is not proposed to give any details regarding actual running clearances in these bearings; this part of the business can safely be left to the " people who know." As regards the small-end bushes, if these are being renewed they must be reamed to size after pressing in. The gudgeon pins should be a free push fit in the bushes after finishing, and this means a diametral clearance of about .0005 in.

CYLINDER BORE CONDITION

If the engine was run before dismantling, its behaviour will no doubt have given some clue as to the condition of the cylinder bores. Some points in connection with bore wear on the P type and similar engines will be useful. Firstly, it should be remembered that these engines have no thermostat control of the warming-up period, and there is inevitably a considerable running time spent in a lukewarm condition. Thus, if the car has been used for the typical town-and-back journey the bores may have suffered. Secondly, the high-revving characteristics of the engine do not make for considerable cylinder life. This is not to say that the bores wear at an excessive rate, but it is fair to state that after 25,000 to 30,000 miles, a rebore is legitimately required.

Two symptoms which cause some owners misgivings, but which of themselves do *not* constitute evidence of a rebore being necessary are piston slap and fume expulsion from the crankcase breather. The P-type engine, thriving as it does on revs, requires adequate piston clearance. This increases with use to a point where the pistons are distinctly audible when starting from cold and when pulling at low revs (which is undesirable practice anyway). Unless the slap is accompanied by excessive oil consumption, and/or loss of power it can safely be ignored. As regards breather fuming, the characteristics of the engine are such that there is a tendency to fairly high crankcase pressure, and the free exit provided from the breather may give the impression that too much fume is being emitted. Here again there is no need to worry unless the other snags aforementioned are also present. The bulkhead and its sealing rubbers are there for the purpose of preventing fumes from reaching the cockpit, and no attempt must be made to extend the breather by means of flexible tubing or other means, in a misguided effort at leading the efflux under the car. Incidentally, if such a fitting is found on the engine it will be as well to look for signs of corrosion caused by excessive condensation, inside the engine. As regards the actual checking of, and work on, the bores and pistons, this extremely important subject warrants a chapter on its own, which will be found later in the book, and which is applicable to all types of M.G. engines.

VALVES AND VALVE GUIDES

Assuming that the cylinder bores and pistons have been dealt with as determined by their condition, and in line with the recommendations detailed in the chapter dealing with this part of the job, attention can next be given to the cylinder head. First examine the valve guides. These wear very slowly, as lubrication is ample. Inlet valve guide wear is in fact often shown up by persistent plug oiling, due to excessive lubricant being drawn down the valve stem during part-throttle operation. Very careful visual examination may show that the guides have worn oval. Trying the fit of a new valve of each type (inlet and exhaust) will show whether clearances are excessive. When making this check, it should be borne in mind that quite a lot of running clearance is necessary, and is not detrimental. If the clearance is too small, a tendency to sluggish valve operation at high speeds may be apparent. For the inlet valves about .003 in. should be right; aim at not less than .002 and not more than .004 in. A shade more can be allowed on the exhaust valves, and .003 to .005 should be satisfactory.

If it is thought after checking that the guides require replacing, the removal of the old guides and refitting of new ones should be entrusted to our friend the M.G. specialist. This is an operation requiring a good deal of care and know-how, and is worth having done properly. It might be as well to suggest here that if, having gone so far in dismantling the power unit, the condition of these small parts—valve guides being typical—leave one undecided whether to renew or not, get them renewed. This will prove most satisfactory in the long run.

If the valves have been subjected to much grinding, the valve seats will in all probability be somewhat pocketed. If this is the case, they should be recut by a professional. This recutting will restore the original freedom of gas flow; it is not generally realized how much power can be lost because of valves which are only slightly pocketed. Recutting the seats also ensures that there are no doubts about the dimensional accuracy of the seat in relation to the valve guide.

Naturally, if any of the valves show evidence of burning or bad pitting they should either be replaced or have the faces recut, again by a specialist. If they are of considerable age it is probable that, in addition to defects on the valve face, some wear of the stem and split-cone groove will have taken place. Possible sources of future trouble in this part of the engine are to be avoided, so if in doubt, the valve should be scrapped.

PORT AND MANIFOLD ALIGNMENT

Before examining the remaining parts of the valve assemblies with a view to refitting, it will be as well at this stage to take a look at the valve ports. These are extremely well finished in the o.h.c. engines, but quite a lot can be done with emery cloth and elbow-grease to obtain a high finish on the inside of the ports. The inlet port is, of course, far more important in this respect than the exhaust, so the inlets should be tackled first whilst enthusiasm is at its height! No attempt must be made to cut away the valve guide protrusions into the ports.

The lining-up of the induction pipe with the inlet ports in the head is a matter of great importance. As the four ports are of circular section, and the induction pipe of light alloy, it is not a difficult operation, but pays dividends in performance. If the inlet manifold is bolted to the head (without any packing washer) the degree of truth in the fit can be gauged to some extent by inserting a flexible " probe " such as a length of Bowden outer casing, through the port and past the flange joint. Such a test is rather of the hit-and-miss variety, and a more satisfactory method is to cut a sheet of white cartridge paper to the shape of the manifold flange, complete with stud-holes but without the port-holes cut. The faces of the cylinder head and corresponding manifold flanges should next be smeared lightly with graphite, and the manifold bolted up to the head with the paper interposed between the flanges. Upon removal, it will be found that the port and pipe apertures are clearly defined one on either side of the paper, and any discrepancy in their relative concentricity is easily seen and corrected. Remember when getting to work on the induction manifold that it is quite soft metal, and it is very easy to remove too much. The same care in lining-up is not so important in the case of the exhaust manifold; just as well, as this component is made of extremely hard iron. If there is any variation in dimensions it is desirable that the entry to the manifold should be of slightly larger diameter than the exit from the cylinder port. This condition can be achieved by enlarging the manifold openings by means of a grinding wheel on a flexible shaft.

COMPRESSION RATIO MODIFICATIONS

Having completed work on the ports, the only other attention likely to be required as regards the head casting, is machining for compression ratio. It may be that the owner will wish initially to get the engine to its peak condition as standard, before doing any tuning. However, there is something to be said for carrying out this machining operation while the head is in a suitable state of undress, particularly since there is little question but that the original compression ratio of the P-type engine—6.4 to 1—is somewhat on the low side, even with present-day fuels. Quite a difference in liveliness can be obtained, without sacrificing any other qualities, by machining off 3/64 in. This raises the ratio to 6.7 to 1, and the total depth of cylinder head after machining should come out at 3 19/32 in. Checking of this depth will serve as a guide as to whether the head has already been

" planed." As a further example, the L-type Magna (six-cylinder) has an even lower ratio—5.7 to 1. Removal of 1/16 in. gives 6 to 1, leaving the total head depth 3 25/64 in.

The above increases in compression ratio are, of course, by no means the limit, but if it is desired to go any higher, the technical press should be consulted, giving full details of the fuel which it is proposed to use. In the middle 1930s many P and PB units were operating quite happily on ratios up to 8 to 1, using Ethyl or Discol, and, of course, fuels at least equal to these are now available in the " Premium " brands.

CHAPTER 4

The Overhead-Valve Mechanism

ATTENTION TO VALVE PARTS. CAM-FOLLOWERS AND CAMSHAFT. CAM-FOLLOWER ADJUSTMENT. ROCKER-SHAFT ASSEMBLY. CAMSHAFT BEARINGS AND DRIVING GEARS. TIMING AND DYNAMO GEARS.

Having completed work on the head casting in regard to lining up the manifolding, polishing the ports, and modifying the head depth as required for the chosen compression ratio, attention can next be given to the valves and their associated parts. The valves themselves can have the stems polished with superfine emery cloth, after which the usual grinding-in process, finishing off with metal polish, will ensure a

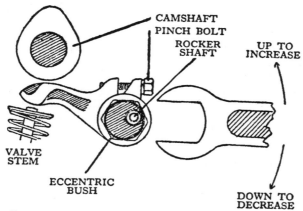

Correct position of eccentric rocker-shaft bushes

perfect seating. Grinding-in is, of course, necessary even if the valve seats have been recut, and regardless of whether the original or new valves are being fitted.

The standard valve springs are satisfactory up to an engine speed quite a lot in excess of peak revs. If the existing springs have seen considerable service, they should be replaced; the specialist spring makers such as Terry's will be able to supply the correct springs, and excessive spring strength should be avoided at this stage. Very high spring pressure can be wasteful of power and puts extra loading on the valve operating gear. Double valve springs are standard, though quite a few engines, probably modified in other directions as well, may be found fitted with triple springs as used on the 750 c.c. Q-type racing cars.

If the spring collars and split-cones are in good condition, no work is necessary here, but if at all doubtful they should be replaced, and are easily obtainable. The main thing to watch is that the cones, when firmly in position are not sunk unduly below the collar face to an extent which indicates a danger of them pulling right through. There is no danger of this unless " pirate " parts have been used, or the engine grossly 'neglected. The rocker-shafts are liable to become very dirty internally with oil-sludge, due to the relatively slow feed at low pressure. This sometimes results in one or more of the oil-feed holes through the cam-followers, or rockers, becoming blocked. The shafts must therefore be thoroughly cleaned internally. The same applies to the cam-followers, and in this case the process will be aided, as far as the very small-bore feed hole is concerned, if an oil-syringe is used, provided with a nozzle small enough to " seat " in the slightly chamfered outlet hole at the follower-tip. If the follower is held in the vice, and the paraffin-filled gun held firmly into the outlet-feed hole, a hearty squirt will clean out the hole better than any lengthy probing with Bowden wire strands.

It is possible for the engine to be run for a long time with one or more of these feed holes blocked, as the rocker-box casting effectively deadens any extra noise. The whole of the oil supply to the face of the cam and the corresponding face on the follower is dependent on an ample feed at this point, and failure of the supply results in scoring of both cam and follower. Fortunately, the depth of hardening on both these components is considerable, and it is often possible to make a good job of renovation by patient work with a carborundum slip. If this has to be done, the utmost care must be taken to adhere as nearly as possible to the original contours. When the engine is on the road again removal of the rocker-box at reasonable intervals, and inspection of the individual oil-feeds with the engine running, will ensure that blocking trouble does not recur. Even with the engine in running condition, it is perfectly feasible to clear a follower-feed stoppage with the oil-syringe and nozzle aforementioned, and this should be regarded as a desirable item of garage equipment.

CAM-FOLLOWERS AND CAMSHAFT

Even if the majority of the cams are not actually scored, they will in all probability benefit from a dressing with superfine emery cloth. As far as any lightening of followers is concerned, however, this should be avoided.

The follower adjustment incorporates an ingenious arrangement of bronze bushes inserted in the heels of the followers, the hole for the rocker-shaft being drilled eccentrically in relation to the outer periphery of the bush. The follower is split and fitted with a pinch-bolt at the point where it embraces the bush, and the bush in turn is provided at one end with a hexagon allowing it to be turned (when the pinch-bolt is slackened) in relation to the follower. Due to its eccentric mounting, any turning of the bush in this manner will cause the follower to move towards or away from the cam, depending on which way the bush is turned, thus allowing correct clearance to be obtained.

If the engine has seen a considerable amount of wear, it is possible for the bushes to be turned so far that the correct adjustment is completely lost. When assembled in the proper manner, and irrespective of which side of the engine—inlet or exhaust—is being dealt with, a downward movement of a spanner placed on the hexagon at the bush end should tend to push the follower towards the cam, or in other words, to take up the clearance. An upward movement of the spanner should draw the follower away from the cam, thus increasing the clearance. A glance at the diagram will show why this is the case, it being noted that the " thick " part of the eccentric is towards the camshaft. Lifting the spanner turns this part, and thus the follower, away from the camshaft, and lowering the spanner does the opposite.

CAM-FOLLOWER ADJUSTMENT

Although the amount of adjustment available by this method is not great, it is perfectly adequate unless the valve stems are abnormally short for some reason. It will, however, be evident that if the bushes are turned through 180 degrees from the correct position it will still be possible to obtain some sort of adjustment although the lie of the follower in relation to both cam and valve stem will be hopelessly out. This point should receive careful attention in consequence, when assembling, and a test with a spanner will ensure correctness.

The rocker-shaft bushes are extremely long-lived, as the loading is very light. If it is decided that the bushes require renewing, the work is not difficult and is well within the scope of an average fitter. The clearance of the bush to the rocker-shaft is not critical, but excessive shake must be avoided, the ideal to aim at being a free running fit without shake. Remember that the act of clamping the cam-follower on the outside of the bush will have the effect of tightening up the bush on the shaft, and therefore the allowed clearance should take note of this. The best method to adopt is to reamer the bush to fit the rocker-shaft, with the cam-follower already in position and clamped tightly on the outside of the bush. The use of an expanding reamer will enable the clearance to be judged to a nicety.

ROCKER-SHAFT ASSEMBLY

If the valve seats have been recut, or maybe for some other reason, it is quite possible that even with the followers correctly set, the lie may be slightly inaccurate, due to too long a valve stem. The ideal to aim at is that with the valve in the half-open position, a line drawn through the centre of the rocker-shaft bush to the follower tip should meet, at right angles, a line drawn vertically through the axis of the valve. In this connection it is important to note that the centre of the rocker-shaft bush is *not* the centre of the shaft, as the bush is eccentric to the shaft. However, a little experimenting with the camshaft and rockers in place will enable the correctness of the dimensions to be judged, and if necessary a small amount should be ground off the tip of the valve stem to get everything perfect. In grinding, take care to keep the surface flat and at right angles to the valve stem, and do not take too much metal off. The valve stem length is not vitally critical within small limits, and unless the aforementioned check reveals that the stem is quite a bit too long, it is preferable to let well alone. At the same time, it is essential that the check should be made, just in case. A temporary reassembly of the camshaft and rocker-shafts will show whether the spacing tubes on the rocker-shafts allow the followers to take up their correct positions. Each follower must lie centrally under its cam, and not to one side. If correct it will be found that the follower tip is absolutely in line above the valve stem. If it is allowed to deviate to one side or the other, irregular and rapid wear of both follower and cam will result. If the existing spacing tubes do not fill the bill in this respect, new ones can easily be made from light-gauge steel tubing. Although, obviously, excessive side-play in the followers is undesirable for the reason mentioned above, sufficient must be allowed to give free running; this should amount only to the merest trace of side movement. If a final check is made when the job is assembled for keeps, and adjustment made if necessary by lightly grinding the spacers, the clearance will be obtained to a nicety. This final check is advisable as small clearances have an uncanny habit of disappearing as assembly proceeds.

Camshaft Bearings and Driving Gears

Assuming that all oilways have received attention (not forgetting the provision of the necessary oil-ducts in the new bushes, if fitted) the valve gear components can be considered as ready for assembly. Attention will have been given to the cams in the way of removing minor scoring. The camshaft bearings should not present any difficulty, but if excessive wear is present no attempt should be made to rectify this by removing metal from the bearing standards or their caps. The bearing shells should be re-metalled and the camshaft bearing surfaces dressed with a lap to remove any scoring. If the wear is reasonable, and there is no measurable up-and-down play when the shaft is in position with the bearing caps tight, leave well alone. The test for up-and-down play should be made at the bevel end of the shaft, and, of course, is done with no components other than the camshaft in position.

The camshaft bearings allow for a definite degree of endplay on the shaft, which is under the control of a large spring washer located between the bevel and the front bearing housing. This spring washer serves to keep the bevel wheel and pinion firmly in mesh, providing smooth running and silence. There is no need to remove the washer if it is in good condition, but obviously if it appears at all doubtful or shows signs of loss of tension it should be renewed.

Examination of the bevel gear teeth should be carefully carried out. Unless some untoward incident has occurred during the previous running of the engine, the teeth should stand up well as they are of ample area, and the spring thrust washer ensures full tooth contact. Chipped teeth cannot be allowed to pass, since if one tooth is chipped the others must be suspect. It is unlikely, however, that such will be found, and the most serious fault will probably be a little roughness at the tooth edges which is readily corrected with a carborundum slip.

There is no need to go to elaborate lengths to check the meshing of the gear teeth. Just note that the inner edges of the teeth on the respective wheels are level with each other at the point of contact, so that the full tooth width is in mesh. If there is any discrepancy here it can be corrected by careful shimming of the vertical shaft housing.

The bearings in the latter have a pretty hard life (they are of the Hyatt roller type). It is often found that considerable shake develops at this point after a big mileage, and neglect to remedy this will eventually lead to trouble with the flexible coupling and the top dynamo bearing, if nothing worse. If this shake is present, it is advisable to have the whole vertical shaft unit complete with housing, renovated by an M.G. specialist, who will, in addition to renewing the bearings ensure that the thrust washer and oil thrower disc are fitted in their correct positions. Incorrect fitting of these components is liable to cause a serious oil leak from the housing, with dire results to the dynamo.

When refitting the vertical drive shaft housing into its location on the cylinder head, try it initially with the same number of shims in position between the flanges, as were present when the housing was removed. It may be found that correct meshing of the bevels cannot be obtained, due perhaps to the camshaft having now been repositioned correctly. In such an event, any adjustment must be done by shimming the vertical shaft housing; the end-location of the camshaft must not be interfered with once it has been fitted to meet the requirements of relationship of cams, followers and valves as already described.

If the correct shims are unobtainable, new ones can easily be made from shim-brass, which is obtainable in various thicknesses. The use of a multiplicity of wafter-like shims is not good practice; use the minimum number of thicker ones, and if you can get the number down to unity, so much the better. When satisfied that the gear meshing is correct, and the assembly is being fitted for keeps, see that the flange faces and shim faces are spotlessly clean, and use the merest trace of jointing compound on the faces. This will ensure an oil-tight joint, but do not overdo it, otherwise the clearances will be affected.

The meshing of the bevels to give the designed valve timing is facilitated by markings on the teeth. These take the form of indentations on the inner ends of the teeth and occasionally are very difficult to spot. However, the relatively large pitch of the gear teeth means that one tooth error shows up in no uncertain manner, and the following method of gear meshing will give the right answer.

TIMING AND DYNAMO GEARS

Set the coupling fork on the vertical drive shaft so that it points across the head, that is, from left to right, or parallel with the front axle. Drop the camshaft into place in its lower bearing shells, positioned so that both valves are closed on the cylinder adjacent to the bevel (No. 1). In this position, the cams on No. 1 cylinder will point upwards towards 10 o'clock and 2 o'clock approximately, or at about 45 degrees on either side of a vertical line drawn through the camshaft axis. The camshaft can be finally assembled thus, the position taken up by the coupling fork representing its correct lie when No. 1 cylinder is at TDC of the firing stroke. It follows from this, of course, that the corresponding dynamo coupling fork will lie at 90 degrees to its fellow, or along the axis of the engine, when coupling up, but naturally it is still necessary to ensure that the dynamo and crankshaft bevels are meshed with the crankshaft in the right position.

The dynamo has a hard life, as it runs at engine speed under the stress of an inherently rigid drive. It is specially designed to withstand

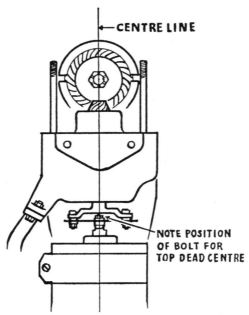

Position of dynamo coupling at t.d.c. of firing stroke
No. 1 cylinder.

rapid acceleration and centrifugal force as well as the considerable load occasioned by driving the valve gear. To ensure reliable service the dynamo requires servicing by the makers at intervals of 20,000 miles, and neglect of this not unreasonable requirement leads to early deterioration. The dynamo bearings are grease-packed, and although oilers are provided additionally on some machines, they are of doubtful utility. Far more bother is caused by excess of oil than otherwise. The bearings have to be carefully watched, as they are heavily loaded, and running with worn bearings sets up a vibration in the whole camshaft drive, as well as accelerating wear of the Hyatt bearings in the vertical drive shaft and the bevels themselves. If the dynamo has the maker's attention as specified, it should not require any maintenance such as brush renewal or commutator cleaning throughout the 20,000-mile period, unless, of course, there is something seriously wrong with the electric circuit. It is a very simple machine, with a normal shunt winding and no external voltage control, and there is little to go wrong.

Although not strictly in correct sequence, it will be just as well whilst we are on the dynamo topic, to deal with its refitting to the front housing. Its location should be obvious, but if in doubt it can be noted that the terminals should point to the off-side of the engine; in other words they are just behind the distributor cover when the engine is assembled. Also, the circular inspection cover on the dynamo is fitted with its securing bolt at this side. Meshing of the bevels is not so vitally important as in the case of the camshaft bevels, due to the valuable quality of inertia possessed by the armature, but a good fit is essential, and can be obtained satisfactorily by the twin processes of feeling the amount of backlash and inspecting the meshing through the flange holes of the oil-pump and distributor mountings.

Correct meshing is again the responsibility of shims, and the same proviso applies as was the case with the vertical shaft housing. It is absolutely necessary to allow an appreciable amount of backlash in the bevels which can be felt on the top of the dynamo shaft at the coupling fork (without the coupling disc being connected). If there is little or no backlash an unbearable whine will be set up by the bevels. This, apart altogether from the noise aspect, spells wear and vibration. On the other hand, this does not mean that so long as there is plenty of play all is well. Too much backlash will overload the gear teeth. The ideal is the least amount of play that is noiseless.

CHAPTER 5

The Lubrication System

The oil-pump is the next component to receive attention. This is of the normal gear type, and has a by-pass relief valve self-contained in the body of the pump. The valve comprises a spring-loaded plunger which seats on a port in the pump body, the spring and plunger being enclosed by a screwed-in cap.

The pump body cover will in all probability have already been removed at the time the complete pump was taken off the engine. Further dismantling merely involves taking out the two gear wheels, disassembly of the relief valve aforementioned, and unscrewing of the inlet and delivery unions if these appear in need of attention through ill-usage.

Particular attention should be paid to the pump gear teeth. Whilst the actual running clearance between the two meshed wheels is not critical, and will not affect the volume or pressure to any extent, the condition of the teeth is naturally important. Pitting or chipping can hardly be caused otherwise than by foreign matter in the oil, but if any such defects are found, careful work with emery cloth and a carborundum slip should remedy matters.

SIDE CLEARANCE OF GEARS

The body and cover of the pump having been thoroughly cleaned, the fit of the gears in the body should be checked. As already mentioned, the running clearance between the teeth of the gears is not critical. The side clearance of the gears to the body and the cover is, however, most important, as too much clearance at this point will allow pressure to leak across the gearwheel sides. The clearance at this point therefore should be the absolute minimum consistent with free running. Obviously, excessive clearance can be caused by using too thick a washer between the cover and the body. The thinnest possible paper washer only should be used, with the merest trace of jointing compound. Before fitting, make sure that the mating surfaces are perfectly flat, and if necessary ensure this by the use of grinding paste on a flat plate. Incidentally, a sheet of plate glass makes an excellent flat surface for such jobs as these.

The side clearance of the gears should be about .001 in. It is, of course, not easy to check this when everything is assembled, but one excellent method is to assemble the pump without a packing washer

30

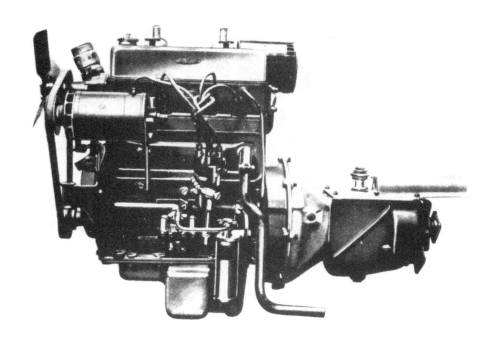

The TA-type engine, nearside.

The TA-type engine, offside.

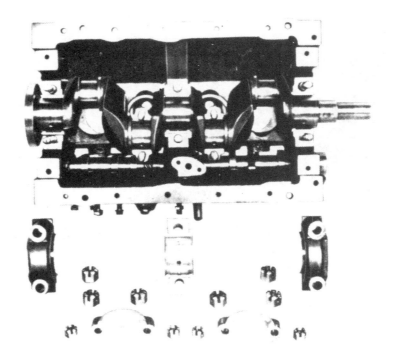

The TA crankshaft and bearings.

The TA cork-insert clutch dismantled.

on the cover, bolting up temporarily with suitably sized nuts and bolts. If it is found that, having done this, the gears are just trapped between the body and the cover, it follows that by using a packing washer of .001 in. thickness, the requisite clearance will be obtained. If too much clearance is evident even without any washer in at all, the height of the joint face on the body can be reduced the required amount by rubbing down on the above-mentioned plate. If a lot of metal has to be removed, a sheet of emery cloth on the plate will get the " rough " off quickly, using grinding paste for the final fit.

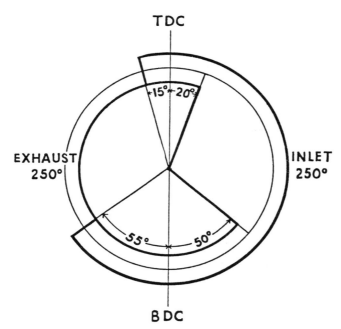

Valve timing diagram, PA and PB engines

Assembly of the gears and pump body in this manner will enable a really first-class performance to be obtained from the pump. It is surprising how much pressure can be lost through unduly light-hearted assembly, and attempts to restore this by packing up the relief valve are foredoomed to failure.

THE RELIEF VALVE

The relief valve comes next on our list. If any packing pieces are found in its spring housing, scrap them. It may be difficult to determine whether the spring is standard or not, but this will show up when the engine is started, and adjustment can be made accordingly. The valve plunger invariably gets all the wear rather than the oil-port against which it seats, but in any case it wears very slowly. If it seems to have grown ridges, ease them down carefully, taking care to keep the seating surface absolutely square. If in doubt about your capabilities in this direction, obtain a new plunger or have one made to pattern. It is important to make sure that the relief valve is absolutely oil-tight under normal conditions, thus the point is stressed.

If the pipe unions are damaged in any way they should be replaced with new ones, otherwise oil-tight connections will be difficult to obtain. Use red fibre washers of the correct size between the union flanges and the pump body. A trace of jointing compound on the union threads before screwing them into the body will also help to

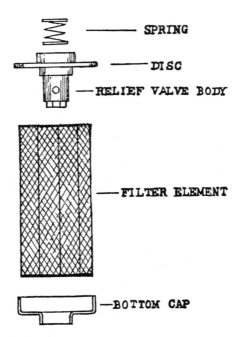

Correct assembly of components in oil filter

make an absolutely tight job. Use a box spanner to put them in, and make a good strong-arm effort when tightening, so that there will be no tendency towards unscrewing when the pipes are removed at any time.

The external oil-pump driving gear should be examined in the same manner as other engine gears. It meshes with a worm gear on the crankshaft, and this latter can with advantage be examined at the same time, so that any faults can be checked on both wheels. There should be nothing wrong that a carborundum slip cannot rectify, as the gears are of adequate size and lubrication is ample. The oil-pump spindle is splined to engage with the driving gear sleeve (which also drives the distributor) and both the shaft splines and the internal splines in the gear should be examined for wear, which usually results in sharpish edges on the splines and sometimes makes them difficult to withdraw. The splines can be dressed if thought advisable.

FILTERING ARRANGEMENTS

The remaining items of the lubrication system to be considered, comprise the gauze filter on the suction side, which is housed in the sump, the Tecalemit pressure filter between the pump delivery and the oil distribution circuit, and finally the various pipes. The suction filter comprises a gauze cylinder built up on a tube which locates in suitable registers in the sump casting, being screwed in from the front end. This filter is very robust, and can only be damaged through carelessness. Apart from thorough cleaning in petrol, it should not require any other attention, but if the gauze is in any way damaged, this is, buckled or holed, it must be renewed. Anyone possessing reasonable dexterity with a soldering iron will have no difficulty in fitting a new gauze. The Tecalemit pressure filter comprises an alloy housing with a top cover secured by four studs and nuts. The housing has an inlet union to take the pump delivery pipe, and also two outlet unions. One of these—the small one—connects to the oil gauge, whilst the other leads to the front main bearing and overhead valve gear via external pipes. A hole in the housing flange which bolts to the crank-case, leads the oil supply to the centre and rear main bearings. The big-ends are, of course, fed by drillings in the crankshaft in the usual way.

The Tecalemit filter element is renewable, the "throwaway" mileage being 10,000. A new element will, of course, be fitted as a matter of course during an overhaul of the kind under discussion. Before doing this the whole of the filter housing must be cleaned meticulously. The element seats on a spun metal cap at the bottom, whilst at the top, under the alloy cover, is a relief valve which comes into action in the unlikely event of the filter being so neglected that it chokes with debris. The bottom cap and the relief valve are both designed to fit properly on to the element, providing an oil-tight joint, and care must therefore be taken, when renewing the element, to see that these components are positioned properly. As far as the bottom cap is concerned, its rim fits round the outside of the element, and its centre protrusion registers in a recess in the bottom of the filter housing. As for the relief valve, the valve body must point downwards into the centre of the element, so that the metal disc fits snugly over the top of the element with the light coil spring above this and under the cover. Although to those in the know, the manner of assembly of these bits and pieces may seem obvious, some people seem to find unusual ways of getting them back; hence the reason for this full explanation. It is vital for the well-being of the engine that oil fitration is above reproach, and wrong assembly will allow serious leakage past the filtering element.

Before refitting the filter housing to the crankcase, make sure that all the pipe unions are really tight, using similar methods to those employed on the oil-pump unions; do not overdo the tightening, of course, as you are working on alloy threads in this instance. A thin paper washer is required between the fixing flange of the filter body and the crankcase, and this can be treated with jointing compound to ensure an oil-tight joint; every care must be taken, as the pressure is considerable especially when the oil is cold.

Assembling the Filter Element

The top cover of the filter requires a packing washer of thin Hallite or similar material. Before fitting, make sure that the joint faces on both body and cover are registering correctly. Uneven tightening-down can result in distortion of the alloy cover, making it impossible to get an oil-tight joint. Slight distortion can be corrected by grinding the faces with valve paste, but any serious errors must be corrected by use of a scraper. Having got the faces to the required degree of accuracy, see that the four studs are undamaged, and that their nuts run freely thereon. This will ensure that when tightening-down the cover, the correct degree of tension on the nuts can be gauged without errors caused by binding threads. A trace of jointing compound on the washer, and spring washers under the four nuts, will complete the job, and ensure a leak-proof filter that really does its stuff.

The Oil-piping

Although the pipes will not be fitted until a late stage in the final assembly, it will be as well to deal with the salient points while we are on the particular subject. The suction pipe from sump filter to pump is of very large diameter on P-type engines (on some earlier o.h.c. types it was not so large), and in consequence does not take too kindly to forcible fitting. In other words, bend it to line up with the unions before fitting, and do not attempt to pull it into position with the union nuts. Bending will be assisted by heating the pipe to nearly red heat and quenching in water. This also anneals the pipe, which is all to the good. Get it lined up absolutely true with the two unions, and then pull up the nuts firmly. This will ensure freedom from suction leaks, a point which is all-important because of the high level of the oil-pump compared with the oil in the sump.

The same care must be taken with the delivery pipes. The pipe leading to the front main bearing includes a T-piece brazed in, which feeds the valve gear. See that the brazing is sound at this point; and also at the top fitting which connects with the cylinder head feed hole.

CHAPTER 6

The Ignition System

The next assembly to receive attention is the ignition distributor of the standard coil system. The main requirements when dealing with this component are use of the correct tools and cleanliness. Many of the parts are easily damaged, particularly screw-threads. It is not proposed to describe normal maintenance procedure, which will be familiar to readers, but rather to give emphasis to the "little extras." Having dismantled the unit, cleaning must be done with a dry cloth, no liquid aids being allowed. Examine the moulded distributor cover for cracks which, while unlikely, can be caused by careless removal and refitting. If any such are found, the cover must be scrapped, as makeshift repairs are not good enough. The electrodes in the interior of the cover should be trimmed with a fine file to remove pitting, and the central carbon brush must be quite free in its holder, with the spring making good contact and gripping it firmly.

The rotor of the distributor is arranged to clear the electrodes by a few thousandths of an inch, the actual degree of clearance not being critical. Some P-type engines (or maybe some rotors of the period) seemed to suffer from burning of the rotor to a remarkable degree, demanding frequent renewals, but rotors are not expensive, and if trimming with a file does not produce a serviceable rotor, a new one must be fitted. If too much metal has to be removed from the rotor edge, excessive electrode clearance will result, and a decision should be made on this basis. Just to finish off, polish the rotor contact arm with metal polish all over.

The contact-breaker unit complete with its base will have been removed, and after completely dismantling the components, and cleaning the points in the usual way, finishing off with superfine emery cloth on the points, the items can be reassembled. The older type of blued contact-breaker spring was apt to break after a moderate mileage, but the modern type, of bright steel, which will doubtless be fitted, has a very long life. The fit of the rocker-arm should be checked on the pivot. This should be quite free, but without side rock. A trace of engine oil on the pivot assists in free movement.

As regards the fixed contact, there are no particular snags here, except to ensure that the tongue carrying the contact is at right angles to the base when the fixture is clamped down. Judicious bending will get this right, and obviously any error will give faulty lining-up of the two contacts and prevent them meeting squarely. With the unit on the bench it is an easy matter to get everything " just so " as far as the make-and-break is concerned.

Before re-making electrical connections, such as, for example, those to the condenser and L.T. terminal, polish the metal to afford the minimum electrical resistance.

CONTACT-BREAKER ACCURACY

The opening of the contact points on all four lobes of the cam should be checked, as equality of opening is important, because any variation means that the spark timing will vary as between individual

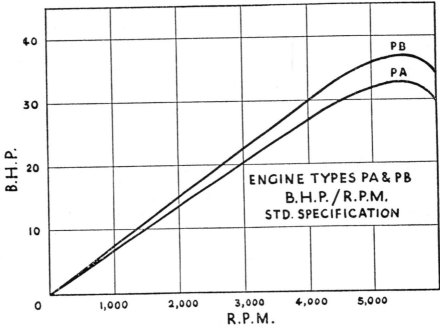

B.h.p. curves, PA and PB engines

cylinders. Any discrepancy can be corrected by carefully easing the appropriate lobe with a carborundum strip. The actual fully open gap was originally specified as 15 to 18 " thous," but it is considered that something nearer .012 in. gives just as good results and results in an easier time for the mechanism.

The automatic advance-and-retard mechanism, housed below the contact-breaker, is easily dismantled for cleaning. If it has been neglected, a good deal of dirt will probably be found in the housing, but apart from that, trouble is rare, as considerable freedom is allowed in the pivot mechanism. Should a broken spring be found, be sure to fit the correct replacement, as the tensions vary. The normal method of lubrication of the device is via an oil-duct which is revealed after removing the distributor rotor-arm. It is doubtful if this is really adequate for the purpose, though the makers probably consider that too little oil is better than too much. With the mechanism exposed fully by removal of the contact-breaker baseplate, however, it is easy to give every pivot the right amount of oil, and, by oscillating the cam with the driving shaft held firmly, to see that everything is working as it should.

LUBRICATION OF THE PARTS

The main driving shaft wears very slowly, and a little extra clearance in the bearings is not critical, providing it does not amount to real sloppiness. There is an oiler on the side of the housing, which is all too frequently neglected, and even allowed to get full of dirt. If this appears to have happened, the spindle should be examined very carefully for scoring, and rectified with fine emery cloth if necessary.

When reassembling the unit, make sure that the screws securing the contact-breaker baseplate to the main body are correctly fitted with spring washers, as they form an earth connection to the body, and must go home adequately tight. When tightening up the adjustable contact after finally setting the gap, do not overdo things; the point will not slacken off if normal effort with the small spanner or screwdriver is used.

HIGH-TENSION WIRING

If the high-tension wiring is of the original type, it will repay renewal with one of the modern classes of cable, which embody many improvements in insulation and are impervious to oil and heat. The fitting of the H.T. cables into the distributor demands some care to ensure that full contact is made with the metal electrode, and that the cable is absolutely secure so that it will withstand unintentional pulls during a hectic plug change! It is frequently found that moisture lodges in these terminals, creeping down between the bakelite union nut and the cable, and causing corrosion. To combat this, it is a good idea to run some jointing compound or shellac varnish between the cable and the union nut after tightening the latter.

CHAPTER 7

Reassembly of Major Items

MISCELLANEOUS ITEMS.   ASSEMBLING CRANKSHAFT AND BEARINGS.
FITTING THE FLYWHEEL.   BOLTING UP THE BIG-ENDS.
CHECKING OIL CIRCULATION.

Having dealt with the various assemblies, it is almost time to get down to the job of reassembly of the engine. Before doing this, it is necessary to mention one or two miscellaneous items which may warrant attention, and which might as well be dealt with during a major operation of this nature. The first concerns the flywheel. If the starter gear-ring teeth show signs of wear on the engaging edges, it may be advisable to have them built up and recut, or otherwise renovated. If, however, only a degree of raggedness is present, this can be removed with a carborundum stone. These gear teeth last a very long time, and there is no need to worry about a moderate amount of wear on the edges so long as there are no teeth actually broken or badly chipped.

Another item concerns the water-jacket cover plates on the near-side of the engine block. These are of sheet steel, and are subject to corrosion by water action, eventually developing holes right through. This particularly applies to the plate having the water inlet pipe attached thereto. New plates are easily manufactured either of sheet steel or alloy. The maker's plates are dished and flanged at the edges for strength, and are of fairly light-gauge metal. If replacements are made in the home workshop, perfectly flat material will do, but in view of the absence of a flanged edge, the thickness should be sufficient to ensure freedom from distortion. About $\frac{1}{8}$ in. in the case of steel, and $\frac{1}{4}$ in. for aluminium alloy, will be all right. When fitting the plates, use a thin Hallite packing (or similar) plus jointing compound, and tighten the set-screws up firmly but not so heartily as to distort the plate, particularly if alloy is used.

ASSEMBLING CRANKSHAFT AND BEARINGS

Reassembly of the crankshaft is a perfectly straightforward matter. Before finally assembling the centre bearing block thereon, give all the crankshaft oilways a final squirt through with petrol. The same applies to the oilways in the bearing. Having fitted the centre bearing to the shaft, the assembly can be positioned in the crankcase, with the centre housing in its circular register.

In case of difficulty in obtaining packing washers for the joints between the crankcase and the front and rear housings, these can be

38

made from good quality paper; excellent for this purpose is white drawing paper as used in engineering drawing offices. The washers should be carefully cut.

The front and rear housings are positioned with the packing washers between the flanges, a thin coating of jointing compound being used to ensure an oil-tight joint. Bolt up the flanges with even pressure, and finally replace the long bolts which retain the centre bearing, using new tab washers to lock them in position. Test the shaft for free rotation, with just a shade of end-play. This latter is governed by the centre bearing, and obviously if bearing renovation has been carried out in the approved manner, the end-play will be " just so." Finally, give the oilways another squirt through for luck.

When keying up the drive gears at the crankshaft nose, have a good look at the keys. These should fit really well. This does not imply excessive tightness, which will merely make the parts difficult to assemble. A good fit means that the key should contact the keyway on all sides, not just on the top. If any of the keys do not meet this condition, make new ones of good quality key-steel.

FITTING THE FLYWHEEL

At the other end of the crankshaft is the most important key in the whole engine, that securing the flywheel flange. Really accurate fitting here is time well spent. First of all, check the fit of the tapers on shaft and flange boss. If they do not mate perfectly, grind them in with fine grinding paste, applying moderate pressure and taking time over the job. This will ensure a perfect fit. Then fit the key. When finally assembling the flange on the shaft, there is no need for fancy methods, or brute force. Tighten the large crankshaft nut as tightly as possible with the outsize spanner used for removing same. Then obtain a short piece of stout tubing large enough to fit over the nut, and to abut against the flange face. Hold this against the flange, and give it a hearty blow with a block of wood—just one good wallop. Tighten the nut again. Repeat the process until it is impossible to tighten the nut any more, and there will be no trouble with the flange shifting.

The secret of carrying out the above operation is to do it methodically. It is much easier to write about than to do, as it must be remembered that after each blow, the tube has to be removed, the box spanner inserted, and the tightening-up process carried out. There is naturally a temptation to give the tube several outsize blows while it is in position. Such action will lead to trouble, as there is quite a possibility that some distortion will occur either of the shaft or housing. Therefore, tighten after each single blow, and strike the blows squarely and with moderate force.

Fitting the flywheel to its flange does not present any particular snags. The bolts must be a good fit, and new ones must be used if there is any doubt. Wash the centre ball bearing in petrol and re-pack with high-melting-point grease before reinserting it in its housing, which is clamped under the flywheel retaining nuts. Tighten the nuts evenly and very firmly. If the split-pins will not register, grind the nuts until equal pressure is obtained—don't slacken the nut to bring the holes into line, likewise don't over-tighten with the same object. Cut off the split-pins to the correct length, and bend the legs at right angles.

Having assembled the crankshaft and bearings, together with the flywheel and auxiliary drive gears, attention can now be given to the connecting rods and pistons. The connecting rods are not provided with an oil-spray hole to the cylinder walls as on the push-rod T-type engine and it is therefore immaterial which way round they are replaced. This remark, of course, applies on the assumption that re-metalled rods are being installed; if the rods are being replaced unaltered, they should be put back the same way round as they were removed. The connecting rods are inserted from the bottom and pushed up the cylinder bores until the small-end protrudes sufficiently far out of the top of the bore for the piston to be put in place over the rod and the gudgeon pin inserted. The skirt of the piston can then be gently slid into the bore, having first been liberally anointed with engine oil. Space the piston ring gaps evenly around the periphery of the piston and then slide the piston the remaining distance into the bore until the big-end top half locates on the crank journal.

BOLTING UP THE BIG-ENDS

The operation of getting the rings into the cylinders is sometimes a bit tricky because of the absence of a radius at the top of the bore. The job is made much easier if a piston ring compressor is used, this device comprising a flexible circular clamp which encircles the ring and compresses it into its groove with equal pressure all round. The clamp is tightened to just sufficient degree to allow it to slide off the ring as the latter enters the bore. The bottom big-end caps can then be fitted, the bolts having previously been examined to ensure that they are sound and with threads undamaged. Note that the head of the bolt is so formed that it abuts against the connecting rod and is thus prevented from turning while the nut is tightened. Tighten the nuts firmly with a socket spanner and tommy-bar of normal length. Due to the fine-pitch bolt threads it is possible to stretch the bolts if too much force is used. If, with the requisite degree of tightness on the nut, it is found that the split-pin holes will not register, remove the nut and grind the face until, with the nut properly tight, the holes are in line. Take care to keep the nut face square when grinding, and do not remove too much metal—very little makes an appreciable difference in terms of rotary movement of the nut. Engine oil should, of course, be applied to the journals before the caps are fitted.

The split-pins must be of a size which will enter the holes under light persuasion by way of a few taps with a hammer. Sloppy pins are a menace. The length can be rectified after fitting; cut off the legs of the pin until just sufficient is left to bend over at right angles across one flat of the nut. Finally, check that the shaft will rotate freely. If it appears unduly tight, this will invariably be due to one or more of the big-ends rubbing slightly on its end-face against the web of the journal; in other words, a high-spot of white metal, reducing the side clearance, is the culprit. If the shaft is rotated a few times, bright marking will indicate the trouble without recourse to lamp-black on the faces, and careful scraping will give the necessary clearance. Although running-in will, of course, eliminate stiffness caused by such slight inaccuracies in metalling, it is better to do it by hand wherever possible, before the engine is run. It must be emphasized, however, that the side clearance of the big-ends is designed to fine limits and liberties must not be taken with it. The above action is expressly for odd high-spots only, which are occasionally found in remetalled bearings.

This completes assembly of the main components in the crankcase. As regards the external components, we have already dealt with the dynamo and its remounting on the front housing. However, just as a reminder, the dynamo bevels should be meshed with No. 1 piston at t.d.c. and the coupling fork at the top of the dynamo pointing fore and aft along the engine centre line. The use of a little jointing compound on the shims at the dynamo base will ensure an oil-tight joint.

The distributor unit should be fitted in such a position that the two spring clips securing the cap are at about 6 and 12 o'clock, the condenser lying towards the crankcase, and the clamp screw towards the radiator. Check which of the H.T. leads goes to No. 1 cylinder, that is, the shortest lead, and mesh the driving gears so that the distributor rotor synchronizes with the electrode for No. 1 cylinder. The meshing of the gears depends on the relative position of the oil-pump shaft, and a few trial-and-error fits of the oil-pump will probably be necessary to arrive at the correct position of the slot which engages the distributor drive. When finally fitting the oil-pump, a thin paper washer and jointing compound between pump body and crankcase will ensure an oil-tight joint. The long spigot fixing of the distributor body ensures freedom from oil leaks at this point without any special precautions other than cleanliness.

CHECKING OIL CIRCULATION

Whilst checking the assembly for free and correct running, it is worth while carrying out a final check of the oil circulation, so that the sump can be put back before any gremlins get in! To do this, having fitted the oil filter and pipes as previously detailed, place the engine on the bench in such a position that the crankshaft can be turned by hand and the big-ends inspected simultaneously. Turn off the tap on the oil filter which connects to the pressure gauge. Block up the outlet from the overhead-valve gear pipe by means of a small plate and packing washer bolted thereto. Then fit the suction pipe to the pump and prime it with clean engine oil by means of a squirt through this pipe. Immerse the end of the suction pipe in a pan of the same oil, and turn the engine slowly through several revolutions, when, if all is well, the oil will be seen emerging from all four big-ends.

When refitting the oil sump, a paper washer of the type already described should be used between the flanges, together with jointing compound. If the washer is manufactured, make sure that all the necessary holes are cut, in particular those for the oil-drains. Do not use undue force when tightening up the nuts on the sump studs, as they are only $\frac{1}{4}$-in. diameter threads, and see that the spring washers have been replaced thereon.

CHAPTER 8

Replacement in the Chassis

LINING-UP THE CLUTCH. REPLACING THE CYLINDER HEAD.
ENSURING OIL-TIGHTNESS. REPLACING THE INLET MANIFOLD.
CLEANING OUT THE RADIATOR. IGNITION TIMING.
CLUTCH ADJUSTMENT.

It may be considered advisable at this stage of assembly to replace the engine in the chassis, particularly if lifting tackle or a few extra pairs of hands are available to cope with the extra weight of the complete unit. The main thing to watch is in connection with reassembly of the clutch. It is obviously necessary for the clutch-plate splined bore to be co-axial with the flywheel spigot bearing, so that the clutch-shaft will enter without trouble when the housing flanges are lined up. For this purpose it is necessary to use a mandrel of a diameter which will just fit nicely through the clutch-plate bore, with one end reduced in diameter to enter the inner diameter of the ball-race in the flywheel centre. If the mandrel is fitted into the ball-race, and the clutch-plate passed over it, the pressure-plate can be bolted up with the assurance that the parts are in correct relative positions. The mandrel can then be withdrawn.

If the above procedure has been carried out, there will be no difficulty in fitting the engine back in the chassis, in more or less the reverse order to that in which it was removed. Put a spot of oil on the clutch-shaft splines and the end which engages the spigot-bearing, and see that the engine is level on its underneath support. There is no washer between the clutch-housing flanges, and these can be pulled together very carefully by two suitable nuts and bolts, after first ensuring that the clutch-shaft has properly entered the centre of the plate. (Incidentally, reassembly is invariably much easier than disassembly.) When the flange has pulled up properly, the flange bolts can be fitted. The front nose-piece is fitted to the front housing with a paper washer and jointing compound. It will in all probability be advisable to use a new rubber sleeve on the clamp to the front cross-member.

The above procedure is, of course, the same whether the engine is only partially or completely assembled. We will now consider the other work necessary to complete the job of engine assembly.

REPLACING THE CYLINDER HEAD

Unless the cylinder head gasket is damaged, it should not be discarded. There is no virtue in using a new gasket for any other reason. Also, unless the reader possesses uncommonly comprehensive facilities for ensuring absolutely " super " faces on head and block, no attempt should be made to use any form of thin gasket to raise the compression. The proper way to do this is to machine the head as already described. In short, there is nothing to beat a well-seasoned standard gasket. Before fitting the head, apply high-melting-point grease to both faces of the gasket; this will give a 100 per cent. tight joint, with the head perfectly easy to remove next time.

Before finally tightening down the head, examine the camshaft-drive coupling above the dynamo. With No. 1 piston at firing t.d.c., and the dynamo coupling fork pointing fore and aft, the camshaft-drive coupling fork should naturally point left-and-right with both valves on No. 1 cylinder closed. The coupling disc should be perfectly flat, and not distorted in any way. If there is any discrepancy, modification of one or both coupling forks is essential to ensure that there is no end-thrust on the shafts. This condition usually arises if the head has been planed, thus lowering it in relation to the dynamo.

Assuming that all is well in regard to the coupling, the head can be tightened down. The correct order of attack on the holding-down nuts is given on page 12.

When tightening, use the normal ring-spanner, having about a 6-in. length of lever. Use plenty of force on this, and the tension will be right. If the job is done once and for all in the correct manner, there will be no need to " go round the nuts again " in the time-honoured manner. This procedure usually boils down to over-tightening the relatively few nuts that can be conveniently got at when the engine is assembled, and probably does more harm than good. Anyway, it is not necessary.

The camshaft drive having been permanently coupled up, a final check can be carried out on the valve timing, which is as follows:—

Inlet opens 15 deg. before t.d.c.

Inlet closes 55 deg. after b.d.c.

Exhaust opens 50 deg. before b.d.c.

Exhaust closes 20 deg. after t.d.c.

Overlap 35 deg.

A rough check can readily be made by using a circular protractor or " timing disc " attached to a wooden shaft driven into the starting-handle dog centre and protruding through the nose-piece so that it can be seen without difficulty. The check need be no more than rough, as the number of teeth on the bevels ensures that one tooth error makes a lot of difference in timing, although it might be mentioned that the engine can be made to run in this condition! Arrange a pointer attached to the front cross-member in a position that at t.d.c. of No. 1 cylinder the pointer zeros on the protractor. Then check the readings by watching the cam action on No. 1.

Ensuring Oil-tightness

Having checked the valve timing, attention can now be given to the all-important cylinder-head details. First, the oil-feed. As already mentioned, the oil-feed hole in the head which receives the main supply pipe is fitted with a restrictor pin to drop the pressure to a suitable degree for supplying the camshaft and rocker-shafts. If there is any doubt about the correctness of the existing restrictor pin the dimensions should be checked. If the pin is damaged, or has had to be forcibly removed from its hole due to seizure, a new one can be made without difficulty by those with machining facilities from brass rod. The dimensions are as follows : —

Diameter of hole = 0.25 in. Tolerances : plus .0005 in. minus zero.

Diameter of pin = 0.25 in. Tolerances : minus .0005 in. minus .001 in.

A " Flat " is carefully ground on one side of the pin, and obviously the size of this flat determines the quantity of oil which passes. When finished, the width across this flat should be :

.221 in. Tolerances : plus zero. Minus .001 in.

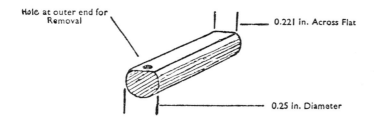

Cylinder head oil feed-restrictor pin. (Tolerances on dimensions are given in the text.)

As regards the length of the pin, this should be such as will allow the pin to protrude appreciably from the head casting when it is fully home in the hole; it should, of course, not protrude sufficiently for it to foul the oil-pipe top junction when this is bolted down. If to complete the job, a small hole is drilled across the pin diameter near this protruding end, this will facilitate future removal, as a piece of wire can be looped through the hole with which to pull the pin out without damage.

When fitting the oil pipe—and this applies also to the various oil-drain pipes from head to sump—use washers made out of thin red fibre plus a light application of jointing compound. The pipes are secured to the cylinder head by through-bolts, and these should have washers of red fibre fitted between the flat steel washer under the bolt-head, and the oil-pipe fitting. These details will ensure oil-tightness.

The alloy water take-off pipe and the exhaust manifold will not present any difficulty. If the makers' packing washers are not available, the appropriate type of heat-resisting material should be used for making the joint for the latter—Hallite or similar. Brass nuts must be used on the exhaust manifold studs to facilitate future removal. Steel ones are almost certain to seize on the threads.

REPLACING THE INLET MANIFOLD

The induction manifold is fitted minus the carburetters, and with a paper washer between the flanges. Air leaks are fatal at this point, so make sure the aluminium face is not damaged, use a light film of jointing on the washer, and tighten up the five nuts evenly and firmly. Flat spring washers are used under all nuts and, in particular, on the nuts which are fitted inside the manifold opposite the carburetter ports. The washers here should be of a size which will allow them to register nicely in the recesses turned to receive them.

The carburetters present no snags in fitting, again using paper washers. Take care that the manifold studs are of correct length, otherwise they may foul the carburetter body and prevent the flange faces from meeting properly. As regards the carburetters generally, a separate chapter is devoted to their overhaul.

CLEANING OUT THE RADIATOR

Before replacing the radiator, give it a thorough swill through with a hosepipe. If there seems to be a lot of foreign matter about, it is worth applying one of the well-known radiator cleaning mixtures.

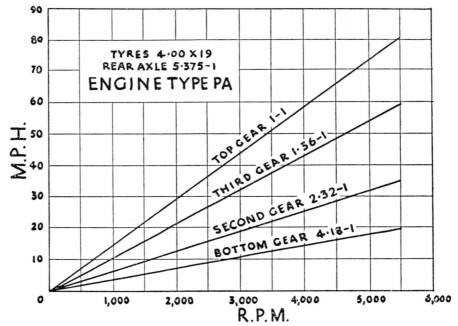

R.p.m./m.p.h. curve, PA type

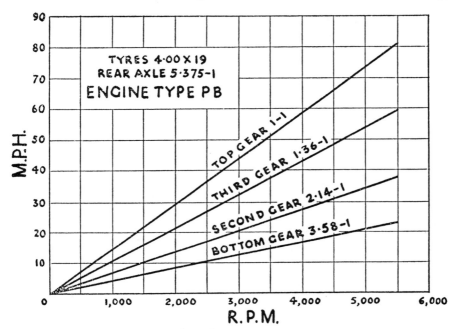

R.p.m./m.p.h. curve, PB type

These are usually specified for insertion in the cooling water when the engine is running, but equally good results can invariably be obtained by plugging the radiator inlet and outlet pipes, filling it with a stiff dose of the mixture in boiling water, and leaving it to do its stuff. A good hosing with clean water will then complete the process.

Radiator hoses should be replaced if at all doubtful. The top hose in particular has a hard life, due to the right-angle bend therein. It will be found that the rubber eventually starts to peel off at this bend, on the inside. The correct type of bent hose is now obtainable, but in the past, cases of scarcity were overcome by making up a metal right-angle adaptor piece for use with two short straight pieces of hose of appropriate diameter. The tip is mentioned in case for some reason a bent hose cannot be obtained. If such an adaptor is used, have a good one made with a proper radiused bend. "Stovepipe" plumbing and right-angles without curves are unsightly.

Use new hard rubber washers for seating the radiator on its bottom platform, and tighten up the nuts moderately so as to leave a little resilience in the rubber. If properly wired or lock-nutted, the fixing will stay put. The attachment of the radiator top plate to cylinder head needs no comment.

Fitting of the hose connections will be facilitated if a light smear of vaseline is put on the inside of the hose before it is slid on to the pipe stubs, and this will do no harm. The pipe stubs should be clean and free from adhering shreds of old hose. When the clips are fitted, do this neatly. Fit the clip at the end of the hose, and do not over-tighten the clips in such a way that the hose is strangled. Remember that if the hose is fitted correctly and is the right size, it should form a leak-proof joint even without a clip.

IGNITION TIMING

With work on the carburetters completed, as detailed in Part III, and their correct fitting to the induction manifold carried out as previously described, we are now just about ready for a preliminary start-up. Before taking this action, there are a few final checks to be made.

Firstly, the ignition timing. Examination of the flywheel through the clutch inspection aperture will show that, approximately 1½ in. in advance of the TDC marking for cylinders 1 and 4, there is an " Ign " marking. If this mark is located centrally in the aperture by movement of the crankshaft, the contact-breaker points should be just about to break on the appropriate cylinder, and if necessary the distributor body must be rotated to arrange this. The final setting will, of course, have to be determined on the road, but this rough timing will be sufficient for the preliminaries.

The contact-breaker gap was originally specified as between .015 in. and .018 in., but it will in all probability be found that a smaller gap, of say .012 in., will give better results. This again can be settled under service conditions.

The owner may have his own pet make of sparking plug, and so long as he uses the correct type for the engine, all will be well. The makers of the car favour Champion L10 for fast work, and a gap of .018 in. to .020 in. gives the best results.

As regards the valve-rocker clearance, this is finally set when the engine has attained its normal running temperature. All we want just now is plenty of running clearance, and if all rockers are set at about .010 in., this will be safe.

CLUTCH ADJUSTMENT

It will be as well to adjust the clutch-withdrawal mechanism at this stage, as the setting will have been disturbed during the overhaul. The disengagement is effected by means of four spring-loaded fingers, or levers, actuated by a fabric-faced disc adjacent to the thrust race. Each of the four levers has its own adjusting screw, and it is essential that all four are equally adjusted. With everything correct, it should be possible to insert a gauge having a thickness of 3/16 in. between the fabric-faced disc and the thrust race. It is also easy to check that the four fingers have been dealt with equally by noting whether the disc wobbles axially when the crankshaft is turned. It should, of course, rotate perfectly true, so that when the pedal is depressed, the thrust race meets it squarely. There is no difficulty in arriving at correct adjustment with a bit of patience, but a worth-while tip when carrying out the setting, is to anchor the spanner, gauge, and any other tools used, with a length of string to some external object. It is extremely difficult to retrieve such objects from the depths of the clutch housing! The gauge required can easily be made from a strip of mild steel filed to the required thickness. Incidentally, the clutch lubrication is by grease gun to the nipple provided, using Duckham's Hardy-Spicer grease, or similar. Do not overdo this; every 2,000 miles is ample, and only a little at that.

Whilst on the subject of clutches, a few notes for owners of older models may be helpful, as these differ from P/PB cars in many respects. Types M, D, J, and F require the clearance measuring at two places; that is, between the extremities of the fingers and the ball-race (3/32 in.), and between the adjusting screws and the thrust pins (.010 in.). Some of these clutches also have oilers for the thrust race, and need attention—a few drops of engine oil—every 500 miles.

So much for the clutch. The rocker-box can next be replaced, but need only be lightly tightened down as it will have to come off again after warming-up. Before fitting it, just have a final look around the head to see that all is correct. Then couple up the tachometer drive, and the other miscellaneous items such as dynamo and starter wiring, controls and so forth.

CHAPTER 9

Starting Up the Engine

UPPER-CYLINDER LUBRICATION.
HEAD OIL PRESSURE.   BEARING CLEARANCES AND OIL FLOW.
RUNNING-IN TECHNIQUE.   ADJUSTING THE CARBURETTERS.   IGNITION
TIMING " SPOT-ON."   LIFTING THE HEAD.

A spot of engine oil, or of your favourite upper-cylinder lubricant, in the fuel, is a good thing. With regard to the latter, it is as well to obtain the M.G. factory's advice, particularly where graphited brands are concerned. It is essential that the battery is in first-class condition for the preliminary start, as the engine may have to be buzzed round for quite a time before anything happens; on the other hand, it may fire immediately. After checking all oil levels and radiator water, a start can be essayed. If nothing happens after a reasonable interval, have a look round, and verify that fuel supply and " sparks " are O.K. Faulty timing is invariably accompanied by easily recognizable " noises off " ; so we will assume that a start is in fact accomplished, and that all four cylinders go into action. Note the oil pressure immediately; this should be about 60 lb. when hot, but with a reconditioned engine will be considerably higher for the first few miles. In any case, do not worry about the reading so long as it is well up; with the oil cold it may go over the 100 mark, but should fall as the engine warms. If it does not, attention to the relief valve spring may be advisable, but that can wait for the moment.

After a few minutes' running, the rocker-box should be whipped off, and the engine restarted with it removed to check that oil is reaching all the cam-follower ends; it is undesirable to run the engine too long, or too fast, with the cover removed, as oil is apt to spray all over the place, and makes the discovery of genuine oil leaks, if any, more difficult. If any of the cam-follower oilways are not passing lubricant, which is most unlikely at this stage, recourse must be made to the squirt and special pointed nipple mentioned earlier. This should do the trick, but if the worst happens and the hole will not clear, there is nothing for it but to dismantle the component. Do not leave it in the hope that the pressure will clear the obstruction in due course. It won't.

HEAD OIL PRESSURE

However, assuming all is well, replace the rocker-box and run up the engine at 1,000 to 1,200 r.p.m. until the oil is nicely warm. Incidentally, the oil pressure in the cylinder head system, i.e., on the " head " side of the restrictor pin, is about 5 lb. per sq. in. Obviously, this pressure is not unduly critical, the only thing being that if the restrictor passes too much oil, it is liable to drop the pressure through-out the system, as well as passing far too much to the camshaft and valve-gear, with the likelihood of oiled plugs as a result of valve-stem leakage. Too low a pressure in the head is again undesirable, but so long as there is visual evidence of plenty of oil on the bevels and cam gear, there is no need to worry.

This point regarding oil pressure in the head is emphasized in case the restrictor pin hole has been brutally drilled out oversize, so that a standard pin, or one made to standard dimensions, will not do. In such cases, it is possible to bush the hole to allow of a standard pin being fitted. A simpler plan is to make an enlarged pin, and grade the " flat " thereon by trial and error, until a pressure of approximately 5 lb. is obtained in the head oilways. This pressure can readily be measured by connecting a gauge to the oil hole which will be found on the right-hand side of the head near the front. This hole, normally blanked by a hexagon plug, is screwed ⅛ in. B.S.P. thread, and fitting a suitable union will enable an ordinary oil gauge to be piped thereto.

To continue with our preliminary " light run " ; when everything is warm, remove the rocker-box again, and adjust the cam-follower clearances. The method of adjustment has already been detailed; very little movement is necessary on the spanner applied to the eccentric rocker-bushes, and the clearance is measured with a feeler gauge between the cam and the follower. Allow .006 in. on inlet cams and .008 in. on exhaust cams. Don't forget the spanner is moved down to take up clearance, and with careful movement the exact setting can be gauged to a nicety. Finally, tighten up the clamp screws with a small spanner; being lock-washered, they do not need undue force.

As already mentioned, with the oil at normal running temperature, the pressure should be 50/60 lb. per sq. in.; if a higher pressure persists, it is advisable to remove the pressure relief valve spring and grind off, say, half a coil to reduce pressure. If this does not bring it down sufficiently, grind off a little more. Theoretically, the relief valve should by-pass at 80 to 90 lb., so that at any oil temperature (except under extremely cold conditions) the pressure should not exceed this. In practice the ideal is rarely attained, and it is sufficient to see that the pressure at normal running temperature is adequate. With new bearings, naturally, the " cold " pressure will be higher than usual, but this does not matter so long as it does not persist. Too high a pump pressure for extended periods may cause undue wear of the pump drive gears, and puts an excessive strain on pipe unions. The writer must ask to be excused if he seems to be labouring the point, but there is a lot of misapprehension regarding oil pressures, and it is sometimes a signal for alarm and despondency when two otherwise identical cars show pressure readings differing by, perhaps, 20 lb. under identical conditions. The point is that there is no particular virtue in running a pressure greatly in excess of the normal figure, and that the latter can vary within surprisingly wide limits without the slightest harm.

BEARING CLEARANCES AND OIL FLOW

Very slight variations in bearing clearances can affect the resistance to flow, and hence the pressure, to a surprising degree, but if circulation is maintained to ensure that the oil film remains intact (which means sufficiently to dissipate the heat) all is well. On the other hand, an abnormally low pressure such as one gets on worn engines, is of no use, since the oil supply escapes through the excess clearance on the non-loaded side of the bearing, whilst the film on the loaded side becomes overheated, and breaks down.

It should be mentioned that pressure gauges are easily damaged, and if there is any doubt about the accuracy of the one fitted, it is essential to check it against an accurate one. Finally, the sump holds one gallon of lubricant, and racing oil (e.g., Castrol R) is not recommended for anything but racing (and this means "real" racing!). Stick to the recommended mineral brands.

RUNNING-IN TECHNIQUE

It can now be assumed that the car is on the road, and that running-in is about to commence in earnest. Most enthusiasts are familiar with the technique of running-in, but a few notes may be of value. The time-honoured notion of 500 miles at 30 m.p.h. and then full-bore *ad infinitum* is still adhered to in some regrettable cases. The correct technique is, of course, to combine a rigid r.p.m. "ceiling" with common sense in the use of the throttle. Do not attempt to accelerate fiercely, and do not hang on to a high gear; just let the engine spin freely at all times, using a small throttle opening for the most part. Occasionally, let it have a good dollop of gas for a few hundred yards, then snap back the throttle so as to get the oil up the bores.

For the first 500 miles, restrict r.p.m. to 2,000; from 500 onwards to 1,000 miles, progressively increase the permitted r.p.m., using a general maximum of 3,500 to 4,000 towards the end of the period; after this, so long as everything feels perfectly happy the car can be cruised at 3,000 to 3,500, and occasionally run up to maximum on the gears for short periods. From then onwards, it is just a question of being sensible until at 2,500 miles the motor should be ready for anything. It is as well to keep the mixture somewhat on the rich side for the first few hundred miles, even if the engine idles somewhat irregularly in consequence. The idling speed should be kept in the region of 1,000 to 1,200 at all times.

ADJUSTING THE CARBURETTERS

After about 500 miles, it is time to adjust the carburetters and to correct them for synchronism. Once set, they should remain O.K. indefinitely, as even if minor adjustment to the mixture strength is dictated later by outside conditions, this will not affect the synchronism, as the degree of adjustment will substantially be the same for both instruments.

Reference has already been made to the special chapter dealing with the S.U. carburetter, and information regarding the correct technique for carburetter synchronism will be found therein, this being applicable to all twin-carburetter M.G. engines.

During the first 2,000 or so miles running of the overhauled engine, while things are getting bedded-in, the rocker-box should be removed once or twice to ensure that the lubrication is satisfactory, and that all the cam-followers are receiving their quota. The valve clearances should also be checked once during the period. When it is found possible to hold high r.p.m. for extended periods without distress, it is time to get the ignition timing spot-on. It is impossible to lay down a hard-and-fast timing; many words have been written showing how to arrive at the theoretical ideal, including the use of flashlight bulbs and batteries to indicate the precise moment at which the breaker points open. Such experiments, while interesting, are valueless for our purpose. The best road performance can only be arrived at by varying the setting under power. The normal timing as indicated by the timing marks already mentioned, serves as a perfectly good starting point, and in fact gives generally good results. Individual engines are, however, sensitive to a particular setting, and this is best arrived at by gradually advancing the firing point, by moving the distributor head a little at a time, between test runs. In this connection, a manual control is a great help, and can readily be arranged by Bowden cable and lever. Alternatively, a vernier type of adjustment can be fitted to the distributor head; this fitting is standardized on later types of M.G. and many other cars.

IGNITION TIMING " SPOT-ON "

It is not too easy to describe in words the " feel " of the correct ignition point. Excessive advance produces roughness which may give a false impression of pep. One should not be misled by this, as it is harmful. Under conditions of excessive advance, it will be found that the engine revs freely on the lower ratios but will not " bite " on the next higher ratio as it should. It will be realized that the engine is not designed to pull at very low speeds, and performance should always be assessed on the top half of the r.p.m. scale, that is, above about 2,700 r.p.m. If more than very slight pinking is evident when pulling away from this engine speed, using moderate throttle, a slightly retarded setting is advisable. Heavy-footedness will always produce pinking on these engines at moderate revs.

Having arrived at the stage where we have a run-in engine with carburetter and ignition in 100 per cent. adjustment, it is advisable, at say 4,000 miles, to remove the head and see that all is well. The removal is mainly for examination of the cylinder bores, but the opportunity should be taken to remove the carbon from piston and cylinder heads. There is no need to remove the valves, as the faces and seats can be examined by rotating the camshaft, using a suitable tool (such as a large adjustable spanner) on the vertical shaft coupling fork, to do this. Unless something is amiss, the valves should not need grinding, under normal usage of the engine, more often than about 8,000 to 10,000 miles. The type of fuel used has, of course, some bearing on the distance.

LIFTING THE HEAD

Readers who may wonder what we expect to find on removing the head, are answered by one word, " Nothing." It will in all probability be either that, or something rather serious such as a tight piston, but the latter is unlikely unless obvious symptoms have shown up when running. A look-see showing that all is well has a powerful moral effect though, and for this alone is well worth while.

Refitting of the head proceeds on the same lines as already described, and valve clearances should be carefully checked and adjusted if necessary at this stage, after which the engine is ready for anything.

The b.h.p. output of the 850-c.c. P-type engine is about 35 at 5,500 r.p.m. with standard compression ratio. The figure will, of course, bear comparison with most other sports engines, but is worth quoting if only for the reason that the earlier o.h.c. engines were given type-numbers, in line with most cars of the period, which were tacitly assumed to represent the taxation rating and the actual b.h.p. For example, the original M type was known as the " 8/33 " while a 1,271-c.c. six-cylinder of similar vintage was called the " 12/70." If one investigates the make-up of these examples, it will be apparent that there could not possibly be any grounds for thinking that the higher figures were the actual engine output, but lots of folk did. Of course, the robust construction of the P-type engine lends itself to considerable increase in output.

The standard gear ratios are as follows:—

| Gear | 850-c.c. P-type | | 939-c.c. PB-type | |
	Ratio	M.p.h./1,000 r.p.m.	Ratio	M.p.h./1,000 r.p.m.
Top	5.375	14.73	5.375	14.73
3rd	7.31	10.83	7.31	10.83
2nd	12.46	6.35	11.5	6.89
1st	22.48	3.53	19.24	4.12
R.	22.48	3.53	19.24	4.12

CHAPTER 10

The P-Type Chassis

THE GEARBOX. ROAD SPRINGS AND SHOCK-ABSORBERS.
THE BRAKES AND OPERATING GEAR. THE CONTROLS AND STEERING.
CONCLUSION.

As far as keeping the engine in a state of satisfactory maintenance is concerned, the requirements do not differ from those demanded by any other good engine. This point is mentioned because there is a wide impression amongst the uninitiated that M.G. engines have to be continually " fiddled with " to keep them in tune. Nothing could be further from the truth, and if M.G. owners do seem at times to spend quite a lot of hours on maintenance, it is simply because they are giving a decent motor-car its due.

Plug- and contact-breaker gaps should be looked at and adjusted if necessary at reasonable intervals, say every 3,000 miles. Fuel filters may need cleaning at much longer intervals, depending on the state of the tank's interior, and the quality of the fuel. Carburetter pistons must be kept free, which implies frequent and moderate oiling with light cycle oil. And that just about covers ordinary maintenance, apart, of course, from the regular changing of engine oil, and cleaning or renewal of the oil-filter element as already indicated.

With regard to the remainder of the chassis, whilst this embodies features peculiar to the car, it is generally of normal construction, and there is no need to go into details in connection with such standard items as, for example, the rear axle and differential. There are, however, a few rather special features which may be worth mentioning, and a few random tips given will be of service.

The propeller-shaft universal joints are of the usual Hardy-Spicer type; earlier cars have a plain bush pattern requiring lubrication at the nipples provided, while later cars have the current needle-roller type which do not require any attention. The former are inclined to develop a " clonk " after a fair mileage, even with adequate lubrication, but no other adverse effects seem to appear, while the noise is only obvious with the hood up. Renovation is easily carried out, and, of course, the needle type can be fitted if the owner desires and funds allow.

The gearbox is an extremely reliable piece of mechanism, with constant-mesh third gear of double-helical type. The sliding-pinion first and second ratios seem impervious to brute force, and it is far easier to break off the gear lever at the roots than to damage the gear teeth. Hence, apart from draining and refilling as specified by the lubrication chart, there should be no need to delve into the internal economy of the box, but if it is desired to investigate, dismantling is

55

a perfectly straightforward operation. This latter remark also applies to the rear axle.

ROAD SPRINGS AND SHOCK-ABSORBERS

The road springs are unusual in that instead of being shackled at one end, they use a sliding trunnion. This is a valuable .feature as it makes for great lateral rigidity. Dismantling of the trunnion is an easy operation, and the construction will be self-evident. Side play is, of course, taken up by removing metal from the face of the bronze block in which the spring-leaf slides. Blocks which are badly worn all round can be readily renewed, new blocks being made up of phosphor-bronze round bar suitably slotted, and not forgetting the oil hole in the block adjacent to the oil pipe.

It is essential for the welfare of these trunnion mountings that they are properly protected from the weather. As fitted originally, each one has a neat rubber gaiter, but these inevitably perish in time. New ones have been obtainable, and although their fitting entails removal of the spring, this must be done. Any short-cuts such as splitting the gaiter with a knife and then taping it into position (frequently done) is an insult to the car, as well as being unsatisfactory, as the result is not waterproof. In case of a dry-up in the supply of rubber gaiters, an extremely satisfactory substitute can be made in the form of lace-up leather covers. The design of these may be left to the ingenuity of the owner, but they are most efficient so long as plenty of overlap is allowed at the lace-up joints, and no attempt is made to produce a neat job at the expense of weatherproofness.

The Hartford shock-absorbers fitted to the front axle are well up to the job, and only need keeping clean and the pivot pins tight. The Luvax rear shockers are not too clever, probably because they are hardly adequate for the short, high-frequency movement. (This refers to those fitted as standard.) Hartfords at the back make a big difference to the car, and are well worth fitting, as, alternatively, are one or other of the latest types of damper now available.

The grouped-nipple lubricating system is grand while it works. Failure, which seems to occur with age, can be traced to bulged pipes, congealed lubricant and faulty nipples. If all these are present, no great hardship is entailed if the pipes are scrapped and nipples screwed direct into the various lubrication points. Restoration of the system to its original efficiency simply involves a lot of patience and work, and the acquisition of the necessary components.

THE BRAKES AND OPERATING GEAR

The cable-operated brakes, working in 12-in. drums, are extremely effective if properly adjusted. Due to their size, the shoes are easily handled for re-lining, and the correct die-pressed linings are readily available. The shoe anchor pins are nutted at the back of the brake plate, and removal of the nuts allows the shoes to be withdrawn without any hub dismantling.

In case of defective brake cables it is preferable to renew the complete unit—cable and casing. If for any reason this is impracticable, and a new inner cable only is fitted to an existing casing, the nipples must be brazed in position, not soldered. Adjustable screwed stops are provided at both ends of each casing, but those at the chassis end must always be screwed right home, and all adjustment of individual cables made at the brake end. The reason for this recommendation is that it is possible very largely to gauge, by the position of the stops, how each brake is sharing the load, but to do this it is necessary for all the stops at the chassis end of the cables to be in the same relative position.

Normally, brake adjustment is done on the single master adjuster on the pedal shaft; the hand brake is similarly adjusted by its appropriate wing-nut. To obtain perfect balance it will in all probability be necessary to make use of the individual cable adjusters, but there should not be very much difference in their positions. A pretty accurate approximation of balance can be obtained with the wheels on jacks in the garage, but for the final touch there is nothing to beat taking the car to a cinder-surfaced space and practising a few crash stops, noting which wheels lock, and the ensuing changes of direction. Careful attention to the individual adjusters will enable a dead-square pull-up to be obtained. In this connection, make sure that the rear brakes do their fair share, and don't be tempted to have the fronts overdoing it. Remember that the front suspension is very stiff, and therefore if the " nodding " effect beloved of modern tinware is remotely present under heavy braking, it is very likely that the front brakes are coming on too soon in advance of the rear. This causes excessive stresses in axle and springs, and must be attended to. It is not in the least difficult to obtain a nicety of balance between front and rear, and once arrived at, the setting need never be lost; all adjustment for wear can be made on the master adjuster.

If rubber gaiters are fitted between the casing ends and the brake cam-levers, these should be kept packed with grease, otherwise they are liable to hold water, to the ultimate confusion of the cable end. There is really no need for such gaiters, so long as the exposed cables are kept liberally greased, and one advantage of having the cables exposed is, of course, that they can be readily examined for fraying or other ills. The hand-brake lever is rather far forwards, and it is possible to make up an extension to clip round the tubular lever, carrying an auxiliary lever back nearer the driver's hand. A much neater method, which is admirable if the driver favours a fairly forward seating position, is to slack back the hand-brake adjuster so that the lever operates only on the last few notches of the ratchet in the " on " position, and to modify the " off " stop at the forward end of the ratchet so that the lever does not go so far forward in the " full-off " position. With this modification, it is necessary to watch the hand-brake adjustment rather more carefully, as the permissible lever movement has been considerably reduced, but this is no particular hardship, and the lever will be found to come to hand much more readily.

THE CONTROLS AND STEERING

As regards the cockpit controls, the remote control gear lever may require attention; a mysterious rattle emanating therefrom on very second-hand vehicles may often be caused by the omission of the long coil compression spring which goes between the underside of the lever ball-joint and the toggle fitted to the horizontal actuating shaft. The lever will actually work without this spring in place, but rather indecisively. The spring required is about 3 in. long when not compressed, and should be quite flexible, and not too strong. Fitting such will cure all rattles from this part.

The slow-running control comprises a horizontal rod along the remote control trunnion, screwed at the bulkhead end and engaging in a tapped hole in the bulkhead bracket. The threads being of small diameter, and rather too fine, are likely to strip after some considerable use. A vast improvement and permanent cure can be effected by re-tapping the hole in the bracket $\frac{1}{4}$-in. Whit., cutting off a few inches of the rod at its screwed end, and brazing thereto the appropriate length of steel rod threaded $\frac{1}{4}$-in. Whit., to engage in the bracket hole. With this modification, it will be found that far less twiddling is necessary to obtain the right slow-running setting.

Steering gearboxes fitted to the P types are of Marles-Weller or Bishop make, the latter being generally most satisfactory. Trouble is mainly caused by using grease instead of gear oil for lubrication, this causing rapid wear of the drop-arm shaft and bearing. Replacing parts, or suitably bushing, will remedy this. Correct adjustment inside the box is obtained by the use of shims under the cover, in the case of the Bishop box, and very fine adjustment can be obtained with the unit on the bench and empty of oil. The aim is to obtain the merest trace of free movement between the conical connection which engages the cam, and the cam itself, with the gear in the position corresponding to straight ahead. If this is achieved it will be found that the degree of free movement increases slightly towards the full-lock positions, due to the shape of the cam which is designed with this in view.

The Marles gear, which was fitted to very early cars of this range, does not lend itself to " orthodox " adjustment for taking up wear, replacement or renovation of parts being the only cure for excessive play.

CONCLUSION

In Part I of this book, we have covered just about the major items concerned with the renovation of a typical small M.G. of the o.h.c. type. Many readers engaged in work on examples of these cars will no doubt come across their own particular snags, and it is obviously not possible to cater for every contingency nor to suggest remedies for all the ills that befall motor-cars which may have been through the hands of several owners. It is considered, however, that sufficient information has been given to enable work to be undertaken on the right lines. To anticipate possible disappointment in regard to the omission of " secrets of tune," it should be mentioned that it has always seemed to the writer that this magic word " tuning " is much abused. Literally, it is suggested that it implies only that all the engine components are working in tune to the maximum advantage. It should not be used to describe drastic modifications or departures from the standard specification such as fitting a blower or mechanical alterations to valve gear. It might be asked, quite naturally, just what there is to do to tune an engine, if such modifications are ruled out.

The answer is that, providing all the components have been dealt with as already described, there will not be much amiss with anything. Careful matching-up of manifolds and ports, and polishing of induction passages and valve ports (without alteration to their shape) will show to good advantage. Suggestions have already been made in regard to compression ratio. Anything beyond this should come under the heading of a " modification," and how far one should go depends entirely upon the use to which the car is to be put.

Such departures from standard are always somewhat experimental, and in any case do not differ in essentials as between one type of engine and another, although naturally, some engines will stand more than others! The P and PB engines lend themselves admirably to the fitting of triple valve springs, blower installations, and so on.

PART II

CHAPTER 11

Push-Rod Engine Types and Characteristics

A MORRIS BASIS.   WHERE THE POWER COMES FROM.
PRELIMINARIES TO ENGINE REMOVAL.   REMOVING THE POWER UNIT.
THE ENGINE MOUNTINGS.

The first M.G. Midget engine using push-rod-operated overhead valves appeared in July, 1936; its introduction was the signal for much heart-burning on the part of M.G. enthusiasts, who had long regarded the overhead camshaft as a traditional feature. Naturally enough, these enthusiasts were not prepared to take the new model at its face value, and it is proof of the quality of the type, that it very quickly won over the most hard-bitten " camshaft " supporters, mainly because, whilst retaining all the desirable M.G. features, its larger engine, providing more pulling power right up the scale whilst losing little in the way of revving ability, made the car more likeable on fast cross-country journeys. The roomier body and more comprehensive all-weather equipment rendered the vehicle, on the whole, a better proposition for the all-round driver, whilst its competition record shows that nothing has been lost on that score.

History repeated itself to some extent with the introduction of the M.G. Midget Series TA, as it was designated. Just as the original M-type Midget of 1929 used a virtually standard Morris Minor o.h.c. power unit, so, in the case of the TA, the current Morris Ten-Four engine formed the basis. Again, as in the case of the M type, the disadvantages of retaining too much of the basic engine, when applied to a sports car, gradually became apparent under the stress of hard usage, and with the passage of time the push-rod T-series engine, originally producing around 45 b.h.p., has been developed to a state whereby, with no alteration to major components, nearly 100 b.h.p. (supercharged) is available.

Shortly after the introduction of the Series T Midget, further additions to the M.G. range were made, all having push-rod engines. The larger engines, however, did not undergo the development work which was applied to the Midget, and were in fact not continued in production after the outbreak of war in 1939. In many respects their design followed the lines of the TA-type engine, so that owners of the larger models will find much of interest and assistance in these pages. As a preliminary, it will be helpful to detail the range of push-rod overhead-valve M.G. engines with which we are dealing.

The last two models above are current at the time of publication. In addition to those listed, there were a few " specials " built for

Year	Maker's model	Mark	Cyls.	Bore mm.	Stroke mm.	Capty. c.c.	B.h.p./r.p.m. (Peak) approx.
1936/9	Midget	TA	4	63.5	102	1292	45/4800
1936/9	2-litre	S.A.	6	69.5	102	2322	80/4800
1937/39	1½-litre	VA	4	69.5	102	1548	55/4800
1938/9	2.6-litre	WA	6	73.0	102	2561	100/4800
1939	Midget	TB	4	66.5	90	1250	54/5200
1945/50	Midget	TC	4	66.5	90	1250	54/5200
1947	1¼-litre	YA	4	66.5	90	1250	46/4800
1950	Midget	TD	4	66.5	90	1250	54/5200
1952	1¼-litre	YB	4	66.5	90	1250	46/4800
1953	Midget	TF	4	66.5	90	1250	57½/5500
1954	Midget	TF 1500	4	72	90	1467	63/5000

competition work but still incorporating components taken from the range; for example, the 1938 " Cream Cracker " trials cars, which used a modified 1½-litre VA-type engine in the Midget chassis. Although such variations from standard did not reach the public in any number, there is no doubt that many conversions have been carried out by enthusiasts, so that buyers of used M.G.s of the pre-war period may occasionally come across an interesting example.

In dealing with the push-rod engines, it is proposed to detail the work on the TA engine, in general, separately from the other Midget types, since, in spite of its superficial similarity, the TA unit differs in many important respects, which call for a different technique in dismantling and so on. The TB, TC, and most TD units are identical except in very minor details which do not affect anything that matters, whilst the 1¼-litre engine fitted to the saloon-bodied Y model is to all intents and purposes a de-tuned version of these engines.

WHERE THE POWER COMES FROM

One of the objections raised by the overhead-camshaft supporters, at the introduction of the TA M.G. was that it was such an " ordinary " engine. This was perfectly true, but its 45 b.h.p. from 1,300 c.c. was very good in 1936, and more than sufficient to endow the car with a lively personality. With its very long stroke, non-counterbalanced crankshaft, and rather heavy flywheel, it was happiest when pulling a fairly high-gear ratio, giving effortless high-speed cruising. Undeniably, however, the factors which provided this most likeable characteristic mitigated against really high revolutions and that capacity for zipping up and down the r.p.m. scale which had been such an outstanding feature of the o.h.c. engines. The basic design was sound enough, and the redesigning carried out in 1939 as the result of three years' experience in the stern field of competition work was sufficient to provide in the TB and later engines, units which, whilst retaining the flexibility and much of the pulling power of their predecessor, have that zest for revs and unburstable feel which M.G. owners consider their birthright.

All T-type engines are compact and rigid constructionally, with ample bearing area. The cylinder-head design provides for good breathing capacity, with large ports giving an easy flow, whilst a " squish " feature promoting turbulence is incorporated in the combustion chamber. As regards the essential differences between the TA unit and the TC (taking the latter as representative of the later types), which lead to such enhanced potentialities in the case of the latter, it will be of interest to tabulate these briefly.

Item	Engine type TA	Engine type TC
Cubic capacity	1,292-c.c.	1,250-c.c.
Bore	63.5-mm.	66.5-mm.
Stroke	102-mm.	90-mm.
Bore-stroke ratio	1.607	1.354
Standard compression ratio	6.5 to 1	7.25 to 1
Standard output (b.h.p.) at peak r.p.m.	45 at 4,800	54 at 5,200
Valve layout	Single row, vertical	Single row, inclined
Camshaft drive	Roller chain, no tensioner	Roller chain, with tensioner
Inlet porting	Two siamesed, no baffles	Two siamesed, with baffles
Exhaust porting	3 ports, central siamesed	4 ports, separate
Exhaust manifold	3-branch	4-branch
Crankshaft	3-bearing, non-counterbalanced	3-bearing, counterbalanced
Main bearings	White-metal, shell-type	White-metal, shell-type
Big-end bearings	White-metal, direct on rod eyes	Thin wall
Oil-pump intake	Floating suction strainer	Rigid suction strainer
Type of clutch	Single-plate, cork-insert in oil	Single-plate, Borg and Beck, dry

The T-type engines can be manhandled without undue trouble, providing some assistance is available; it is also a good idea to reduce the overall weight by partially dismantling, before attempting to take the power unit out of the chassis, and if this is done, special lifting tackle is not necessary.

PRELIMINARIES TO ENGINE REMOVAL

The radiator mounting is similar on all T-type cars. The first operation is to remove the bonnet, and drain the cooling system by means of the taps at the base of the radiator and the off-side of the cylinder block. Should the taps be stubborn to turn, do not force things, but unscrew the whole fitting from its boss and put on one side for attention. Next remove the nuts and bolts which secure the headlamp brackets to the radiator, after which a little " wangling " will enable the brackets to be slipped out of the radiator supports, while leaving the brackets attached to the mudguards. Uncouple the two tubular tie-rods which run from the bulkhead to the top of the header tank, and remove them completely. The two nuts (and locknuts, if fitted) which secure the bottom of the radiator block to the lugs on the front cross-member can now be removed, leaving the radiator perfectly free.

In the case of the TA engine, the top water connection should be broken at the flange joint below the thermostat, leaving the hose in position. It will in all probability be necessary to lift the radiator slightly as the flange nuts are unscrewed, as the nuts may foul the thermostat body as they travel up the studs. Before breaking this joint, the forked metal water-pipe and the three smaller-diameter hose connections between radiator bottom, cylinder-head rear, and by-pass, should be removed completely. If the hoses are stuck, remove the clips completely and apply a thin knife blade between the pipe and the hose, plus a squirt of petrol. This procedure will free the hose without trouble.

In the case of the other T-type engines, a similar procedure is followed in removing the forked pipe forming the bottom connection, water-pump inlet, and by-pass. The top connection is broken at the flange on the cylinder-head front, four bolts securing this. After attending to the above points, the radiator can be lifted clear.

REMOVING THE POWER UNIT

As already mentioned, it is advisable to do some partial dismantling before lifting out the engine, if the latter has to be manhandled. As the task of actual engine removal is very similar in all T types, this will next be dealt with. Engine dismantling will demand different sections devoted to the TA and TC units, and the owner may decide for himself how much of this dismantling can usefully be done before taking the engine out of the chassis.

It may be possible, by bending things and similar clumsy methods, to get the engine out without attention to all the preliminaries recommended here. It is, however, doubtful if any time will be saved in the long run, and it is obviously much more satisfactory to do the job properly and also take the opportunity of having a look at other parts of the chassis even if these are not the direct concern at the particular time.

The first thing, then, is to remove the interior amenities of the body, comprising seats, carpets, gearbox cover, and floorboards. It is no reflection on the car, particularly if it has been well used, to say that an essential tool for this operation is an electric drill of a size taking up to $\frac{1}{4}$-in. diameter hole; this is for use if, as will probably be the case, the nuts and bolts securing the floorboards to the chassis side-members are immovably rusted in place. These can be drilled out in a few minutes, and are easily replaced, preferably with brass ones.

On the inside edges, the floorboards are secured by bolts screwed into bosses on the propeller-shaft tunnel. These may also prove obstinate enough to demand the same treatment. If, in so doing, the threads in the bosses are damaged, bolts with nuts can be used for replacements without detriment to the fixing.

The next item to remove is the ramp-plate, which is the plate surrounding the clutch housing. It will be noted that this is bolted to the bulkhead structure. Before finally lifting it out, after removing the screws around its edge, it is necessary to uncouple the battery wiring, and all harness cables where they are attached to the plate. Detach also the plate securing the steering column rubber muff, and the throttle pedal gear. On TA types the clutch withdrawal rod must be removed from the actuating lever (it can be left hanging on the pedal), whilst on the TC, the operating chain is uncoupled at the pedal end, and the clutch pedal slid off its shaft after removal of the split-pin and washer. It should now be possible to lift the ramp-plate out, though, on TC types in particular it may be necessary to bend it slightly to get it past the brake pedal. However, this is no detriment if care is taken.

The Engine Mountings

Various engine accessories such as manifolds, starter motor, control cables, tachometer drive and so, will have to be removed; details of these operations are given in the chapters dealing with engine dismantling. The gearbox cover complete with remote control is then removed (taking care in the case of the TC not to lose the three selector-lock springs and balls which are housed in the back flange), and also the propeller-shaft tunnel.

Before uncoupling the propeller-shaft flange from the gearbox, mark the two flanges with white paint so as to ensure that they go back in the same relative position. This marking is most important, but use paint, not a cold chisel!

Next, block up under the power unit so as to take the weight; this should be properly done with wooden blocks or similar; a jack is quite useless, and likely to cause damage if it slips. The blocks should take the weight sufficiently for the rear bolts, gearbox to rubber mounting, to be removed. The engine earthing cable, if fitted, and the speedometer drive also have to be uncoupled. Finally, the nuts should be removed from the front mounting, after which the power unit is ready to be lifted clear.

If it is desired to remove the engine without the gearbox, or vice versa, practically the same procedure is followed, except that, at the last, the bolts around the clutch housing periphery are removed. The unit which is to be left in the chassis is supported on independent blocks, and its attachment to the chassis is left in position; the other unit can be removed after parting at the clutch housing flange.

There are no snags to splitting this flange joint in the case of the TC, except to ensure that everything is kept parallel. In the case of the TA, however, it is necessary to take the clutch lever off its shaft, to which it is held by a key, plus a taper pin which can be driven out from the small end. This enables the clutch withdrawal fork to swing clear of the withdrawal ball-bearing as the box is pulled back. Also, the spigot ball-bearing in the flywheel centre may tend to stick, so that a little judicious levering may be necessary, but so long as care is taken all will be well. This does not apply to the TC, as a plain bush bearing is used at this point.

So much for general details regarding power-unit removal which apply to the whole T range. We will next consider the dismantling of the type TA engine.

The TA crankcase, with oil-pump, distributor, camshaft and tappet block dismounted.

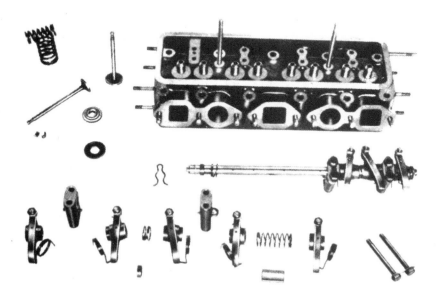

The TA cylinder head and valve mechanism.

TA camshaft drive, showing "timing" links in correct position on marked teeth.

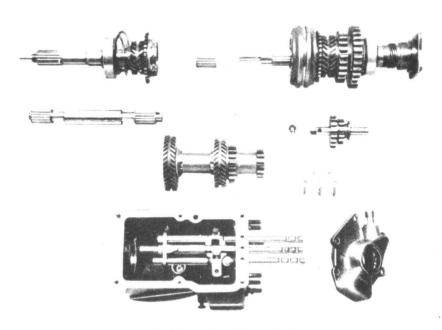

The TA gearbox dismantled.

CHAPTER 12

Dismantling the TA Engine

THE PRELIMINARIES.   CYLINDER HEAD REMOVAL.   THE REMAINING
ACCESSORIES.   CONNECTING RODS AND PISTONS.   THE CRANKCASE
END-PLATES.   CRANKSHAFT REMOVAL.   THE ROCKER-GEAR.

The construction of the TA-type engine is quite straightforward,
and no difficulty will be experienced in dismantling providing a
sensible sequence of operations is followed.

Starting on the off-side of the unit, the first thing to be tackled is
removal of the manifolding.   Fuel piping and float-chamber overflow
pipes come off first, after which the carburetters can be unbolted from
the inlet manifolding (their controls having been uncoupled) and lifted
off as a pair, taking care not to bend the throttle interconnecting
couplings or shaft.   The next item should be to uncouple the exhaust
manifold flange from the pipe, but this often proves obstinate due
to partial seizure of the nuts on the studs, and the difficulty of getting
sufficient spanner leverage.   If this happens, take off the bracket
holding the exhaust pipe to the clutch housing just below the bend;
this will leave the pipe free, as it has a flexible insertion in its length.
If next the manifold bolts are removed, the inlet pipe can be lifted off
and the exhaust manifold pulled away from the engine sufficiently
far to allow of reasonable access for plenty of leverage on the aforementioned flange nuts.   If one of the flange studs is twisted off in
removing there is no need to worry as it can be replaced by a nut and
bolt after drilling out the remnants.   The next components to be
removed are the o.h.v. rocker-box, the water-pump complete with fan,
and the dynamo.   Incidentally, careful note should be taken of the
location of various bolts and studs, when dismantling, as their length
varies, in some cases only slightly, so that they are easily misplaced.

CYLINDER HEAD REMOVAL

The distributor cover complete with H.T. leads can be removed,
and the distributor unit withdrawn; it is secured by one bolt which
anchors the split clamp surrounding the neck of the body.   The spark
plugs should be left in position for the moment.

When the oil-feed pipe from the crankcase to the cylinder head has
been taken off, this will leave the head clear of all external attachments.   Before tackling the holding-down nuts, however, it is necessary
to have the push-rods out of the way.   A special tool is available for
enabling each rocker in turn to be depressed, allowing the push-rod
to be slipped out from under its ball-end at the adjustment end of
the rocker.   This tool is normally for use in cases where it is desired
to leave the rocker-shaft in position, for instance when carrying out a

simple top overhaul. It is considered preferable, and well worth the
slight extra trouble even in those cases, to take off the shaft complete;
this, of course, leaves all the push-rods free to be withdrawn, and
makes the valves much more accessible, as well as facilitating a
thorough examination of the whole rocker assembly.

The four rocker-shaft standards are secured to the head by two
long bolts in each; these bolts have a common locking strip which is
bent over to engage a flat on each bolt-head. After flattening down
these strips with a hammer and drift, the bolts can readily be withdrawn. To prevent the rocker-shaft being unduly stressed under the
influence of the valve-spring pressure, it is best to undo each bolt a
little at a time, so that pressure is taken off the shaft as evenly as

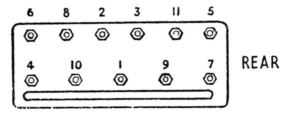

Order of attack, cylinder head nuts, TA engine

possible, and all the bolts are withdrawn together. The bolts should
be left in position in their holes so as to retain the special washers
in the rocker-standards, and the whole assembly put on one side for
future attention. The push-rods can now be lifted out, and kept in
their proper order; this is readily done by punching eight numbered
holes in a sheet of stiff card, and threading the rods through the holes.

The cylinder-head nuts can next be undone, there being eleven of
these. The correct spanner, providing twelve angles of attack is
necessary, and can be obtained from M.G. dealers. The nuts should
be removed in the correct order, which is that used for tightening-up,
and is as shown on the diagram.

If the head is stuck, be careful not to damage the gasket by
unguarded attempts at levering it off with a screwdriver. As the spark
plugs have not been removed, a few turns with the handle will invariably lift the head by compression pressure. If this does not work,
make sure that no nuts have been overlooked! Keep the head level,
and lift it over the studs. Finally, remove the gasket, taking care not
to tear the soft copper as it passes over the stud threads.

THE REMAINING ACCESSORIES

The cylinder head having been removed, it can be put on one side
as a unit for further attention in the future. The next stage in the
dismantling of the engine is the removal of the remaining fitments,
but at this point it might be as well to take out the steering column
on the assumption that the engine is to be removed from the
chassis. The operation of removing the column is quite straightforward. The drop-arm should be slid off its splines, it being necessary

completely to remove the pinch-bolt, as it locates in a groove in the shaft. The column bracket is held to the chassis by three nuts and bolts, and should be taken off at this point. (It is not possible to withdraw the single bolt securing the steering gearbox to the bracket.) After removing the steering wheel, the baffle board and the clamp round the column under the scuttle, the assembly can be withdrawn from the front of the car. The starter motor is next removed after uncoupling its cables and undoing the three securing bolts.

Turning to the other side of the engine, the dynamo bracket, breather pipe, and tappet cover are readily removed in that order, the method being obvious. The oil-pump is secured by six long bolts which also locate its cover. When the pump body is drawn off the crankcase, it is probable that the shaft carrying the pump idler gear will remain in its hole in the crankcase, so that a hand should be kept ready to catch the idler gear in case it slips out. The idler shaft should then be removed (it being an easy push fit), and the whole pump assembly kept together until required. The oil-pipes and filter present no difficulty. After draining the sump, its removal is simple, all the bolts being accessible with the exception of those tucked up at the back behind the flywheel housing; even these, however, being screwdriver-slotted, are readily withdrawn.

At this stage, it will be clear that quite a lot more dismantling, including connecting rods and pistons, can be carried out with the engine still in the chassis. For a thorough overhaul, removal of the unit, as already described, is essential, and if the procedure for removal is carried out at this stage, it will be found that the engine has been lightened sufficiently for it to be manhandled without too much expenditure of energy.

CONNECTING RODS AND PISTONS

The engine should be laid on its side on the bench, and suitably blocked up to bring it level and secure. The floating oil-pickup is best taken out of the way at this stage, so it should be unbolted at its junction with the main casting (two screws). The split-pins should next be removed from all the big-end bolts, and the nuts unscrewed. Mark each connecting rod big-end eye on the two mating halves, with paint, before removing the big-end caps (no centre-punch marks, please!) and keep the caps in the correct order of cylinders when removing. The connecting rods complete with pistons can be withdrawn one at a time, the crankshaft being turned to allow the assembly to come past each crank as required. As soon as the rods are out, replace caps and nuts, each on its own rod, and paint-mark the rods for identification by cylinders.

The gudgeon pins are rigidly held in the connecting rod small-ends, which are split and provided with a clamping bolt for the purpose. This bolt will be pretty tight, and it is essential when unscrewing it not to put any twisting strain on the rod, as would happen if the latter was gripped in the vice. A good method is to obtain a mandrel which is a good push fit in the hollow gudgeon pin, and clamp the mandrel firmly in the vice. The piston and gudgeon pin is then fitted over the mandrel, taking care not to scratch the piston skirt against the vice. The clamp screw can then be removed, using a box or socket spanner. As the clamp screw passes through a recess in the periphery of the gudgeon pin, it is necessary to withdraw the screw completely; the pin can then be pushed right out of rod and piston. An alternative to the mandrel method is to obtain two brass end-pads which can be inserted into the ends of the gudgeon pin, and which have plenty of metal extending beyond the piston skirt, so that the vice jaws can be nipped firmly against the pads without danger of them coming in contact with the piston.

Before the crankshaft can be taken out, there are several preliminaries. First, the flywheel has to come off. The clutch presents no difficulty, as the cover-plate, springs and pressure-plate come away as a self-contained unit, complete with the withdrawal ball-race and hub, after undoing the ring of bolts around the flywheel periphery. The cork-inserted clutch-plate will now be in view, and before this can be removed, the large C-shaped circlip must be sprung off the three long studs which will be seen protruding through the plate near the centre. Then, the plate can be lifted off.

The flywheel is secured to its crankshaft flange by four bolts and two dowels. The former will probably be extremely tight, and nothing but a really first-class socket spanner will look at them. Even with such a tool, much bending of tommy-bars may ensue. If the nuts defy all orthodox efforts, take a man-size chisel and hammer, and " start " them in the brutal manner. Naturally, new bolts will be needed on reassembly, but there is no need to damage any other parts with this form of attack. These same bolts serve to hold the retaining plate for the spigot ball-bearing in the flywheel centre, which plate also carries the three long studs and " pusher " springs which help to free the clutch-plate when declutching. The flywheel can then be prised off its flange and dowels without difficulty.

THE CRANKCASE END-PLATES

Removal of the flywheel provides access to the bolts holding the back end-plate, or flywheel housing, to the crankcase, and this should come off next. There are several retaining bolts, so make sure none is overlooked.

At the other end of the unit, the front end-plate also forms the engine bearer. The fan pulley must first be removed, using a box spanner on the hexagonal starting-handle dog. The pulley is keyed, and is usually a fairly easy push fit, and thus presents no trouble in levering off. The camshaft drive cover is taken off next, exposing the timing chain and wheels. The retaining bolt for the camshaft wheel should be removed; this will allow the crankshaft and camshaft wheels, together with the duplex roller chain, to be drawn off as one unit. The chain must not be uncoupled, but must remain endless. The bolts holding the crankcase end-plate to the case can now be unscrewed, and the plate pulled off its two dowels.

CRANKSHAFT REMOVAL

The front and rear main bearing caps have bridge-pieces over them, to form the necessary continuation of the sump machined joint surface. These bridge-pieces are located by cheese-headed screws recessed flush with the surface, and removable by means of a hefty screwdriver. The bridge-pieces can then be levered out, exposing the bearing caps. Removal of these, including the centre one, demands an adequate spanner, but otherwise is simple. The crankshaft can then be dismounted.

Before removing the camshaft, the two tappet blocks should be removed complete with their tappets. They are dowelled as well as being bolted, but are a light push fit only, on the dowels. The tappets cannot fall out, as they are circlipped at their upper ends. The camshaft centre bearing has to come out with the shaft, and is retained by a screw which will be found just above the oil-gauge connection on the oil gallery. If this screw is withdrawn, the camshaft can be drawn out from the timing-drive end. The shaft will pass through the front bearing and will, of course, pull out of its back bearing. The split centre bearing will come out of its housing along with the shaft, and once clear of the housing it will fall clear. To avoid damage to the bearing surfaces it is as well to arrange some sort of padding inside the crankcase for it to fall on; alternatively, a piece of wire can be passed round it when it is just clear of its housing, and a groove will be found on the outside of the bearing for this purpose. This is, of course, most useful when replacing the bearing.

This completes the dismantling of the main components, and it will be logical to complete the sequence by describing the operations involved in taking down the o.h.v. gear.

THE ROCKER-GEAR

The rocker-shaft and rockers have already been removed to facilitate push-rod removal. The valves can therefore be tackled next. These are of normal type with a split-cone fixing in the top spring collar. The earlier TA types had double valve springs, a subsequent modification, and a worth-while improvement being the fitting of triple springs. (This modification will be described in detail later.) A really hefty valve-spring compressor is necessary. When using this, if considerable screw-pressure fails to shift the collar off its split-cones, give the top of the compressor a light tap, which invariably has the effect of jarring the parts free. At the same time, be careful not to cause the compressor to slip—this can be dangerous.

Keep all the springs, top collar, bottom cap, and split-cones for each valve together, and, of course, keep the valves in the order of removal from the engine. It will be found necessary, before the inlet valves can be dropped out of their guides, to remove from each a spring ring located in a groove just below the collar. This can be sprung out with a knife blade, and its useful purpose is to prevent the valve from dropping in, in the event of the collar letting go. To complete dismantling of the head casting it is as well to take off the rear water-pipe elbow, which will allow the water passages to be cleaned out. The same applies to the oil-pipe union at the rear (near-side).

The rocker-shaft is, of course, hollow for lubrication purposes, and seems to collect quite a lot of sludge which is much better out of the way. It will be noted that, of the four rocker-shaft standards, the two middle ones are slotted sideways, the slot containing a washer which engages a keyway cut in the shaft to prevent it turning. Naturally, the washers are held in place by the through-bolts, and with the bolts out, can easily be shaken free of the standard and shaft. Removal of one of the large hairpin retainers at the shaft end will then enable all the components to be slid off the shaft, care being taken to keep them in the right order for reassembly. A few early cars were fitted with rocker return springs, but they can be left off without detriment on reassembly.

CHAPTER 13

Examination and Renovation

THE CRANKSHAFT AND BEARINGS.   CYLINDER BORES, RINGS AND
PISTONS.   ATTENTION TO THE VALVES.   THE INDUCTION PIPE.
CYLINDER-HEAD MODIFICATIONS.

Before commencing a preliminary inspection, it is necessary to get everything to a proper state of cleanliness, and for this purpose, the outsize metal container referred to in the Introduction at the beginning of the book, should be called on, together with accessories such as stiff paint brushes of various sizes, oil-squirt, and so on.

There is no objection, of course, to leaving certain items, which are not immediately concerned, to " soak " while others are being dealt with, so long as, when their turn comes, cleanliness is above reproach.   Examination of components may well commence with the crankshaft and its bearings.   If the shaft has done a biggish mileage, it will show signs of scoring on both main and big-end surfaces.   It is false economy in such a case to renew the bearing shells only (plus a connecting-rod exchange), as such a step will give only a very temporary improvement in smoothness of running.   Incidentally, excessive bearing wear is recognizable not only by a considerable drop in oil pressure, to around 20 lb. hot, but also by a periodic vibration at high speeds which seems to run through the engine in a regular rising-and-falling rhythm.   A competent M.G. specialist will be able to grind the shaft, and provide a set of service connecting rods and main-bearing shells metalled to suit.   Make sure that the work is entrusted to someone who appreciates the necessity of maintaining the correct bearing clearances.   As in the case of the P-type engines, the connecting rods must not be machined on the cap faces, but should be handed in for exchange; the new ones must be metalled to the required depth to suit the reground crankpins.

The small-ends, which, of course, have no bearing surfaces to worry about, have one point of note, in that when unscrewing the gudgeon-pin clamping bolt, the latter sometimes loses all its threads in the process.   This is due to the fact that the bolt engages a recess in the pin, with very little clearance, against which the threads may chafe when removing.   It is sound practice to renew these clamping bolts whenever they are disassembled.

The connecting rods, as standard are well finished, and unless the engine has obviously been in the wars, and shows signs of a major mishap, correct alignment of rods may be taken for granted.

CYLINDER BORES, RINGS AND PISTONS

Some clue to the condition of the bores and pistons will, of course, have been given by the behaviour of the engine before dismantling.

71

Thanks to the rapid warming-up provided by the thermostat in the cooling system, and the layout of the water circulation, not forgetting also the positive oil spray to the cylinder bores on the thrust side, from the big-ends, the TA engines are able to put up extremely good mileages before requiring reboring, 45,000 miles being quite a common figure before oil consumption becomes excessive and oiled-up plugs troublesome. Piston slap when cold will, of course, have been noticeable before this, but is not in itself a handicap to performance.

However, the best way of deciding what attention is required to this part of the engine is to do some checking-up. This process is substantially the same irrespective of the type of engine, and thus a section devoted to the technique will be found later on in Part III of this book.

As regards the pistons, some early cars, up to and including engine number MPJG 696, were fitted with pistons having a plain skirt and four rings, comprising two compression rings and an oil ring with angle ends (all above the gudgeon pin), plus a second oil ring, with square ends, and pegged to prevent it rotating, below the pin. Engines with numbers commencing MPJG 697 had the familiar Aerolite pistons with three rings, two compression and one scraper. The latter are, in general superior, and there is, of course, no objection to fitting the later type when reconditioning the bores.

ATTENTION TO THE VALVES

Assuming that the cylinders and pistons have been dealt with as determined by their condition, attention can next be given to the cylinder head. The valve guides should be examined, bearing in mind that quite a lot of clearance is permissible between stem and guide, and unless ovality is obviously present, should not be taken as excessive wear. By far the best way of settling any doubts is to obtain a new guide of each type, plus a new valve, and compare the clearances thus obtained with those existing on the engine. If the difference does not amount to more than about .002 in. wear on the existing guides compared with the new (checked, of course, as *new* valve and guide against *old* valve and guide), there should be nothing to worry about in this direction. Should it be decided that renewal of the guides is worth while, the removal of the old guides and refitting of the new ones should be entrusted to an M.G. specialist, who will have the necessary special tools and press.

Naturally, should any of the valves show signs of pitting or burning, they should be renewed. Exhaust valves are rather prone to this, particularly if long mileages are covered between top overhauls. Valve seats last a very long time without being recut, but if excessive grinding has resulted in them being pocketed, they should be recut by a professional, otherwise there will be much restriction of gas flow.

While this part of the engine is under review, it will be as well to take a look at the valve ports. These are perfectly smooth as standard, but time is well spent, as far as the inlet ports are concerned, in polishing with emery cloth. The same can be done with the exhaust ports, but these are not nearly so important.

The Induction Pipe

The alignment of the induction pipe with the two cylinder ports may leave a little to be desired. Due to the shape of the former, it is not easy to determine just how far " out " the flanges are in relation to one another. However, a good method is to bolt the flanges together, with a sheet of white cartridge paper between, having first smeared the flanges with graphite. The pipe apertures will, upon parting the flanges, be found clearly defined one on either side of the paper, and this will show where metal should be removed to give the best alignment. It should be noted that if it is just not possible to obtain a perfectly smooth passage from pipe to port, any " step " should be " down " into the port, i.e., the port should be larger than the pipe opening. This will ensure that globules of fuel do not pile up against a ledge, as would happen if the error was the other way round.

As regards the exhaust side, the same work can be carried out in matching-up the exhaust ports and manifold. There is no need to go to extremes in obtaining accurate lining-up, so long as the entry ports to the manifold are a shade larger than the cylinder exit ports. As the manifold is of very hard material, a flexible-shaft grinding wheel equipment is much to be desired at this stage.

Cylinder-head Modifications

The combustion chambers are machined very satisfactorily as standard, but are of a shape lending itself to quite a bit of extra polishing, which is a matter for the patience of the reader. A more important point, which might well be considered while the head is free from accessories, is the question of compression ratio. The original compression ratio of the TA, like that of its o.h.c. forebears, was rather on the low side at 6.5 to 1. A ratio of 7.3 to 1 is not too high even for " pool " fuel, so long as the car is driven intelligently, and not expected to slog. This ratio is obtained by machining off sufficient metal to give a head depth of 3.292 in. instead of 3.386 in., or, strictly speaking, 0.094 in. However, it is much simpler to request the machinist to plane off 0.1 in., and the difference is negligible.

This increase will provide a worth-while addition to the performance, but it is not recommended that any higher ratio is attempted, as it may lead to unduly rapid bearing wear with the standard (non-counterbalanced) crankshaft.

In 1938-9, some TA types used ratios as high as 8 to 1, but special fuel was necessary, and in addition, counterbalanced shafts were generally fitted. Unless, therefore, really drastic modifications are contemplated, it is better to be content with the figure given earlier. This completes the work on the head casting, it being assumed that the water and oil passages have been cleaned out satisfactorily. Quite a lot of scale can, incidentally, be removed from the former by digging with a sharp probe to loosen it, and then flushing with one of the chemicals marketed for the purpose.

CHAPTER 14

The TA Overhead-Valve Mechanism

ASSEMBLING THE VALVES. THE ROCKERS AND ROCKER-SHAFT.
ASSEMBLY OF THE ROCKER-GEAR. THE CAMSHAFT AND
ASSOCIATED PARTS.

Having renewed any valves which are beyond redemption, we can now consider the assembly of these items. The first step is to polish the valve stems with superfine emery cloth, and then to grind them in, following the usual course and finishing off with metal polish. Grinding is, of course, necessary even if the valves are new, or the seats have been recut.

Early cars had rough-finished valve springs which were apt to break, and these were superseded by polished springs which cured this particular defect. However, a further trouble which was very prevalent on engines fitted with double valve springs was valve bounce and sticking, which could be a most annoying fault. This was completely rectified by the fitting of triple springs, which also gave a useful increase in performance. The modification is, of course, easily carried out on engines which have double springs, and merely involves obtaining and fitting the new parts, which are as follows (per valve) : —

Part No. M.G.	734/261	Spring, outer.
,, M.G.	735/262	Spring, middle.
,, M.G.	735/263	Spring, inner.
,, M.G.	706/444	Top cap.
,, M.G.	706/443	Sealing ring.
,, M.G.	735/265	Seating washer.
,, M.G.	706/76	Push-rod.

The push-rods are modified to take the extra loading of the triple springs, and no attempt should be made to economize by retaining the existing rods, otherwise breakage will result.

The split-cone cotters should be examined to ensure that they seat firmly in the top caps, and are not sunk unduly below the cap surface to an extent which makes pulling right through a possibility. Trouble is unlikely, as the standard parts last indefinitely, but if makeshift spares have been fitted previously, there is a possibility of undue wear, and the cones should be replaced. The fit of cones, valve stem and cap can, of course, be tried prior to assembly on the head. When assembling, make sure that the seating washer, or bottom collar, is firmly down on the head casting, the wire rings are replaced on the inlet stems, and the springs are properly located on both top and bottom collars. Also, a most important point is the fitting of the small synthetic rubber rings on the valve stems below the top caps. These rings are sometimes found to be missing on second-hand engines, but they serve a most important purpose in preventing undue leakage of oil down the valve guides. The easiest way of fitting is by pushing them well down the valve stem initially. Then, when the valve assembly has been completed, apply gentle pressure to open the valve, until it is absolutely fully open. This will ensure that the rubber ring is pushed up the stem to its proper location right under the split-cone.

THE ROCKERS AND ROCKER-SHAFT

As already mentioned, the rocker-shaft is apt to contain quite a lot of sludge; it should be most carefully cleaned, and examined to ensure that its considerable number of oil-holes are clear. The shaft can also be tested for straightness by rolling it on a flat surface. There should be no trouble as regards its accuracy, but occasionally shafts are bent slightly due to incautious removal, or slackening-off one of the rocker-shaft standards.

The rockers are provided with drill-ways for lubrication, which communicate with the rocker-shaft oil-holes via the bushes. The force-feed oil-can should be used to check that the drill-ways are clear, and any bockages must be remedied—a strand of Bowden wire will work wonders in this direction, as the passages are fairly straight. If the rocker-ends which contact the valve stems show signs of much wear, the offending rockers should either be built-up and ground to the original shape, or replaced; preferably the latter. It is possible, when there is not too much wear, to lap the rocker-end on a carborundum stone to provide a better contact surface, but too much lapping will go through the hardening. It is, however, essential to get this contact point right even if it means renewing all the rockers, as otherwise it will be quite impossible to obtain accurate rocker clearance measurements, and side-thrust on the valve stems will be increased.

If the valve seats have been recut, it may be desirable to grind a little off the top of the valve stems, so that the rocker and stem assume the correct relationship. This point can be checked when the rocker-gear is reassembled on the head. Within reasonable limits, the valve stem length is not critical, and unless some discrepancy is obvious it is better to leave well alone. If, with the valve in the half-open position, the contact face of the rocker tip is squarely across the centre of the valve stem, all should be well.

The rocker-shaft bushes have a long life, but, of course, take considerable loading, and shake is disguised somewhat by the presence of the spacing springs, or " silencing springs " as they are aptly termed. Too much play must not be tolerated; the rockers should oscillate freely on the shaft, but side play (in the sense of being able to grip the rocker tip and move it from side to side without sliding the fulcrum along the shaft) must be the absolute minimum. The bushes are easily renewed if necessary, removal being effected by the method of using a long draw-bolt with suitable washers and tubular distance-pieces. The new bushes can be fitted in the same manner, taking care to provide the necessary oil-hole and to line this up with that in the rocker itself. The bushes will require reamering to fit the shaft after pressing-in.

There is unlikely to be any work required on the " adjustment " ends of the rockers, as the ball-ended adjusting screws last indefinitely. They are readily renewed if very much worn, otherwise, an examination of the threads and locknuts is all that should be required.

ASSEMBLY OF THE ROCKER-GEAR

After ensuring that all the rocker-shaft spacing springs, distance tubes and so on, are sound, and all parts perfectly clean, the components can be assembled on the shaft. Examine the back standard to ensure that the main oil-way is perfectly clear, and that this lines up with the hole in the shaft. The correct shaft position is ensured by the two keyways in the shaft, which lie inside the two central standards and are engaged by washers fitted to the bolts passing through these two standards. Once everything is tightened up, the shaft cannot turn. When refitting the large hairpin retaining spring on the shaft end, make sure it is firmly in its groove, but that it can be readily turned round the shaft without any tendency to leave its location. If the compression ratio has not been altered, which can be checked by confirming the head depth as 3.386 in., the rocker-gear is ready for bolting back to the head, the only point needing checking being that the drilled standard has been fitted at the back to line up with the oil-way from the head casting. If the ratio has been raised as already described, however, it is necessary to insert packing pieces under the rocker standards, to bring the rockers to the correct " lie." These packing pieces can be made of mild steel, and must be $\frac{1}{16}$ in. in thickness. The one fitted under the rear standard must, of course, be drilled to coincide with the oil-way.

This completes work on the cylinder head and rocker-gear; it will be appreciated that refitting of the latter to the head must wait until the head is back in position on the block. Attention can next be given to the other parts of the valve mechanism.

THE CAMSHAFT AND ASSOCIATED PARTS

The wearing surfaces of the camshaft are of ample area, and should not show signs of distress even after a big mileage. If new camshaft bearing bushes are considered necessary, it is preferable for these to be fitted in the crankcase by an M.G. specialist, as far as the front and back ones are concerned. The split centre bearing is, of course, readily renewed. However, in view of the large diameter, wear is usually negligible. The cam surfaces may be touched with superfine emery cloth if any minute scoring is seen, but here again, this is most unlikely to be serious. Camshaft end-float is controlled by a flat spring riveted to the timing chain cover interior, and bearing against the shaft-end bolt; this should be examined to ensure that it is secure and sound.

Examination of the gear teeth for oil-pump and distributor drives should be carefully carried out. It is most unlikely that any chipped teeth will be found, unless something very serious has happened inside the engine. Slight roughness on the tooth edges can be dressed with a carborundum slip. Correct meshing of the gears is, of course, automatic, providing reassembly is carried out properly.

The camshaft drive comprises a Renold .375 in. pitch duplex roller chain running on wheels having 25 and 50 teeth, the chain being 64 pitches in length. No tensioning device is provided, so that undue chain slackness must be avoided. Actually, the chain becomes noisy when considerably worn, and is quite audible at idling speeds. About 40,000 miles can be considered a reasonable mileage at which a new chain may be called for. The chain is supplied endless, and must not be uncoupled; there is no difficulty in refitting it complete in position along with the wheels. As regards the latter, they need not be renewed with the chain unless they show very obvious signs of deviation from the correct tooth shape, which can be judged by comparing the shape of the sides of adjacent teeth on both angles. Considerable wear results in a hooked formation being given to the edge of the tooth which is " pulled " by the chain roller.

The camshaft chainwheel is provided with oil holes which lead oil on to the chain from the camshaft bearing, and these should be oil-squirted through to ensure cleanliness. Some engines have a blanking disc against the outside of the wheel to encourage the oil to go where it should, and this should not be overlooked. It is secured underneath the camshaft end-bolt.

The push-rods repay careful examination, as breakages have been known to happen. Test them for straightness, using a steel rule or similar edge, and polish them all over with emery cloth, when, if they are free of hair-lines or other doubtful signs, they can be passed as 100 per cent. reliable. Do not attempt to straighten bent rods; new ones are the only remedy, and these should be tested and polished before installation.

The tappets should give no cause for comment, the large size and ample lubrication making them practically everlasting. The circlips round the upper ends should be checked to make sure they are secure. If desired, they can be removed altogether, but if this is done, refitting the tappet blocks will be a slightly trickier operation.

CHAPTER 15

The Lubrication and Ignition Systems

CHECKING THE OIL-PUMP COMPONENTS. LUBRICATION SYSTEM
DETAILS. THE IGNITION DISTRIBUTOR. REASSEMBLING THE
CONTACT-BREAKER. MISCELLANEOUS ITEMS.

The oil-pump can next receive attention. It is of the usual gear-type with a spring-loaded relief valve housed in the body. The valve is of the ball pattern, its spring being enclosed by a screwed cap.

As the bolts securing the pump to the engine also hold the pump cover to its body, the whole assembly will already be dismantled and open for investigation. Unless foreign bodies have been allowed to get into the pump, there should be no cause for complaint in the condition of the two pump gears. If traces of foreign matter have resulted in slight chipping, this can invariably be remedied by using a carborundum slip. Running clearance between the gears is not unduly important, but a point to watch carefully is the side clearance, which must be the absolute minimum consistent with free running. The side clearance can be tested by temporarily bolting-up the pump to the crankcase using the fixing bolts, which locate in tapped holes in the crankcase casting. Having ensured that everything is absolutely clean, when assembled in this manner without a packing washer between body and cover, the gears should be just a little tight, being nipped between the cover and the body. The use of a packing washer about .001 in. thick will then give the correct clearance. It is worth while spending a lot of time in arriving at the correct clearance, as it can make quite a difference to the oil-pressure. The pump cannot, of course, be permanently reassembled until it is actually being fitted on to the engine, but when this is done the slightest trace of jointing compound should be used on the cover packing washer. If, even without a washer in place, there is too much side clearance, the face of the pump body will have to be reduced in depth. This can be done by rubbing down, using grinding paste on a perfectly flat plate, or, if initially a lot of metal has to come off, a sheet of emery cloth against the plate. Needless to say, in the latter case, the job must be finished off with grinding paste.

A careful investigation must be made of the interior of the cap over the relief valve spring, as this may easily contain an assortment of washers used to pack up the spring. If any are found they must be removed, and the spring replaced without them. If on starting the engine, the oil-pressure is found to require adjustment, steps can be taken to do this legitimately, in the knowledge that all bearings, etc., are in perfect condition. The ball and its seating should be in order, but if the ball seems to have become discoloured due to seating in one place for a long time, it is worth replacing in case leakage is occurring due to it being worn.

The oil-pump driving gear should be examined in the same manner as was detailed for the camshaft gear, and similar treatment applied if necessary. Finally, all threaded holes for pipe flanges, and any other minor " cleanliness " points should receive examination. This completes the work on the oil-pump.

LUBRICATION SYSTEM DETAILS

Apart from oil-pipes and passages, the items concerned with the oil-circulation system comprise the floating pick-up on the suction side, and the Tecalemit filter on the delivery side. As regards the former, this has a hinged elbow which allows a swivelling action constituting the essential feature of the device. It is possible for a suction leak to develop at this point, but it is also difficult to determine just how much effect it is having on the oil-pressure. It is a good plan to let well alone at this stage as far as this point is concerned, unless, of course, there is evidence of a lot too much shake, which is unlikely.

The gauze suction filter, which is under the float when the device is in position, is protected by a metal cover; this is readily removed by carefully prising back its locating lugs. When it is off, it will be possible to remove quite a lot of sludge both from the inside of the plate and from the gauze. Very careful cleaning of the latter is well repaid, as it need be done only at very long intervals, or " major overhaul " occasions.

The pressure filter is a very simple type, with the housing located by a long through-bolt passing upwards through the centre of the renewable filter element. The top of the assembly, which bolts on to the crankcase, contains the oil passages, and also has a spring-loaded disc which normally holds down the element, but which also forms a relief by-pass in case the element becomes solidly clogged. If this happens, the plate is forced upwards, allowing unfiltered oil to pass from the inside of the element to the outside. This will not happen if the element is renewed, as it should be, every 10,000 miles. (After a major overhaul, a new element should be fitted when the first 1,000 miles is up.)

Apart from thoroughly cleaning all parts, and providing a new element, there are no complications in this design of filter. The joint ring in the top, against which the removable pressed-steel body locates, can be renewed if necessary, whilst the fibre washer on the central main bolt should be checked to see that it is sound.

With the crankshaft and camshaft out of the way, it is an easy matter to clean out all the oil passages in the crankcase block, using the force-feed oil-can and plenty of paraffin followed by engine oil. Oil-pipes should be similarly treated, not forgetting the pipe to the oil gauge, which should, of course, be removed completely. The short flexible portion of the oil-gauge line should receive very careful examination, as it is liable to develop a leak after a long time, since there is quite a lot of engine movement to cope with. It should be replaced if at all doubtful, otherwise the sump will be found empty at an inopportune moment.

The oil-pipes will not, of course, be refitted until a late stage in final assembly, but it is worth mentioning here that it is essential always to line them up with their unions before fitting, and not to attempt to pull them into position forcibly by tightening up the union nuts. The only pipe likely to need much pre-bending is the fairly large diameter one from pump to filter, and as this is not very long it should be annealed before bending, by heating to nearly red heat and plunging into cold water. Finally, all brazing on the pipes should be carefully examined, and the obvious remedy applied to any doubtful items.

THE IGNITION DISTRIBUTOR

The next assembly to merit attention is the distributor of the standard coil-ignition system. Use of the correct tools, gentle handling, and absolute cleanliness, are the main essentials in dealing with electrical components, particularly in view of the very small dimensions of many parts. Normal maintenance procedure will, of course, be familiar to readers, and consideration will therefore be given here to the extra attention which puts the seal on a good job.

Having dismantled the unit, all cleaning should be done with a dry cloth, liquid aids being barred. Examine the moulded cover for suspicious cracks, which can be caused by careless removal and refitting. Scrap the cover if these are found, as any repair will not be sufficiently reliable. The internal electrodes should be trimmed with a fine file to remove pitting, if any is present. The central carbon brush should also be checked to make sure that it is firmly gripped by its spring, through which the electrical contact is made, and that it is quite free to slide in its housing.

The rotor should be dressed with a fine file if it shows signs of burning, though T-type engines do not exhibit this trouble to the same extent as earlier models. The rotor clearance to the distributor contacts is not critical, but obviously too much clearance is undesirable, so that a new rotor should be fitted if there is any doubt on this point. The rotor contact area should be finally polished with brass polish all over.

The contact-breaker unit, complete with its base, will have been removed complete, and dismantling will enable all the components to be cleaned. The breaker points should be trued up in the usual way, finishing off with superfine emery cloth. There is no need to renew the spring just for the sake of doing so, as it retains its tension indefinitely, and being of the " bright " type, breakages are very rare. The fit of the rocker arm on its pivot should be checked, so as to be quite free but without side rock. The fibre washer fitted below the rocker arm on the pivot determines the lining-up of the points, and care must be taken that its thickness is such as to allow the points to

The TC crankshaft and bearings.

The TC clutch dismantled.

The TC-type engine, nearside.

The TC-type engine, offside.

meet squarely in line. A trace of engine oil on the pivot will provide a perfect action.

The fixed contact does not call for any particular comment, except that the tongue carrying the contact point which is bent at right angles to the fixing plate, should be lined up at a true right angle to its base when clamped down. If any bending is required to get this right, do it carefully. It is not difficult with the unit on the bench, to get everything absolutely correct, so that the two points meet squarely over their whole area.

All electrical connections such as, for example, that between the condenser and L.T. terminal, should have their contacting areas polished to reduce resistance to the minimum. The opening of the contact points on all four lobes of the cam should be measured, equality of opening being important inasmuch as too great a discrepancy between individual lobes will mean a variation in timing as between cylinders. Carborundum strip can be used to correct this, and if, with a nominal breaker opening of .012 in., there is no greater variation than .010 in. to .013 in., this will be good enough.

The automatic advance mechanism, housed below the contact-breaker, should be cleaned and oiled; otherwise, it is unlikely that any more involved attention will be required. Broken springs in the mechanism are rare, but if one is found, be sure to fit the correct replacement. The main driving shaft wears very slowly, and a small amount of side shake is not very serious. There is an oiler on the side of the housing which will probably repay a good clean-out, and frequent attention subsequently.

REASSEMBLING THE CONTACT-BREAKER

When reassembling the unit, make sure that the screws securing the contact-breaker baseplate to the housing are of the correct length, so as not to " bottom " in the holes, and are fitted with spring washers. This is important, as the screws form an electrical connection. In all cases when tightening small screws, including those securing the contact points, do not overdo things. If normal effort with a small spanner or screwdriver (as required) is employed, nothing will shift subsequently.

The high-tension wiring should be examined carefully. It is very long-lasting, and unless it has been doused with oil, or suffered some such unorthodox mishap, it should not require renewing. If there is any doubt, the replacement material is inexpensive, and it is worth using one of the modern types of cable which have a semi-glazed finish and are impervious to oil and normal heat. When fitting the H.T. cables into the terminals, allow plenty of bare cable end to make adequate contact with the electrodes; surprising ignition troubles can emanate from neglect of this rather elementary point. It is also rather easy for moisture to get down between the milled bakelite union nut and the cable, causing corrosion of the contact beneath. To prevent this, a little shellac, run down between the bakelite and the cable, will make everything waterproof, and assist in further securing the cable.

Similar care in connecting must be taken when attending to the spark-plug connectors. These are frequently cracked during hectic plug-changing, and any found in an unsound condition should be renewed. It is most important that these snap-on connectors fit really tightly on the plug terminals, and a combination of terminal and connector must be found which ensures this.

MISCELLANEOUS ITEMS

There is little difficulty in disposing of the remaining assemblies, comprising the dynamo, starter motor, and water-pump. Apart from the usual commutator-cleaning every 10,000 miles or so, and periodic oiling at the lubricators provided, the dynamo needs no further attention. Neglect of this simple routine may cause more serious trouble. If there is anything amiss, such as a badly ridged commutator, or worn bearings, let " Mr. Lucas " have the job. If on the other hand, all seems well apart from an excess of carbon dust and rather worn brushes, a good clean and brush replacement will be an adequate tonic. Do not touch the commutator unless this is badly blackened, which, if all is well, should not be the case. A commutator in good order with brushes bedding properly, assumes a healthy mahogany colour, and emits a steady whine when running. As regards the starter motor, much the same advice holds good. Thanks to oil picked up by the flywheel gear-ring, the starter pinion and quick-thread have a relatively easy time, and the starter engagement is of unsurpassed smoothness. Unfortunately, these merits are sometimes rather offset by oil finding its way into the starter and gradually creeping along to the commutator end, where it combines with copper-carbon brush dust to form a highly objectionable mixture. This is not always apparent until the starter begins to jib, after which the only cure is a thorough overhaul. Even if this stage has not been reached, and attention to the commutator and brushes is all that seems necessary, it is still better to have the job done by the maker. Due to the heavy current, the commutator invariably needs skimming in a lathe after much use, whilst the brushes are not designed for easy replacement, being provided with sweated connections to the windings.

The water-pump is of the normal type having a carbon-ring sealing-gland. This remains water-tight for a very long time. When it finally gives out, the pump must be changed for a service unit, as a complete assembly. Renewal of the carbon-ring only is a fiddling job, and not worth the trouble in view of the ease of obtaining a replacement pump at little expense.

Assuming there is no trouble with this part of the pump, the only other attention necessary is a good clean, and washing-out and repacking the fan ball-bearing at the front end of the housing. To gain access to this it is, of course, necessary to remove the fan and its nose-piece, and the shaft nut which is exposed after removing the latter. There is no need to extract the bearing; it can be washed out in position, by immersing the end of the housing in petrol and revolving the shaft. It should then be repacked with medium grease. At the same time, the oiler adjacent to the impeller of the pump should be cleaned out. (In early cars, a grease cup was fitted at this point.)

We have now dealt with the various assemblies, and it is almost time to tackle the job of reassembling the engine. Everything should now be in first-class order; all water spaces cleaned up as well as possible, with the aid if necessary of one of the chemical solutions marketed for the purpose. Such cleaning will, of course, include components of the circulation system such as the thermostat, and connecting elbows and metal pipes.

Any doubtful screw-threads, whether on nuts, studs or bolts, should be renewed. A set of the necessary jointing washers and gaskets can be obtained from the works, and it is at all times preferable to use these instead of making them up. If non-availability makes the latter course necessary, use good quality white drawing paper for joints where this type is specified, and other materials as called for. Such washers must be cut to size carefully.

CHAPTER 16

Reassembly of the TA Engine

CRANKSHAFT AND BEARINGS. FITTING PISTONS, CONNECTING RODS AND BIG-ENDS. ASSEMBLING THE CAMSHAFT DRIVE. CLOSING UP THE CRANKCASE. REFITTING THE FLYWHEEL. ASSEMBLING THE CYLINDER HEAD.

With the crankcase upside-down on the bench, the three bearing shells should be introduced into their housings, taking care that they locate accurately, and that their oil-holes line up with the crankcase drillings, feeding the bearings. Run a little engine oil on to the bearing faces, and carefully lower the crankshaft into position, rotating it slowly to ensure that it drops properly home and turns freely.

The bearing shells are next fitted into the bearing caps, care being taken that they register correctly, and the caps slipped over their crankcase studs and pushed down on to the crankshaft. Needless to say, the caps must be put back on the same bearings, and the same way round, as they came off. Before they are right down on the shaft, squirt a little engine oil between shaft and bearing shell, then push the cap home, and run the six nuts on to the studs.

Tighten the nuts slightly, and test the shaft for rotation. It may be a little stiff, assuming that remetalling, etc., has been carried out, but so long as such stiffness is not excessive, and is uniform throughout the shaft rotation, all is well. If stiffness is apparent at one or two points only, it will be due to high-spots on the flanges of the centre bearing, which locates the shaft endwise. These high-spots can be eased down with a scraper, but under no circumstances must the main bearing surfaces, which embrace the shaft journals, be touched in this manner. The cap nuts must next be tightened evenly and thoroughly, using a socket spanner with about a foot length of tommy-bar, assuming average muscular power. When all is tight, lock the nuts with copper wire through the holes in the studs, and twist up the wire with care; tightly, but not so that it is liable to fracture.

The bridge-pieces can next be placed in position over the front and rear bearing caps; they will go in quite easily if they are kept level as they are pushed home. Their locating screws must be tightened well and truly with the largest possible screwdriver.

The camshaft can next be installed. The only snag here is the split middle bearing, which must be put on the shaft after the latter has been inserted through the front bearing. The two halves of the middle bearing are then encircled with wire or string (which must be right) in the groove provided and the whole induced to enter its central housing. As soon as it is well inside, the strings can be untied, and the shaft pushed right home. The centre bearing is then secured by its locking screw from the outside. If the hole for the latter, in the bearing, is difficult to find, it will be necessary to " wangle " the bearing about in its housing, at the same time probing for the hole from the outside of the crankcase, via the locking screw hole. After tightening the locking screw, it must be wired.

The front end-plate and rear clutch housing can next be fitted, using paper washers between them and the flanges, with a moderate application of jointing compound. Bolt up with even pressure, and use lock-washers on the bolts.

FITTING PISTONS, CONNECTING RODS, AND BIG-ENDS

The pistons can next be fitted to the connecting rods. As already mentioned it is advisable to use new clamp screws if the threads are in the least degree damaged. Apply a little oil to the gudgeon pin, and slip it through the piston bosses and small-end of the rod. Very carefully line up the recess in the pin with the clamp-screw hole in the small-end; this is most important, otherwise it is impossible to get the screw home without damage. See that the screw is provided with its spring washer, and when finally tightening, use the same technique as was applied when dismantling, to avoid stresses on the rod or piston. Tighten the clamp screw adequately but not ferociously. Using a box-spanner, a tommy-bar which can be grasped with one hand, T-wise, will be quite sufficient to give all the force necessary.

Before refitting the pistons in the bores, space out the ring gaps equally so that they are as far apart as possible, and anoint the rings and grooves generously with engine oil. With the crankshaft turned to the most advantageous position to allow maximum room, each piston is inserted in its cylinder bore from below. The bore immediately concerned should be given a final pull-through with a hefty wad of felt immediately before inserting the piston, in case there are any stray bits of foreign matter adhering to its surface. Make sure that the gudgeon-pin clamp bolt is towards the off-side (the side remote from the camshaft) of the crankcase, so that the oil spray holes in the connecting rods face the correct way. The holes are, of course, on the same side of the rod as the clamp bolts. After liberally oiling the crankpin, each big-end can be seated, and the cap pushed over the bolts. Make sure the latter are properly down on their registers, which prevent them from turning, and run on the nuts. The latter must be tightened with even pressure and quite firmly, but note that the threads are not large and it is possible to stretch the bolts or damage the threads by too Herculean efforts. In particular, do not be tempted to over-tighten the nuts in an attempt to register the split-pin holes with the nut castellations. If adequate tightening fails to obtain the correct register, remove the nut and lightly grind the surface until the fit is correct.

After fitting each rod, test the crankshaft for free rotation. It is possible, if the rods have been remetalled, for a slight degree of raggedness or overhanging white-metal on the rod edges, to cause undue tightness. The offending area will be readily apparent on removal of the big-end, and very careful scraping will soon remedy matters. It must be emphasized, however, that very great care is necessary here, as the oil-flow through the bearings is largely controlled by the big-end side-clearance. Unless the stiffness is really serious, therefore, it is better to let well alone, as it will soon disappear with the first few revolutions under light load.

When split-pinning the big-end cap nuts, use pins of as large a diameter as possible; cut off the legs to a reasonable length, and bend them back securely round the nuts. Do not leave a superfluous length of pin festooned all over the place.

ASSEMBLING THE CAMSHAFT DRIVE

The keys securing the crankshaft chain pinion and camshaft wheel should be carefully examined. Ragged edges should be trimmed with a fine file, otherwise difficulty may be experienced in refitting the wheels. As already mentioned, the timing chain can be expected to be good for up to 40,000 miles before wear makes it audible. With a new chain, the amount of " slack " when in position is very slight indeed—about $\frac{1}{8}$ in. only. On balance, it is preferable to fit a new

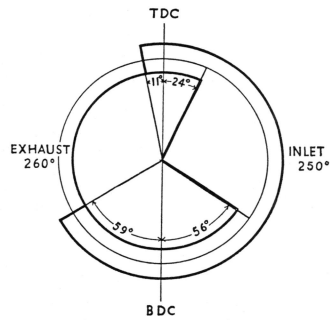

Valve timing diagram, TA engine

chain unless it is obvious that this has already been done fairly recently. Wear on the wheel teeth can readily be gauged by wrapping the chain around as much of the periphery as possible, and judging the amount of play by plucking the chain away from the teeth at one point. Another useful guide is to compare the tooth form with that of a new wheel.

The wheels and chain must be fitted as a unit; before this is done, it is necessary to assemble the chain on the wheels to give the correct timing. The standard chain incorporates two " bright " links, i.e., links with side-plates finished metallic instead of the usual blue colour. Each wheel also has one tooth stamped with a T. The chain must be fitted on the wheels so that the two T-marked teeth engage the two bright links when the shortest length of chain between the bright links is on the upper run of the drive. Actually the number of chain links in the short run is 29: counting the first bright link as No. 1, the second bright link will be No. 29. If by any chance it is necessary to use a chain without the timing links, therefore, it is quite a simple matter to mark two of the links with paint, as above, and then carry out the fitting as already described.

Having assembled the chain and wheels, and ensured that the wheel bores and shaft ends are spotless and their keys in position, slide the wheels carefully on to the crankshaft and camshaft, keeping everything parallel. Although there is very little slack on a new chain, no difficulty should be experienced in carrying out this operation, as all the fits are accurate. However, if real trouble ensues, it is possible to obtain a little more play by washing the chain in petrol before fitting, thus removing all the lubricant. If this is done, liberally oil the chain as soon as it has been fitted. The chain *must* be riveted endless, without a spring connecting link.

The camshaft wheel is secured by its set-screw, which should be fitted with a new lock-washer if the old one is at all damaged. One side of the lock-washer is hammered up over a flat of the set-screw head, whilst the washer is also punched into the hole provided for the purpose in the wheel hub. Do not pierce the washer when doing the latter operation; a deep pimple which goes adequately into the hole, is all that is necessary. In tightening the set-screw, use plenty of force, wedging the crankshaft with a block of wood between a crank and the case to prevent it from turning. It is not possible to fit the fan pulley which finally secures the chain pinion on the crankshaft, until the timing cover is on, and there are a few other points to attend to first.

CLOSING UP THE CRANKCASE

The tappet blocks complete with their tappets can next be fitted; if the locking strips under the bolts show signs of cracking, fit new ones. Then, having carefully reassembled the floating oil intake pick-up, this unit may be refitted, using a new fibre washer on the stand-pipe flange, and locking the flange bolts with wire after tightening them firmly. Give the crankcase interior one last good look round, and refit the sump; if a washer for this has to be made, use a paper one with jointing compound. See that all the sump bolts are fitted with spring washers, and do not forget the screwdriver-slotted ones at the back, behind the flywheel housing. It will now be feasible to mount the engine in an upright position for the remainder of the assembly. In this connection, it might be mentioned that it is usually not too difficult to put the engine back in the chassis, as opposed to taking it out, almost completely assembled. The reason being, of course, that the replacement is assisted by gravity! Naturally, some help is required, but a few boxes at different heights, plus a rope slung over a beam, will serve quite well in preventing control being lost.

Before refitting the timing chain cover, the timing should be checked. This is as follows: —

> Inlet opens 11 deg. before t.d.c.
>
> Inlet closes 59 deg. after b.d.c.
>
> Exhaust opens 56 deg. before b.d.c.
>
> Exhaust closes 24 deg. after t.d.c.
>
> Overlap 35 deg.

A rough check can easily be made by using a circular protractor or timing disc attached in some way to the crankshaft. Any error will be readily apparent, as one tooth makes a lot of difference.

Assuming all is well, the cover can be refitted. A thin cork washer, plus jointing compound, is used for the joint. Before refitting, examine the leaf-spring inside the cover, which controls the camshaft end-play: see that it is riveted firmly to the cover, and shows no signs of cracking. If in doubt, make a new one. When the cover has been reassembled, the fan pulley can be keyed to the crankshaft, giving the same attention to the key as has been described for the timing-wheel keys. Do not overdo tightening-up the starting-handle dog which secures the pulley, as the thread diameter is relatively small considering the size of hexagon, and is quite easily twisted off.

Refitting the Flywheel

Before refitting the flywheel, give it a final examination as regards the condition of the starter-gear teeth. These actually last almost indefinitely, as they receive ample lubrication, and nothing more than a little attention with a carborundum strip should be necessary. After ensuring that all parts are clean, the flywheel may be placed on the crankshaft flange. If, as is probable, the four securing bolts were damaged when removing them, new ones must be fitted: in addition, new dowels are advised, as the removal prejudices the close fit of the original ones. The dowels should be driven in after the bolts have been moderately tightened. Don't forget the spigot bearing and its retaining plate, the latter being held under the bolts. Finally, tighten the bolts with a hefty socket spanner and a foot-long tommy-bar, and when all is tight, pass a locking wire through the holes provided in the bolt-heads.

The clutch plate may be found to have lost a few of its corks. These are secured in their holes in the plate by a special process, and it is not very satisfactory to try to fit odd new ones. A much more satisfactory job is to renew the whole plate, or have it re-corked by a specialist in this class of work. Never replace a clutch plate, the corks of which have worn almost flush with the metal, even if otherwise the plate is perfect. It will only have to be renewed at an early date.

When passed as correct, the plate can be fitted over the three spring-loaded pins protruding from the spigot retaining plate, and the large circlip refitted over the slots in the pin-ends. When refitting this circlip, do not bend it more than necessary. On the other hand, make sure it is properly home in the grooves. It is quite a light fit, but perfectly secure, so long as it is not distorted.

The cover plate, plus the pressure plate, which were, of course, removed in a unit complete with the withdrawal bearing, should not require dismantling unless one or more of the clutch springs are broken—a most unlikely contingency. Assuming that all is well, therefore, replacement is merely a matter of registering the pressure plate on the three flywheel driving dogs and bolting-up the cover plate to the flywheel rim. Centralizing of the clutch plate is not necessary, as it runs in the machined centre of the cover plate, and thus cannot slip out of line except by an amount equal to the clearance at this point. This is not likely to be sufficient to cause difficulty in entering the clutch-shaft. The cover-plate bolts should be tightened with even pressure, and must have lock-washers thereon.

ASSEMBLING THE CYLINDER HEAD

Attention can now be given to refitting the head on the block. There is no advantage whatever in using a new gasket unless this is unavoidable due to damage of the existing one. Also, do not be tempted into trying any kind of " fancy " gasket: there is nothing to beat the standard pattern. Apply high-melting-point grease in a thin film to both sides of the gasket. This, while making a perfect seal, will leave the head in a condition facilitating easy removal in the future.

Order of attack, cylinder head nuts, TA engine

When tightening down the head, follow the proper sequence (as already detailed when dealing with head removal). Use the standard ring-spanner having a leverage of about six inches, and apply plenty of force. Do the job once for all, and there will be no need for further tightening, a difficult procedure in any case when all the valve gear is in position.

The push-rods may next be slipped into position, in the same order as they were removed, and the rocker-shaft fitted. Check, once more, that the rear rocker-standard is the one with the oil-hole, and also, if the compression ratio has been modified, that the packing pieces are in place. Unless the existing locking plates fitted under the heads of the long holding-down bolts are in good condition, new ones must be fitted. Tighten the bolts firmly, then bend the ends of the plates up and against one or more flats of the bolt-heads. As an alternative, the bolt-heads can be drilled and wired, instead of using the plates. It will be evident that as the rocker-shaft is pulled down, some of the valves will be lifted off their seats by their rockers, so that considerable stress is put on the rocker-shaft. So as not to concentrate this, the shaft must be pulled down evenly by tightening the eight bolts in a proper sequence having regard to which valves are causing the pressure.

After finally checking the push-rods for correct location in their tappets, the push-rod cover can be replaced, using a cork gasket. This joint can be troublesome as regards oil leakage, and it pays to be fairly generous with jointing compound. Over-tightening of the holding nuts merely distorts the pressed-steel cover, leading to worse leaks: a fairly thick washer, plus jointing compound and moderate pressure on the nuts, will result in an oil-tight job.

Refitting the oil-pump calls for no particular comment: use a thin paper washer between the pump body and the crankcase, plus a little compound. The importance of the fit of the pump-cover joint has already been emphasized, and due care must be taken. The oil-filter can also be refitted to the crankcase, using a thin fibre washer, and the pipes, with similar washers, connected up.

When refitting the distributor, it will naturally be necessary to mesh the gears to give the correct timing. Examination of the cover will indicate which electrode corresponds with No. 1 cylinder. Turn the distributor driving shaft until the rotor is pointing to that electrode, and mark the body with paint in case the position is " lost." Then turn the crankshaft until No. 1 cylinder is at t.d.c. of the firing stroke, that is, with both valves closed. (In contrast, No. 4 cylinder, also at t.d.c., will have both valves slightly open.) The distributor can then be pushed into its housing, but it is quite possible that one or two trials will be necessary before it is positioned correctly, as the skew gearing causes the shaft to rotate while being pushed home. It is thus necessary to allow a slight margin between the rotor and the timing mark so that the two line up when the gears are fully meshed. Actually, one tooth error makes a lot of difference, which is obvious on sight. The locking screw can then be fitted, and the vernier adjustment set to the half-way mark. With the piston at t.d.c., the contact-breaker points should be just breaking. Final adjustment will, of course, be made on the road.

CHAPTER 17

Engine Replacement and Starting-up

THE CLUTCH-HOUSING JOINT. ATTENTION TO DETAILS.
STARTING UP THE ENGINE. RUNNING-IN TECHNIQUE.
ALTERNATIVE GEAR RATIOS.

At this stage it is advisable to replace the unit in the chassis, as otherwise handling will be made more difficult. In any case, it is necessary to couple up the exhaust manifold to the pipe before the induction arrangements are fitted. Assuming that the engine has been man-handled into a position between the chassis members as far forwards as possible, the next step, and the most difficult, is to fit the paper washer around the flywheel housing flange. A washer is necessary here, of course, because of the fact that the clutch runs in oil, and as the joint is of large diameter, leakage is not easy to avoid unless great care is taken.

The best method of tackling the job is to anoint the flywheel housing joint face with compound, and then carefully fit the washer thereto, smoothing it down with the fingers. Next, get the engine as level as possible and within an inch or so of the clutch housing, the clutch-shaft having been entered in the clutch-centre after ensuring that the withdrawal fork has been correctly positioned so that it slips between the clutch and the withdrawal bearing. A little patience may be necessary to ensure this, but positioning is simplified if it is appreciated that the fork " pulls " on the bearing when the fork shaft is rotated clockwise looking on the operating lever end, or off-side. The clutch-housing joint face can now be anointed with compound, the engine levelled, and slid towards the gearbox. Some wangling will be needed to get the joint faces to close up, but as soon as they are near enough to allow of a few bolts being inserted, these should be put in and tightened a few threads. Incidentally, three or four bolts longer than standard, but having the same thread as the flange bolts, are a great help in keeping things lined up while the clutch-shaft is finally persuaded to enter the spigot bearing. All the time, keep an eye on the paper washer in the housing joint to ensure that it is not getting out of place. When the flanges have closed up, insert the remaining bolts and tighten them moderately. Then fit the front engine mountings. When these are secure, tighten up the flange bolts fully and wipe off any surplus jointing compound.

If the engine was removed complete with the gearbox, and it is desired to replace as a unit, the same general procedure as detailed is used in coupling up engine and gearbox on the bench. To handle the combined weight, of course, special lifting tackle is essential, and equipped with this, there is no difficulty in replacing it in the chassis, it

being merely a matter of fitting the front and rear mountings. No
doubt, however, in the majority of cases, the engine will have been
parted " at the clutch."

ATTENTION TO DETAILS

Various items, such as starter motor, dynamo, clutch-operating
lever and rod, and oil pipes to o.h.v. gear and gauge, can be assembled,
and do not present any particular snags. The water-pump requires

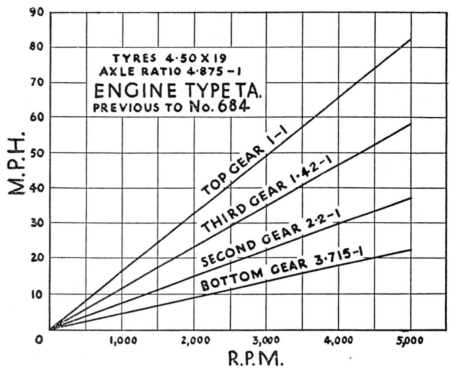

R.p.m./m.p.h. curve, early TA type

a thin Hallite joint washer, and the same material should be used on
the water elbow at the rear of the head. The inlet and exhaust
manifold washer is of one-piece form, and must be of heat-resisting
material. Thin Hallite or paper washers are used between the
carburetters and the inlet manifold. Special care must be taken at this
point, and also on the main manifold joint with the induction pipe, to
avoid air leaks, and a little jointing compound should be used. There
is no need, however, to smear this all over the washer adjacent to the
exhaust ports. As regards attention to the carburetters, a special
section is devoted to this important part of the work.

When refitting radiator connections it is advisable to use new
hoses. A little vaseline will help in getting them over the pipes. As

regards the large-diameter top hose, this must be of an adequately flexible type, as it is very short. If a stub of ordinary stiff hose is used, it may prove incapable of absorbing the engine movement *vis-à-vis* the radiator, causing leakage in the latter. Thin Hallite should be used for all water-joint flanges such as that on the thermostat.

When refitting the radiator, use new rubber washers for it to seat on if the existing ones are showing signs of age. Do not tighten the nuts too much, and lock them either with lock-nuts or wire.

The exhaust pipe will need a new copper-asbestos joint between it

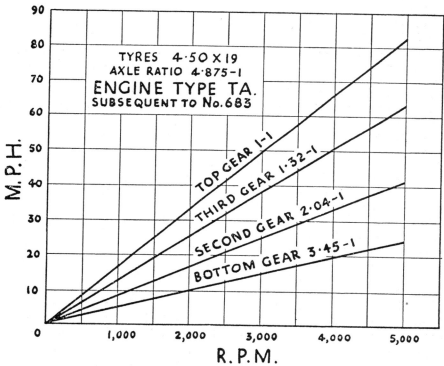

R.p.m./m.p.h. curve, later TA type

and the manifold. If any of the joint studs are broken or otherwise damaged, it is a good plan to replace them with nuts and bolts, the former of brass for preference.

STARTING UP THE ENGINE

Assuming that the carburetters have been attended to as detailed in Part III, and other minor items completed, such as coupling up controls, wiring, fitting the dynamo belt, and tachometer drive, we are just about ready to try a preliminary start-up. First of all, however, it is essential that a few checks are made. First, the ignition. See that with No. 1 cylinder at firing t.d.c. the distributor arm is pointing to the correct electrode, and the points are just breaking. As regards spark plugs, the owner may have his own pet make, and so long as this is one specified by M.G.s, there is no objection. Champion L10 give good results, with a gap of .018 in.

The rocker clearance can be set to .015 in. for both inlet and exhaust, for a start: accuracy in this direction can wait till things have bedded down. The clutch-withdrawal fork should be clear of its bearing when the pedal is right back. Adjustment which gives about 1 in. free movement at the pedal pad will achieve this. Fill up the sump, using S.A.E. 40 winter and 50 summer grade. A spot of engine oil in the fuel is a very good thing, but if you fancy any particular make of upper-cylinder lubricant as an alternative to plain engine oil, get the M.G. factory's advice before using it.

The battery must be in first-class condition, particularly if the engine bearings and bores have received attention, as it is desirable to buzz the engine round with the plugs out for a few minutes before trying a start. While doing this, inject a squirt of engine oil through each plug hole to ensure that there is plenty of lubricant on the bores. As the plugs may become fouled, it is as well to use an old set for the first attempt at a start. Having fitted these, and checked oil and water levels and fuel supply, but without the air manifold and cleaner in position, start up. If this is easier written than done, verify ignition and fuel supply. Faulty timing is usually accompanied by peculiar noises. Assuming that a start is accomplished, and that all four cylinders go into action in due course check the oil-pressure immediately. Do not worry about the reading so long as it is well up, say 60 lb. or above. Then check the overhead rockers, to see that oil is flowing from each one. If all is well, fit the rocker cover, using a cork washer. Don't employ any jointing compound, as otherwise difficulty will be experienced in removing the cover, and it will have to come off quite soon. Restart the engine, and let it run at about 1,000 r.p.m. until the oil is nicely warm. Then note the pressure again. This should be about 60 lb., and if a higher pressure persists, the pump relief-valve spring should have half a coil ground off to shorten it. If this does not reduce the pressure sufficiently, grind off a little at a time until the desired result is obtained. It is advisable, however, to wait until the car has been run on the road before getting really critical in this matter of exact oil-pressure, as all engines vary in this respect. The oil sump capacity is 1½ gallons. The use of racing oil of the Castrol R variety should be confined to " real " racing, the recommended mineral brands being absolutely suitable for all normal (and most abnormal) uses to which the car may be put.

RUNNING-IN TECHNIQUE

With the car on the road, and running-in under load about to commence, a few notes regarding procedure at this important stage will be useful. The time-honoured notion of so many miles at 30 m.p.h. and then go-as-you please is, of course, dead, but it is necessary to maintain a rigid standard of discipline in the matter of maximum r.p.m. For the first 500 miles, restrict this to 2,000, and do not let the engine slog in a high gear or accelerate fiercely. From then onwards to 1,000 miles, increase the permitted revs progressively, as the engine feels to be loosening up. Occasionally, give it the gun for a few hundred yards, then snap back the throttle to get the oil up the cylinders. Use a maximum of 3,500 towards the end of the first 1,000 miles for short periods only, and, for the second 1,000, hold

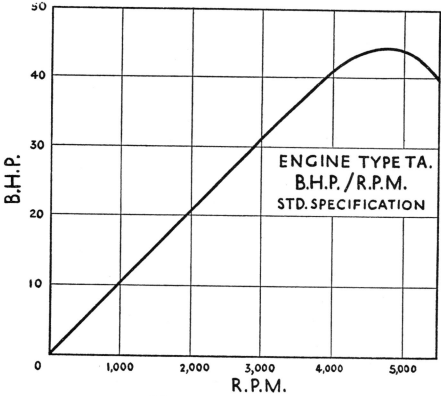

B.h.p. curve, TA engine.

these revs for progressively longer periods of time. Increase the ceiling thereafter until the unit feels perfectly happy at maximum, but if long-bearing life is desired, peak revs should be kept sternly at 4,800, even when the engine is fully run-in. This long-stroke engine is not happy at " screaming " point, and has no reason to be, for there is plenty of power low down.

During the running-in period, the mixture should be kept rather on the rich side, and the minimum idling speed held to 1,000 r.p.m. Towards the end of running-in, the carburetters should be synchronized as detailed in Part III. Minor adjustments to mixture strength will not, of course, affect the synchronism.

Also during the period, the rocker cover should be removed to check lubrication, and the valve clearances can be adjusted if found necessary. After running-in, the ignition timing should be experimented with, the vernier adjustment making this a simple operation. Do not be tempted to over-advance: this produces a rough feel which may well be mistaken for power, but which is likely to cause harm to bearings. A point should be aimed at which gives good pulling from about 30 m.p.h. in top gear, whilst at the same time allowing the engine to rev up quickly when opened up on the lower ratios. Very slight pinking is permissible when pulling away from about 2,500 r.p.m., but it must only be slight. It is worth while lifting the cylinder head at about 6,000 miles, even if all appears well. It has a good moral effect, and allows the welfare of the bores to be checked. There is no need to remove any valves, of course, but the opportunity can be taken to clean the carbon from the piston and cylinder heads. Normal decarbonizing periods are at about every 16,000 miles, this being dependent to some extent on the use to which the car is put, and the fuel used. Fast road work produces less carbon than traffic motoring. The oil-pressure should remain steady at from 40 to 60 lb. hot. Variation of rocker clearances from a standard of .015 in. is alleged in some quarters to improve the performance, .019 in. being the figure mentioned for speedy going. It is doubtful if any perceptible advantage is gained, while the noise is considerable. It will be found that an inlet setting of .010 in. and exhaust setting of .015 in. will result in a quiet valve operating gear with no detriment to performance.

The maximum b.h.p. output with standard compression ratio of 6.5 to 1 is 45 at 4.800 r.p.m. A large variety of gear ratios have been used at various times, and it may be of assistance to detail these.

Alternative Gear Ratios

The standard axle ratio of 4.875 was perpetuated throughout the tenure of the TA, an alternative " trials " ratio of 5.375 being available. The earliest cars, with non-synchromesh boxes, and based on the standard axle ratio, showed overall ratios of 4.875, 6.92, 10.73, and 18.11. A little later, boxes with synchromesh engagement for top and third gears were introduced, the ratios being 4.875, 6.459, 9.847, and 16.477. Early in 1937, these synchromesh boxes had their ratios altered to 4.875, 6.44, 9.95, and 16.84, these ratios remaining unchanged subsequently. The non-synchromesh boxes ceased at engine No. MPJG 683.

A set of wide competition ratios was also available, these being 4.875, 7.46, 11.56, and 19.5.

The gearbox is not likely to need much attention, and in any case follows the usual design of synchromesh boxes in regard to the part of the mechanism which presents a puzzle in dismantling—the synchromesh unit. This has six balls and springs which retain the top and third-gear dog on the sliding hub. The sliding hub can be pushed out from the dog if sufficient pressure is used to overcome the

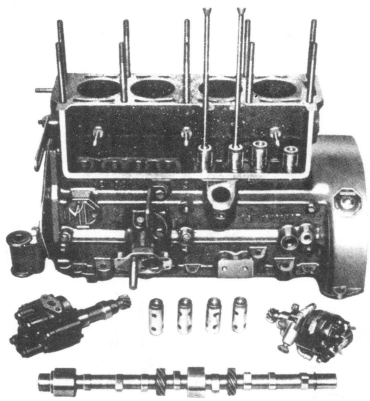

The TC crankcase, with oil-pump, distributor, camshaft and tappets removed.

TC camshaft drive, showing "timing" links in correct position on marked teeth.

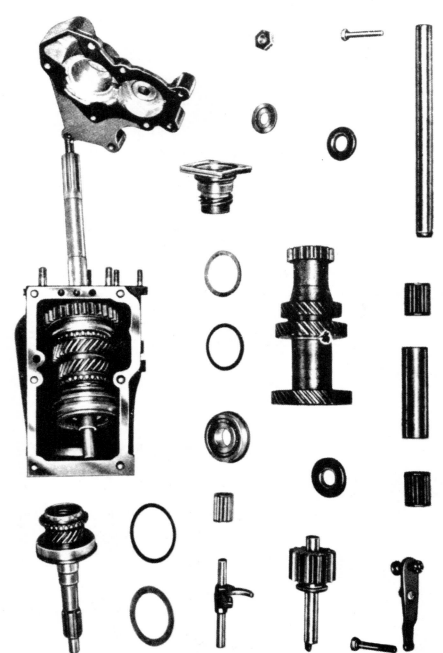

The TC gearbox dismantled.

springs. When reassembling, there is no need for a special tool to persuade the balls and springs to re-enter. The sliding hub should be just engaged in the dog, one spring fitted into place, and the corresponding ball retained in the hub by means of a piece of steel about $\frac{3}{16}$ in. wide by .015 in. thick. Push the steel down between the hub and the dog. Repeat the operation for the remaining springs and balls, using a separate piece of similar steel for each one. A hearty shove will push the sliding hub home, and the balls will register in the ground indentation in the centre of the teeth.

If the propeller-shaft flange is removed from the gearbox main-shaft, it is essential that it is replaced in the same position, and the parts should therefore be marked with paint before removal.

CHAPTER 18

Dismantling the TC and Allied Engines

CONNECTING RODS AND PISTONS. CRANKSHAFT REMOVAL.
THE ROCKER-GEAR.

The construction of the TC-type engine (and also the TB and TD units, which are virtually identical) is, like that of the TA, quite straightforward. As far as removal of the cylinder head, and accessories associated therewith, are concerned, the operations as detailed for the TA generally apply. The head is held down by ten nuts, which should be unscrewed in the order given on the diagram.

The remaining accessories such as starter, dynamo, oil-pump, and so on, are also dealt with as indicated previously, the water-pump being mounted on the front of the cylinder block on this engine. The sump incorporates the bottom half of the flywheel housing and part

Order of attack, cylinder head nuts, TC engine

of the timing chain enclosure, but presents little difficulty in removing, once all its fixings have been withdrawn.

On the assumption that the engine has been taken out of the chassis at approximately the same stage of dismantling as was described in the earlier section, and is now on the bench, further work can be proceeded with.

The engine should be laid on its side on the bench, and suitably blocked up to bring it level and secure. The oil-pump intake strainer should be removed with its attachments, the split-pins drawn from the big-end cap-nuts, and the nuts unscrewed. Mark each connecting-rod big-end eye on the two mating halves, with paint, before removing the caps, and also take similar steps to ensure that the thin-wall bearing halves will be returned to their original positions if it is desired to refit them. The connecting rods complete with their pistons can be withdrawn one at a time, the crankshaft being turned to allow the assembly to come past it on the off-side, that is, the side remote from the camshaft. When all the rods are out, mark each one with paint to identify it for replacement in the correct cylinder.

The gudgeon pins are rigidly held in the connecting-rod small-ends in a manner identical to the TA fitting, so that the instructions already given for piston removal will apply here.

There are a few preliminaries before the crankshaft can be removed. The clutch will cause no trouble in dismantling. The cover plate is secured to the flywheel by a ring of bolts. When these are unscrewed, pull away the cover, and catch the clutch driven plate as it drops out. The flywheel fixing will then be exposed, consisting of four bolts and two dowels. The spigot bearing consists of a plain bush, so that there is no ball-race or retaining plate to worry about. Removal of the bolts in the manner described for the TA will enable the flywheel to be withdrawn.

At the other end of the crankshaft, the starting-handle dog should be unscrewed with a hefty box spanner, and the fan pulley drawn off its key. The timing chain cover may then be removed, exposing the spring-loaded, oil-pressure fed chain tensioner which is held by two bolts. This should be taken off complete, being careful not to lose the internal spring. The set-screw in the centre of the camshaft can then be withdrawn. This will allow the chainwheel and pinion complete with the endless chain, to be pulled away as a unit. The oil-thrower which is normally between the fan pulley and the chain pinion will come away with the pinion.

CRANKSHAFT REMOVAL

The crankshaft is now practically ready for removal, the only remaining operation being to remove the three main bearing caps. The nuts should be extremely tight, so that an adequate spanner is necessary. The crankshaft can then be lifted out.

The tappets slide directly in the crankcase casting, there being no separate tappet blocks. They can be withdrawn upwards, taking care to keep them in sequence of removal. The thrust plate, which controls the camshaft end-float, should also be removed from the front camshaft bearing, and the dowel screw, which secures the centre bearing, taken out. This will be found located just forward of the distributor aperture on the outside of the crankcase. The camshaft is now free to be withdrawn from the front end; it will bring the split-centre bearing with it, and the bearing should be removed from the shaft for safe keeping until it is time to replace it.

THE ROCKER-GEAR

The rocker-shaft and rockers have already been removed to facilitate push-rod removal. The valves can therefore be tackled next. These are of normal type, non-interchangeable (the inlets being larger than the exhausts), and having a split-cone fixing in the top spring collar. Double valve springs are standard. To remove the valves, a good hefty spring compressor is needed. When using this, if considerable pressure fails to shift the collar off its split-cones, give the top of the compressor a light tap, which will jar the parts free. Be careful, when doing this, not to let the compressor slip. Keep all the components for each valve together, and keep the valves in order of removal from the engine. The valves will slip out of their guides freely, as there are no stem circlips.

The rocker-shaft is hollow, and collects quite a lot of sludge in the normal course of events. There are four rocker-shaft standards, the two central ones being slotted and fitted with washers which, carried on the holding-down bolts, engage in keyways in the shaft and thus prevent it from turning. With the bolts removed, these washers can be shaken or picked out. Removal of the hairpin retaining spring from one end of the rocker-shaft will enable all the components to be slid off the shaft. They should be kept in the right order for reassembly.

CHAPTER 19

Examination and Renovation

THE CRANKSHAFT AND BEARINGS.
CYLINDER BORES, RINGS AND PISTONS.   ATTENTION TO THE VALVES.
CYLINDER-HEAD MODIFICATIONS.

Before commencing a preliminary inspection, it is necessary to get everything to a proper state of cleanliness, and for this purpose the cleaning accessories referred to in the Introduction at the beginning of the book should be called upon.   There is no objection, of course, to leaving items which are not the immediate concern, to languish in fluid while others are being dealt with, so long as eventually all items are above reproach.

Examination of components may well commence with the crankshaft and bearings.   The latter comprise, for the mains, thick steel shells lined with white-metal, the end-float being controlled by flanges on both sides of the centre bearing.   The big-ends are of thin-wall steel-backed white-metal lined type located by tabs.   If the shaft has done a biggish mileage, it will show signs of scoring on both main and big-end surfaces.   It is false economy in such cases to replace the bearing shells without giving the shaft proper attention.   The shaft should be handed to a competent M.G. specialist for grinding to a standard undersize, new bearing shells for mains and big-ends being obtainable, of the correct dimensions for the reground diameters.   No hand-fitting is, of course, necessary, or indeed permissible, with these bearings.

The gudgeon-pin clamping bolts in the connecting-rod small-ends are liable to lose some of their threads when removing.   This is due to the fact that the bolt engages a recess in the gudgeon pin with very little clearance, against which the threads may chafe.   The bolts should therefore be renewed when reassembling.   The standard finish of the connecting rods is excellent, and correct alignment can be taken for granted unless the engine has obviously been through the mill.

Data relating to the crankshaft and bearings is given below:—

Diameter of main bearings: Nos. 1 and 2, 52 mm.; No. 3, 52 mm.
Length of main bearings: Nos. 1 and 2, 38 mm.; No. 3, 40 mm.
Diameter of crankpins: 45 mm.
Length of crankpins: 28 mm.
Main bearing running clearance: .0005 to .002 in.
Big-end bearing running clearance: .0005 to .002 in.
Main bearing end-float: .0015 to .004 in.
Big-end bearing end-float: .004 to .006 in.
Standard bearing undersizes—(mm.): .3, .5, .75, 1.0, 1.25.
Connecting-rod centres: 7 in. or 178 mm.

CYLINDER BORES, RINGS AND PISTONS

Some clue to the condition of the bores and pistons will, of course, have been given by the behaviour of the engine before dismantling. Thanks to the rapid warming-up provided by the thermostat in the cooling system, the layout of the water circulation, and the use of relatively thin oil, taken to where it is wanted by a large-capacity pump, extremely good mileage figures are habitually put up before a rebore is necessary. The best way of deciding what attention is required is, of course, to do some careful checking. A section devoted to this will be found later on in the book.

The pistons fitted are Aerolite aluminium alloy type, with oval skirts. Replacements are supplied in five ranges of sizes, dimensions as follows:—

Marking	Size
A	Standard.
C	.5 mm. oversize.
D	.75 mm. oversize.
E	1.0 mm. oversize.
F	1.25 mm. oversize.

The above are nominal sizes, which are identified by the letters OK, i.e., AOK means standard bore of 66.5 mm. DOK means 66.5 plus .75 mm. In addition to the nominal sizes there are two further oversizes of .020 and .040 mm. If these are used, the letters OK are omitted and the relevant dimension is added. Thus, A + .02 would mean standard bore of 66.5 mm. plus .02 mm. D + .04 would indicate oversize of 66.5 plus .75 plus .04 mm. The sizes are stamped on both bore and piston, and obviously the markings should correspond on each component. They are useful to know, as they indicate, in the case of a used engine, the precise dimensions of the bores, which is a guide to the feasibility of further renovation.

The following table gives the standard piston data:—

Clearance: .0022 to .0028 in.
Weight with rings and gudgeon pin: 12.75 oz.
Gudgeon pin diameter: 18 mm.
Fit in piston: Two-thumb push.
Compression height: 45 mm.
Number of rings: 2 compression; 1 oil control.
Gap: .006 to .010 in., for all.
Side clearance to groove: .001 to .002 in., for all.
Width of ring: Compression 2.25 mm.; Oil control 4 mm.

ATTENTION TO THE VALVES

Assuming that steps have been taken to have the cylinders and pistons attended to as required, the cylinder head can be tackled. Quite a lot of clearance is permissible between valve stems and guides, and unless ovality is obviously present, this should not be mistaken for excessive wear. The best way of settling any doubts is to borrow a new valve and guide and compare the clearances of the combination with those existing on the engine. If the difference does not amount to more than about .002 in., there should be nothing to worry about. If renewal of the guides is decided upon, the work should be entrusted to an M.G. specialist equipped with the necessary tools. The guides have no shoulder, and are fitted with the smaller outside diameter at the top. They are pressed in until there is a length of 24 mm. projecting above the face of the head. The overall length of the inlet guides is greater than that of the exhausts.

Should any of the valves show signs of pitting or burning, they should be renewed. However, the TC and allied engines are not prone to this trouble unless mixture strength has been outrageously incorrect. The valve seats last a long time without being recut, but should this require doing, have the job attended to professionally, as pocketing can cause a serious restriction of gas flow.

Modification to the valves in the interests of higher power is permissible, using components supplied by the M.G. Company, and details will be given later. For purposes of comparison, the data applicable to the standard valves is given here. Using the standard springs, valve-crash occurs at about 6,000 r.p.m.

		Inlet.	*Exhaust.*
Head diameter of valve	...	33 mm.	31 mm.
Stem diameter	...	8 mm.	8 mm.
Face angle	...	30 deg.	30 deg.
		Inner spring.	*Outer spring.*
Free length of spring ...	...	2.565 in.	2.927 in.
Fitted length of spring ...	...	1.438 in.	1.532 in.
At load of	...	43 lb.	80 lb.

While we are dealing with this part of the engine, it will be a good idea to look at the valve ports. These are commendably smooth as standard, but time is well spent in grinding and polishing. A flexible-shaft grinding equipment is a very desirable piece of apparatus at this stage, but in its absence much can be done with emery cloth and rifflers. When attending to the inlet ports in this manner, take care not to alter the valve port dimensions. It will be noted that the siamesed inlet ports have a separating boss dividing them. This can be ground away on each side, being careful to maintain the streamline shape of the boss. If about 1/16 in. is removed from each side of the boss, it will be possible to obtain, on either side of the boss, two nicely shaped inlet ports of oblong formation measuring 1³⁄₁₆ in. in height and 21/32 in. in width. It must be emphasized that under no circumstances should the separating boss be removed altogether, as it has a most important effect on the correct distribution of mixture between the ports.

The alignment of the inlet manifold may leave a little to be desired, and if necessary the manifold and ports should be lined-up, using the method already described in the case of the TA unit. The degree of finish to be obtained on the ports and manifold interior depends largely on the patience of the operator and the equipment at his disposal, but the work is very well worth while. The exhaust side is the least important of the two, but even here the ports should be matched with the manifold, though a high degree of polish in the latter is superfluous.

The combustion chambers are machined very satisfactorily as standard, and any extra polishing must be done very carefully, as the shape must not be altered. More important is the question of modifying for increased compression ratio. This alteration can be carried out to various degrees, and is very much tied up with other modifications to the valves, carburetters, and so on. Full details of such work, and particulars of special parts supplied by the M.G. works, are given in a later chapter.

CHAPTER 20

The TC Overhead-Valve Mechanism

ASSEMBLING THE VALVES.   THE ROCKERS AND ROCKER-SHAFT.
ASSEMBLY OF THE ROCKER-GEAR.   THE CAMSHAFT AND
ASSOCIATED PARTS.

Having dealt with any valves requiring treatment such as refacing or renewal, the assembly of these items can be considered.   The valve stems should be polished with very fine emery cloth, and the valves ground-in, in the normal way, finishing off with metal polish.

Grinding is, of course, necessary even if the valves are new or have been refaced.   For holding the valves when grinding, the suction type of grinding tool is most satisfactory, though some people prefer the type with a T-handle which has a shank arranged to grip the valve stem.   This type has the disadvantage that the head cannot be laid flat on its back.

Alternative strengths of valve spring are available, the stronger ones enabling higher r.p.m. to be employed before valve-crash intervenes.   There is no advantage to be gained by fitting these stronger springs, unless other modifications, designed to enhance the engine's performance, are undertaken at the same time.   Details of such tuning are given in a later chapter.   The valve springs should be tested for dimensions in line with the data given earlier in this section.   They should be renewed if their free length is appreciably below the standard figures.

The split-cone cotters should be examined to make sure that they are seating firmly in the top caps.   Trouble is unlikely here, unless makeshift parts have at any time been fitted.   The fit can, of course, be tested prior to assembly.   When reassembling the valves, it should be noted that the spring cap at the bottom goes over the guide, between the springs and the head, and the shroud fits inside the inner spring at the top.   The synthetic rubber sealing rings must be replaced on the stems, it being advisable to fit new ones whenever they are disturbed.   If they are pushed well down the stems initially, they can be persuaded to take up their correct positions after complete assembly of each valve, by applying gentle pressure to the top of the valve so as to push it fully open.   This will result in the sealing ring being pushed up to its correct location just under the split-cone.

THE ROCKERS AND ROCKER-SHAFT

Careful cleaning and examination of all the rocker-gear components is necessary to ensure that all the various oilways are cleared. Test the shaft for straightness by rolling it on a flat surface.   The rockers have drillways for lubrication, and these can be cleaned with the force-feed oil-can, plus a strand of wire if necessary.   Rocker-ends which show much signs of wear must be renovated by building-up and regrinding to the original shape. Slight wear can sometimes be lapped out, but obviously too much lapping will go through the hardening. It is, however, important that the contact point between rocker end and valve stem is not " hollowed," as otherwise it is impossible to arrive at correct valve clearance, and side-thrust on the valve stems will be increased.

The rocker-shaft standards are almost identical, except that the back one is drilled for the oil-feed to the valve-gear. The oil-feed holes to the rockers are at the top, the rockers being bushed. They are of four types. Nos. 1 and 8 are nearly " square " but have their bosses offset to rear and front respectively. Nos. 2 and 7 are considerably offset in opposite directions. Nos. 3 and 6 are again offset in opposite directions not only in relation to each other but also in relation to Nos. 2 and 7. Nos. 4 and 5 are practically straight, but have their bosses offset to front and rear respectively. As regards the spacing springs on the rocker-shaft, the shortest pair go between the extreme ends of the shaft and rockers 1 and 8. The two medium-length springs go between Nos. 2–3 and 6–7. The single long spring goes between Nos. 4 and 5. The assembly is quite straightforward, and any incorrect placing of a rocker is apparent from its relation to the valve stem.

If the valve seats have been recut, it may be desirable to grind a little of the top of the valve stem so that the rocker and valve assume the correct relationship. Unless the discrepancy is very marked it is best to leave well alone. The aim is, of course, that, with the valve in the half-open position, the contact face of the rocker tip should lie squarely across the centre of the valve stem.

Too much play in the rocker-shaft bushes must not be tolerated. It is disguised to some extent by the spacing springs. The rockers must, of course, oscillate freely on the shaft, but it should not be possible to rock their ends sideways to any appreciable extent. The bushes are readily renewed, using the method for withdrawal already described in relation to TA engines. Bushes will, of course, need reamering after pressing-in.

The ball-ended adjusting screws at the rocker-ends last a long time, and are easily renewed if necessary.

ASSEMBLY OF THE ROCKER-GEAR

As already mentioned, assembly of the rocker components on the shaft presents little difficulty if the foregoing notes are followed. It is, of course, not possible to fit the rocker-shaft to the head until the latter is assembled on the engine, but everything can be assembled into one unit. The two washers in the slots of the two centre rocker standards should be engaged with the keyways in the shaft, and located by the long bolts. Check again that the rear standard is the one with the oil-feed hole. Any alteration of compression ratio will necessitate the provision of suitable packing pieces under the rocker-shaft standards, to raise the shaft, thus bringing the rockers to the correct " lie." Dimensions of these packings will vary according to the amount of metal removed from the head, and details are given in a later chapter.

THE CAMSHAFT AND ASSOCIATED PARTS

The camshaft wearing surfaces are of ample area, and usually show little shake even after a large mileage. If new bearing bushes are considered necessary, it is best for these to be fitted by an M.G. specialist, as far as the front and back ones are concerned. The split centre bearing is, of course, readily renewed. The cam surfaces can be touched with superfine emery cloth if considered necessary to eliminate minute scoring, but this should not be present unless foreign matter has been in the oil.

As already mentioned, the end-float of the camshaft is controlled by a thrust plate at the front end, which is located between the chainwheel and the bearing. Details of clearances are as follows:—

Bearing.	Front.	Centre.	Rear.
Diameter	41 mm.	23 mm.	23 mm.
Length	29 mm.	25 mm.	29 mm.
Clearance	.0015 to .004 in.		
End-float	.005 to .013 in.		

The camshaft drive comprises a Renold .375 in. pitch duplex roller chain running on wheels having 21 and 42 teeth, the chain being 60 pitches in length. A spring-loaded hydraulically damped slipper tensioner bears on the back of the chain on the non-driving side, so that chain wear is automatically taken up, and slack does not intrude as wear takes place. The chain has a very long life, and need not be considered as having reached the end of its useful service until the elongation due to wear is 2 per cent., or about $\frac{1}{4}$ in. in a foot length. In order to measure for this elongation it is necessary to uncouple the chain by extracting an outer link with a special extractor tool of the type used by motor-cyclists. The chain must then be washed in paraffin, and measured against a suitably graduated rule when dry and unlubricated. If it is considered that there is plenty of life left, the chain must be riveted up again, using a new outer link of the type supplied specially for hand-riveting. (The old link which was extracted must not be put back.) The chains and wheels are, of course, replaced as a unit when reassembling the drive.

As regards the wheels, they need not be renewed unless they show obvious signs of wear, which causes a hooked formation of the teeth on the edge which takes the pull of the chain.

The chain tensioner spring should be examined, and its length checked. This should be 71 mm. free, or 48 mm. loaded to $1\frac{1}{4}$ lb.

The push-rods should be examined carefully, and polished all over. Test them for straightness, using a suitable straight-edge. Do not attempt to straighten a doubtful rod, but renew it. Also, the end-fittings should be examined for firmness in the rods. Loose fittings can be sweated in place with tinman's solder, but it is an expert's job. The tappets should not require any attention, in view of their large size and ample lubrication.

CHAPTER 21

The Lubrication System and Miscellaneous Items

ATTENTION TO THE OIL-PUMP. LUBRICATION SYSTEM DETAILS. THE IGNITION SYSTEM AND OTHER COMPONENTS.

The next component to receive attention is the oil-pump. In general construction it does not differ materially from that fitted to the TA engine, and therefore the details already given cover much of the work to be carried out. If it is desired to withdraw the main driving shaft, the pump gear on this shaft can be extracted by removing the spring retaining ring, and tapping the pump body on a wooden block to detach the gear. The woodruff key must then be picked out of the shaft, otherwise the bearing bush will be damaged when attempting to pull the shaft out of the body drive housing. The spindle for the driven pump gear is pressed into the crankcase, and should not need removing. It can be withdrawn if desired, however, as its end is tapped for a draw-bolt with 8-mm. thread.

In addition to the normal pump relief valve, there is a further by-pass valve which comes into operation if the main oil filter becomes completely choked, when it allows unfiltered oil to pass direct from the pump to the main oil gallery. This valve is located in the crankcase behind the pump. Its spring, cage, and ball are retained by the ball seating which is pressed into the crankcase. The valve can be withdrawn by pulling out the seating, which is tapped for an 8-mm. draw-bolt. It should then be checked in the same manner as for the pump relief valve.

The normal pump pressure is 50 to 60 lb. The pressure falls, of course, when idling.

LUBRICATION SYSTEM DETAILS

Apart from oil-pipes and passages, the items concerned with the oil-circulation system comprise the gauze intake strainer on the suction side of the pump, and the full-flow filter on the delivery side. The former should not need any attention apart from cleaning, but if by any chance the gauze is damaged, this must be remedied. The pressure filter is of that most efficient type which comprises a canister of sealed pattern having inlet and outlet unions and a simple clamp for attachment to the engine. No cleaning is necessary, the whole canister being thrown away at regular intervals. A new one should, of course, be fitted after a major overhaul, and after the first 3,000 miles thereafter. From then on, with a run-in engine, the filter should be good for 10,000 miles between renewals.

All passages in the crankcase should be cleaned out using the force-feed oil-can and plenty of paraffin, finishing off with engine oil. This is most important, as paraffin must not be left in oil passages. The oil-pipes should have similar treatment, including that to the gauge. The short flexible connection to the oil-gauge junction union on the bulkhead should receive careful examination, as it may develop a leak after a long time.

Always line up the oil-pipes with their unions before fitting, and do not attempt to pull them into position with the union nuts. If any drastic bending is found necessary, anneal the pipe before doing the job, by heating it to nearly red heat and plunging it into cold water. Any doubtful brazing on the pipe unions must be attended to at this time.

THE IGNITION SYSTEM

The next assembly to receive attention is the distributor of the coil ignition system. This equipment is almost identical with that fitted to the TA-type engine. Thus, the details already given should be followed.

The automatic timing mechanism, of the usual centrifugal type, gives a range of 28 to 32 degrees (crankshaft). The mechanism comes into operation at about 500 to 800 r.p.m., advancing progressively to 4,400 r.p.m., when the fully advanced point is reached.

As regards the remaining assemblies, such as dynamo, water-pump, and starter, these again are dealt with as described for the TA unit. The starter motor in the present case, however, is not prone to oiling trouble, as the clutch is, of course, "dry." The quick-thread engagement mechanism should be well cleaned with paraffin, but the merest trace of oil only should be applied, to avoid sticking of the pinion. The pinion itself, and the flywheel gear, are, of course, designed to run unlubricated.

The fan spindle, which is combined with the water-pump, runs on two ball-bearings lubricated from an external nipple. Assuming that the spindle runs smoothly and without shake, there is no point in disturbing these bearings. If the pump shows signs of leakage from the gland, a pump-service exchange should be made.

CHAPTER 22

Reassembly of the TC Engine

CRANKSHAFT AND BEARINGS. FITTING PISTONS, CONNECTING RODS
AND BIG-ENDS. ASSEMBLING THE CAMSHAFT DRIVE. REFITTING
THE FLYWHEEL. ASSEMBLING THE BASE CHAMBER. ASSEMBLING
THE CYLINDER HEAD.

We have now dealt with the various assemblies, and it is time to start reassembling the engine. Everything should be in ship-shape order, with water passages cleaned, including connecting pipes, thermostat, and so on. Any doubtful screw-threads should be renewed. A set of the necessary jointing washers and gaskets can be obtained from your M.G. Agent, and these should be used in preference to making them up. If non-availability renders the latter course necessary, use good quality white drawing paper for joints where this type is required, and other materials as called for.

With the crankcase upside-down on the bench, the three main bearing shells should be introduced into their housings, taking care that they locate accurately, and that their oil-holes line-up with the crankcase drillings. Run a little engine oil on to the bearing faces, and carefully lower the crankshaft into position, rotating it slowly to ensure that it drops properly home and turns freely.

Fit the remaining bearing shells into their respective bearing caps, registering them correctly, and then slip the caps over their crankcase studs and push them down on to the shaft, first oiling the journals. As emphasized previously, the caps must go back in their original locations, and the same way round. Run the six nuts on to the studs and tighten slightly. The shaft may appear a little stiff after a regrind and remetalling of bearings, but so long as this is uniform there is nothing to worry about, as it disappears in the first few revolutions under power. Tighten the bearing nuts finally, using a good-fitting socket spanner and a foot-long tommy-bar. Apply pressure evenly and alternately to the two nuts on each cap, to ensure equal stressing throughout the material. Lock the nuts with wire carefully, when satisfied that all is correct.

The camshaft can next be installed, sliding it in from the front end. The middle bearing must, of course, be put in position on the shaft just before the latter is right home. Every care should be taken to get this bearing into position with its locating-screw hole opposite the corresponding hole in the crankcase. If this is got somewhere near, it will be possible to insert a scriber from the outside for the final lining-up of the holes. The locking screw should then be inserted, tightened up, and wired. If this screw does not enter easily, do not force it, but check the alignment of the holes, otherwise the screw thread may be stripped, or the bearing distorted.

FITTING PISTONS, CONNECTING RODS AND BIG-ENDS

The pistons can next be fitted to the connecting rods. As already mentioned, it is advisable to use new clamp screws if the threads are in the least degree damaged. Apply a little engine oil to the gudgeon pin and slip it through the piston bosses and small-end of the rod. Very carefully line up the recess in the pin with the clamp-screw hole in the small-end. This is most important, otherwise it is impossible to get the screw home without damage. See that the screw is provided with its spring washer, and when finally tightening use the same technique as was applied when dismantling, to avoid stressing the rod or piston. Tighten the clamp screw adequately. Using a box-spanner, a tommy-bar which can be grasped with one hand, T-wise, will give all the force necessary.

Before refitting the pistons in the bores, space out the ring gaps so that they are as far apart as possible, and anoint the rings and grooves generously with engine oil. With the crankshaft turned to the most advantageous position to allow maximum room, each piston is inserted into its cylinder bore from below. The bore immediately concerned should be given a final pull-through with a hefty wad of felt immediately before inserting the piston, in case there are any stray bits of foreign matter adhering to its surface. Make sure that the gudgeon-pin clamp bolt is towards the off-side (the side remote from the camshaft) of the crankcase, so that the oil spray holes in the connecting rods face the correct way. After liberally oiling the crank-pin, and carefully fitting the thin-wall bearing shells so that their locating tabs register correctly, each big-end can be seated and the caps pushed over their bolts. Make sure that the latter are properly down on their registers which prevent them turning, and run on the nuts. The latter must be tightened with even pressure and firmly, but note that the threads are not large, and it is possible to stretch the bolts or damage the threads by too great an effort with a long tommy-bar. In particular do not be tempted to over-tighten the nuts in an attempt to register the split-pin holes with the nut castellations. If adequate tightening fails to obtain the correct register, remove the nut and grind the surface lightly until the fit is correct.

After fitting each rod, test the shaft for free rotation. There should be no cause for complaint if the shaft renovation has been carried out properly. In case of anything seriously wrong, such as undue stiffness, the dimensional data already given for crankshaft and bearings will enable the fault to be tracked down.

When split-pinning the big-end cap nuts, use pins of as large a diameter as possible; cut off the legs to a reasonable length, and bend them back securely round the nuts. Do not leave a superfluous length of pin festooned all over the place.

ASSEMBLING THE CAMSHAFT DRIVE

The keys securing the crankshaft chain pinion and camshaft wheel should be carefully examined. Ragged edges should be trimmed with a fine file, otherwise difficulty may be experienced in refitting the wheels. As already mentioned, the timing chain, being automatically tensioned, has a very long life, and the amount of wear can be readily measured. It is as well to fit a new chain if the degree of wear present indicates that one will be required in the remote future, as quite a lot of dismantling has to be done to fit this component in the normal

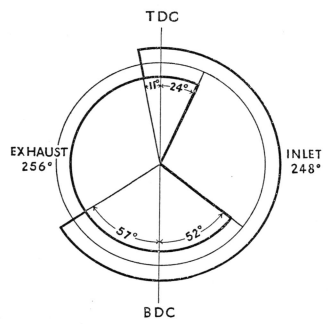

Valve timing diagram, TC engine

course of events, and chains are not expensive. The wheels and chain must be fitted as a unit; before this is done, it is necessary to assemble the chain on the wheels to give the correct timing. The standard chain incorporates two " bright " links, i.e., with side-plates finished metallic instead of the usual blue colour. Each wheel also has one tooth stamped with a T. The chain must be fitted on the wheels so that the two T-marked teeth engage the two bright links with the shortest length of chain between the bright links at the top, or on the " tensioner " side of the assembly. Actually, the number of chain links in the short run is 29. If by any chance it is necessary to use a chain without the bright timing links, it is quite a simple matter to mark two of the links with paint. Calling the first outer link to be marked No. 1, count 29 from there, and mark another one, which will again be an outer link. The marked links are then engaged with the T-marks on the wheels in the normal manner. Before finally

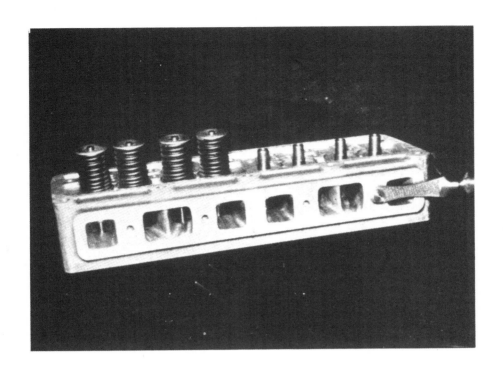

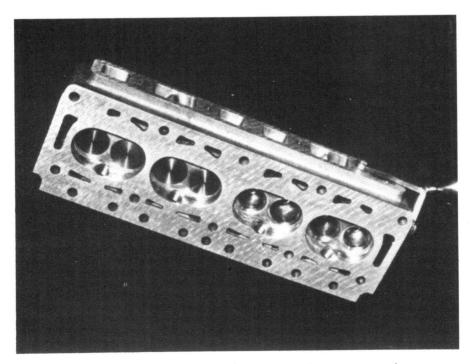

*The Laystall alloy cylinder head for TB/TF engines enhances extra performance
obtained by various tuning stages.*

1,250-c.c. TD-type engine, offside.

1,250-c.c. TD-type engine, nearside.

assembling the chain and wheels, fit the camshaft wheel temporarily, and check for end-play. This is controlled by the thrust plate located between the camshaft shoulder and the chainwheel. The float limits have already been detailed, and as these are very generous, there should be no trouble. The float can, of course, be corrected to a nicety by attention to the thrust plate.

Having ensured that the shaft-ends and wheel bores are spotless, and keys firmly in position, the chain and wheels can be slid on to the shafts as a unit assembly. The camshaft wheel can then be secured by its set-screw, a new lock-washer being fitted if the old one is at all damaged. Hammer one side of the washer up against a flat of the screwhead, and engage the tongue in the hole in the chainwheel. The chain tensioner can then be fitted, after checking that its oil-holes are clear. It is emphasized that the chain must be riveted endless, and no type of fastener (such as a spring connecting link) can be allowed.

It is not possible to fit the fan pulley, which secures the crankshaft chain pinion, until the timing cover has been assembled, and before this is done the timing should be checked. Replace the tappets, so as to have an indication of the cam movement. Any error will be readily apparent, as one tooth makes a lot of difference. A circular protractor or timing disc attached to the crankshaft will provide a ready indication of the crank angle, the timing being as follows:—

Inlet opens 11 deg. before t.d.c.

Inlet closes 57 deg. after b.d.c.

Exhaust opens 52 deg. before b.d.c.

Exhaust closes 24 deg. after t.d.c.

Overlap 35 deg.

Assuming that the timing is found in order, the chain cover can be fitted. There is an oil-seal made of composition, located in a groove in the cover where it embraces the top half of the crankshaft diameter. If a new seal is fitted, take care that the ends protrude slightly beyond the groove. A thin cork packing washer, with jointing compound, is used for the timing cover joint to the engine. Having fitted this, the crankshaft oil-thrower and fan pulley can be pushed on to the shaft, keyed, and secured by the starting handle dog. The peripheral position of the latter can be varied if necessary, to bring the handle into the most advantageous position for swinging over compression. This is done by fitting a shim or shims on the shaft between the dog and the pulley boss. Shims having a thickness of .005 in., .010 in., and .020 in. are available for the purpose.

REFITTING THE FLYWHEEL

Before finally refitting the flywheel, the starter gear ring should be inspected. The ring has 93 teeth, and is a shrink fit. It lasts a long time, but if repairs are considered advisable it is best to have a new ring shrunk-on, rather than attempting to furbish up odd teeth.

New dowels should be used on the flywheel flanges, and if the bolts were removed by drastic methods, they should be renewed also. The dowels should be driven home after the bolts have been tightened moderately. The latter are then tightened really hard, using a stout spanner with a foot-long tommy-bar.

The amount of wear left on the clutch linings can be gauged readily, but renewals are cheap, and if it has had say 20,000 miles of use, a new one, while the going is good, will save a dismantling job at a later date. New linings have a thickness of $\frac{1}{8}$ in., the plate type being Borg and Beck AG-G, $7\frac{1}{4}$ in. diameter.

It will probably not have been necessary to dismantle the clutch pressure plate, or cover plate and springs, unless, of course, spring breakages were apparent, which is most unlikely. Reassembly on the flywheel will merely entail mounting the clutch plate against the flywheel face, with the long boss outwards, and putting the clutch cover plate complete against it, at the same time inserting a few of the cover plate bolts to the flywheel. The clutch plate must then be centralized on the flywheel, otherwise the clutch shaft will not engage properly. This operation of centralizing is easily done by pushing a round bar through the clutch centre until it enters the spigot bearing bush, and then moving it sideways (using the spigot bearing as a fulcrum), so that it pushes the clutch plate in the required direction. By gauging the angle of the bar at various positions, the centralization can be judged to a nicety. The bolts should then all be inserted and fully tightened, after which a final check should be made with the bar. The clutch withdrawal bearing is of the carbon block type. See that there is plenty of depth of carbon still protruding from the metal housing of the block, and renew the part, if it does not pass on this point.

ASSEMBLING THE BASE CHAMBER

Attention can now be given to refitting the oil-sump. Before this is done, the oil-suction pipe and strainer should be reassembled. Next, examine the composition oilseal at the front end of the sump, which corresponds with that in the timing cover. As already mentioned, if this needs renewing, the ends of the seal should be left standing slightly proud of the groove so as to make a firm joint. The fitting of the sump gasket is a tricky operation, and plenty of jointing compound is necessary, especially in the vicinity of the front oilseal and rear collector housing behind the back bearing. The gasket is of cork, and is in two equal halves. Its ends must fit snugly over the ends of the seals at front and rear, noting that there is a cork strip fitted into a groove in the back bearing cap, around which the rear wall of the sump fits. When all is in place, insert the various holding bolts and tighten evenly.

ASSEMBLING THE CYLINDER HEAD

There is no advantage whatever in fitting a new cylinder-head gasket unless this is unavoidable due to damage of the existing one. Also, there is nothing to beat the standard gasket. Apply high-melting-point grease to both sides of the gasket in a thin film. This will facilitate easy removal in the future and will at the same time effect a perfect seal.

When tightening down the head, follow the proper sequence as detailed on page 98 dealing with head removal. Use the standard ring spanner having twelve angles of attack, and a leverage of about six inches, and apply plenty of force. Do the job once for all, and there will be no need for further tightening, which is in any case difficult when all the valve gear is in place.

Order of attack, cylinder head nuts, TC engine

The push-rods may next be slipped into position, in their order of removal, and the rocker-shaft fitted. Check once more that the oil-drilled rocker standard has been fitted at the back, and, if the compression ratio has been modified, that the necessary packing pieces are in position. Unless the existing locking plates under the heads of the long holding-down bolts are in good order, new ones must be used. Tighten the bolts firmly, then bend up the ends of the plates against one or more flats of the bolt heads. As an alternative, the bolt-heads can be drilled and wired, instead of using locking plates. It will be evident that as the rocker-shaft is pulled down into position by the bolts, some of the valves will be lifted off their seats by their rockers, so that an unequal stress is put on the rocker-shaft. So as not to overdo this, the bolts should be tightened a little at a time in a proper sequence having regard to which valves are causing the pressure.

After finally checking the tappets and push-rods for correct location, the push-rod cover can be replaced, using a cork gasket. This is unusual in that it covers the whole of the area of the metal cover instead of being merely a flange washer. Four large holes are punched in the washer, two near the top edge and two near the bottom, to allow of passage of pressure to the breather pipe. It will be evident that this large cork sheet acts as a baffle between the push-rod housing and the breather pipe. It is, of course, also punched with three smaller holes to allow the cover studs to go through.

It pays to be fairly generous with jointing compound on the edges of the packing, otherwise oil leaks are likely. Also, the three holding nuts must not be over-tightened, in case the cover becomes distorted.

Refitting the oil-pump calls for no particular comment. The by-pass valve must be assembled in the crankcase before the pump is put on, but otherwise, the previous comments regarding the TA engine will generally apply. The same remark holds good for the oil filter and distributor.

CHAPTER 23

Engine Replacement and Starting-Up

REPLACEMENT IN THE CHASSIS. STARTING UP THE ENGINE.
RUNNING-IN TECHNIQUE. ALTERNATIVE GEAR RATIOS.

At this stage, it is advisable to replace the unit in the chassis, as otherwise handling will be more difficult. In any case, it is necessary to couple up the exhaust manifold to the pipe before the induction arrangements are fitted. Uniting the engine and gearbox is an easy task compared with the TA engine, as there is no oil-tight joint to worry about at the clutch housing, and the bush-type spigot bearing is easily lined up and entered. Otherwise, the remarks already made in connection with replacement of the TA unit will be found helpful. The various items such as starter motor, dynamo, and oil-pipes can be assembled, and do not present any particular difficulty. A simple but effective improvement which can be carried out at this stage is to replace the clutch-operating chain, which is of the welded-link type, with a short length of 0.625 in. pitch Renold roller chain (this is the usual motor-cycle rear chain size). The result will be considerably smoother clutch operation, providing the chain is always kept coated with grease to protect its bearings.

The water-pump and other water connections to the cylinders' and head will require thin Hallite joint washers, plus a little jointing compound. The inlet and exhaust manifold washer is of heat-resisting material, in one piece. When fitting the induction pipe to this, use a little jointing compound in the region of the inlet ports only, to discourage air leaks. Paper or thin Hallite washers are used between the carburetters and the induction manifold, and jointing compound should, of course, be used at this point. It is also advisable to drill the carburetter fixing bolts for locking wires, as their rather coarse threads make them liable to slacken off unless they are checked for tightness fairly often, which is not too easy a job. Attention to the carburetters is dealt with in a special chapter.

When refitting radiator connections, radiator, and exhaust pipe joints, attention should be given to the points already made in connection with the TA engine.

STARTING UP THE ENGINE

Assuming that the carburetters have been attended to as detailed elsewhere, and other minor items completed, such as coupling up controls, wiring, fitting the dynamo belt and tachometer drive, we are just about ready to try a preliminary start up. First of all, however, a few checks should be made. See that with No. 1 cylinder at firing t.d.c. the distributor arm is pointing to the correct electrode, and the points are just breaking. As regards spark plugs, the owner may have his own pet make, and so long as this is one specified by M.G.s there is no objection to it being used. The plug gap should be .020 in. to

116

.022 in. The rocker clearance should be set to .020 in. for both inlet and exhaust for the preliminary start. Accuracy in this direction can be left until a little later. The clutch should be adjusted so that there is 1 in. free movement at the pedal pad before the carbon block touches the thrust plate: this can be felt easily on the operating lever. The operating-lever stop on the housing should then be adjusted so that the pedal can move 3 in. to push the clutch out (the latter measurement being positive movement, not including the 1 in. play).

Fill up the sump, using S.A.E. 30 oil irrespective of the weather, unless the latter is below freezing, in which case S.A.E. 20 is correct. A spot of engine oil in the fuel is also a good thing. If you have ideas about upper cylinder lubricant as an alternative to the latter, get the M.G. factory's advice regarding your particular brand before using it.

The battery must be in first-class condition, particularly if the engine bearings and bores have received attention, as it is desirable to buzz the engine round with the plugs out for a few minutes before trying a start. While doing this, inject a squirt of engine oil through each plug hole to ensure that there is plenty of lubricant on the bores. Use an old set of plugs for the first start, in case they become fouled. Having fitted these, and checked oil and water levels and fuel supply, but without the air manifold and cleaner in position, start up. If nothing happens, verify ignition and fuel supply. Faulty timing is usually accompanied by peculiar noises. Assuming that in due course all four cylinders go into action, check the oil-pressure immediately. Do not worry too much about the reading, so long as it is good and high, say 60 lb. or above. Then check the overhead rockers to see that oil is flowing from each one. If all is well, fit the rocker cover, using a cork or similar washer. Don't employ jointing compound for the moment, as the cover will be coming off again very soon. Restart the engine and let it run at about 1,200 r.p.m. until it is nicely warm. Then check the oil-pressure again. It should be about 50 to 60 lb. on TC engines, 40 to 50 lb. on TD. If a higher pressure persists the pump relief valve spring can be shortened to bring it down a little. It is as well, however, not to do this haphazardly, but to give the engine a few miles to settle down before deciding that the pressure is going to remain at too high a value. The very large pump capacity enables the pressure to be maintained even when the bearings have considerable wear. The oil-sump holds 9 pints, and the recommended mineral brands of oil should be used at all times.

RUNNING-IN TECHNIQUE

With the car on the road, and running-in under load about to commence, a few notes regarding procedure at this important stage will be useful. For the first 500 miles the maximum r.p.m. should be restricted to 2,000, and the engine must not be allowed to slog or labour in any way. From then onwards to 1,000 miles, the permitted revs can be increased progressively as the engine feels to be loosening up. Occasionally give it the gun for a few hundred yards, then let back the throttle sharply to get the oil up the bores. At the end of the first 1,000 miles a maximum of 3,000 to 3,500 should be permissible for very short distances only, and for the next 1,000 miles the periods during which these revolutions are held should be progressively increased in length. The TC and allied engines show no distress at really high r.p.m. and it is easy to go over the mark, so a lot of restraint is called for. In general, the last 1,000 (from say 4,700 to 5,700) should not be indulged in until the engine has done at least 3,000 miles, the mixture will be kept rather on the rich side during the running-in period, and the minimum idling speed held to 1,200 r.p.m.   Towards the end of running-in, the carburetters should be synchronized as detailed in Part III. Minor adjustments to mixture strength will not, of course, affect synchronism.

In addition, during the period, the rocker cover should be removed to check lubrication, and the valve clearances adjusted. When doing this the engine should be turned until the valve being checked is fully open. From this position the crankshaft should be given one complete turn, and in this position the valve will be fully closed, with the tappet on the base circle of the cam. The clearance should then be set to .019 in. hot, with a feeler between the rocker tip and the valve stem top.

After running-in, the ignition timing should be experimented with. A small amount of pinking is permissible, even on premium fuel, but this must not be too obtrusive, as otherwise it is a definite indication of too much advance.   It should not be present at any

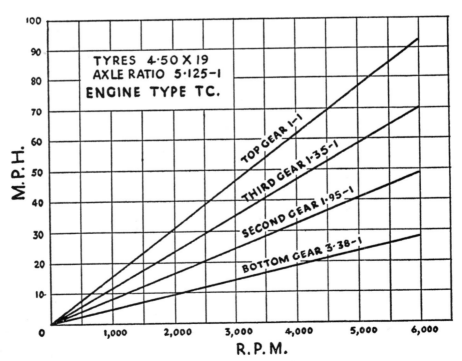

R.p.m./m.p.h. curve, TC type

revolutions above about 2,500 when accelerating in the correct ratio; obviously if the engine is pulling hard on too high a ratio, pinking is inevitable. The vernier device makes adjustment of the timing very easy, but a hand-operated control of Bowden type or similar, is an extremely useful fitment if used intelligently.

After about 6,000 miles it is worth while lifting the cylinder head and having a look inside, if only for reassurance. Advantage can be taken of the opening-up to clear out any carbon which may be present, but, of course, the valves should not be disturbed unless there is something which needs attention. Normal periods between decokes will be around 10,000 to 15,000 miles, depending on the use to which the car is put, and the fuel used. Really fast road work produces less carbon than any other kind of driving, while traffic work has the opposite effect.

Should oiling of plugs suddenly become chronic for no apparent reason, the rubber sealing rings on the valve stems should be suspected. These give no trouble if correctly fitted in the first place, but can be a nuisance if, when fitting, they are damaged in any way which leads to early failure.

ALTERNATIVE GEAR RATIOS

The standard axle ratio is 5.125 to 1, the gear ratios corresponding to this being 5.125, 6.93, 10.0, and 17.32. An alternative axle ratio is available giving 4.875 to 1, but this is too high for the normally tuned engine to give of its best, and should be reserved for use with engines which have been modified to give a really considerable increase in b.h.p.

The gearbox is not likely to need much attention, and follows the usual construction of synchromesh boxes. There are few snags associated with dismantling. When removing the lid, take care to catch the selector springs, and when the selector rods are pushed out (to the rear), catch the selector and interlock balls as they drop. To remove the layshaft it is useful to make up a mandrel 7 9/16 in. long and ¾ in. diameter. Using this, the layshaft can be pushed or tapped out to the rear after removing the set-screw from the lower rear corner of the gearbox.

If the propeller-shaft flange is removed from the mainshaft, or the splined shaft withdrawn, the parts should be marked so that they are replaced in the same position.

The clutch withdrawal mechanism is of a very simple type, comprising a shaft running through the clutch housing, carrying a fork which engages the carbon thrust-block. The shaft oscillates in " self-lubricating " bearings, which may on occasion be none too clever in this respect. Any mysterious tightening-up of the clutch operation should be investigated to see if these bushes are the cause. It is well worth while, if at any time the unit is out of the chassis, to remove the shaft and fit small spring-lid oilers to the bushes.

CHAPTER 24

The T-Type Chassis

GENERAL CONSTRUCTION. ROAD SPRINGS. BRAKES.
STEERING GEAR.

The chassis construction of TA-, TB- and TC-type cars is almost identical, the type TD with independent front suspension having several differences in design from its predecessors. It will be useful to detail a few items which repay special attention.

The road springs on the TA type have the sliding trunnion mounting of a similar type to that fitted to P-type cars, and the maintenance routine applicable should be followed. Early cars had independent lubricating points on the springs, while 1939 models used a grouped nipple system. TB and later cars have rubber-bushed

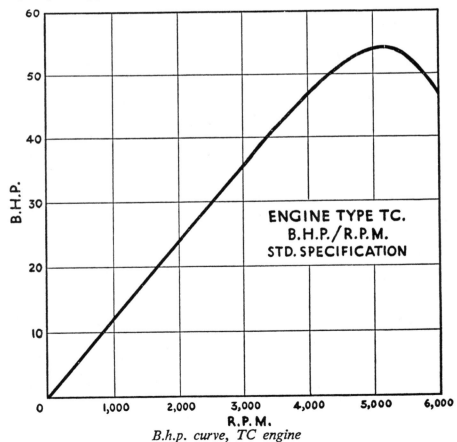

B.h.p. curve, TC engine

120

shackles, which require no lubrication, with the exception of the front ends of the front springs. Owners will have their particular ideas about the best treatment for leaf-springs, but the writer considers the perfect answer to lie in wrapping each spring with the specially prepared, impregnated tape sold for the purpose by accessory houses. This is not to be confused with ordinary insulation tape, which is insufficiently flexible and has no lubricant-retaining properties. The covering should, of course, be applied over a perfectly clean and oiled spring, and lasts indefinitely. The various types of hydraulic shock-absorbers fitted to later models stand up to the job extremely well. The brakes, of normal Lockheed type, are very effective indeed. The brake-fluid reservoir is in a somewhat inaccessible place under the floor near the pedals. It must none the less be inspected regularly to ensure that the fluid level is correct. Suspicious oil drips on the garage floor can quite easily originate from the brake master cylinder, with dire results if neglected.

THE STEERING GEAR

The Bishop cam gear fitted to the TA, TB, and TC cars is delightfully simple to adjust. It is preferable when carrying out such adjustment, to have the steering column and box on the bench and empty of oil. The different thicknesses of shims under the cover of the box enable the amount of free movement to be obtained to a nicety. The aim should be to have practically no play in the straight-ahead position. The shape of the worm is such as to allow a progressive amount of play at each end of the travel toward the full-lock positions. When replacing, make sure that the drop-arm is put on the right spline, and use gear oil in the box.

CHAPTER 25

The TD/TF Engines

SPECIAL FEATURES. ENGINE RECTIFICATION. THE LUBRICATION SYSTEM.
HEAD AND BLOCK MODIFICATIONS. CAMSHAFT AND VALVE-GEAR.

While the general construction of TD and TF engines follows the lines of the TB and TC types, there are differences which may cause confusion, in view of the fact that there is a popular impression that all post-war M.G. Midget engines are identical. Modifications have been introduced periodically, perhaps the most important being the altered valve-timing on the later TDs, and which is standard on TFs. It is therefore advisable to devote a chapter to these points of difference.

The engine mountings differ from previous models, but there is no difficulty in removal. The power unit is somewhat more flexibly mounted, below the centre line of the crankshaft, this feature necessitating the use of a torque-reaction link at the front end. The rear mounting consists of two rubber blocks under the gearbox, these being loose in a cradle formed on the chassis cross-member. There is a rebound-rubber washer under the cradle, and the whole assembly is secured by a single split-pinned nut which pulls down a pivoted link, so compressing the rubber mounting blocks. The diagram 1, part IV, page 178, will make the construction clear. The front mounting is simplicity itself, comprising merely a large rubber block bonded to steel plates which are bolted in position.

The torque-reaction link is anchored to a bracket on the side of the chassis, its other end engaging a lug on the front of the cylinder block below the water-pump. A right-and-left-hand turnbuckle with lock-nuts enables the length of the link to be adjusted to a nicety. With the engine " sitting " properly on its mountings (and therefore upright), the adjustment of the link must be such that it is not tending to push or pull the engine over ; in other words, it must not be used to correct mal-alignment of the engine. The rubber washers fitted both sides of the brackets at each end of the link, i.e., four in all, should be just nipped by the end nuts; there is no need to tighten up until the washers are solid, as this causes engine vibration to be transmitted. Also, do not omit the cups from the washers, otherwise the latter will spread.

It will be found that the control link can be inserted into the bracket holes without taking it to pieces, by first shortening it to its minimum possible length, on the central hexagonal barrel, and then inserting one end, with its cup and rubber fitted, into the hole on the engine bracket. By rocking the engine on its mounting it will be found that the other end can be slipped into its hole in the frame bracket, not forgetting the cup and rubber at this end also. While finally adjusting for length, the engine should be "rocked" from time to time to ensure that everything is central.

ENGINE RECTIFICATION

Dismantling of the engine follows almost exactly the lines laid down in the preceding chapters dealing with the TC. Bearing wear is best rectified by the fitting of a complete service-reground crankshaft with main and big-end bearings, supplied from the M.G. works. The diametral clearance on big-ends is from .0005 to .002 in., with side clearance of from .004 to .006 in. The mains have diametral clearance of from .0008 to .003 in. and side clearance of from .0014 to .0037 in. on the centre journal, which determines the end-clearance of the shaft. The end main bearings have, of course, no end-location.

Pistons are marked on top with an indication of the size of cylinder bore with which they correspond, the running clearance having been allowed for in machining. There are four gradings for bores and pistons, as follows:—

Nominal size bore ±.000 to +.00049 in.   Marked STD.
Nominal size bore +.0005 to +.00099 in.   Marked +.0005.
Nominal size bore +.0010 to +.00149 in.   Marked +.0010.
Nominal size bore +.0015 to +.00199 in.   Marked +.0015.

The piston-to-bore clearance is .0021 in. minimum to .0029 in. maximum, measured immediately below the oil-control ring and at right-angles to the gudgeon-pin axis. It should be noted that this location is important, as the piston skirt is tapered and oval.

It will be useful to detail the range of sizes for standard and over-size pistons, and these are given in the appended table. It should be noted that genuine M.G.-reconditioned engines have only two over-sizes, +.020 and +.040 in. each with four gradings.

Piston Size (across thrust faces below oil ring)		Piston Marking	Suitable for Bore Size	
in.	mm.		in.	mm.
2·6156 2·6160	(66·436) (66·446)	To suit " STD " bore	2·6181 2·6185	(66·500) (66·510)
2·6161 2·6165	(66·449) (66·459)	To suit + ·0005 bore	2·6186 2·6190	(66·513) (66·523)
2·6166 2·6170	(66·462) (66·472)	To suit + ·0010 bore	2·6191 2·6195	(66·525) (66·535)
2·6171 2·6175	(66·474) (66·484)	To suit + ·0015 bore	2·6196 2·6200	(66·538) (66·548)

Standard Piston Sizes

Note.—Production engines having bores .002 in. oversize or over are made into .010-in. bores and graded in the same steps as the standard-bore engine.

Piston Size (across thrust faces below oil ring)		Piston Marking	Suitable for Bore Size	
in.	mm.		in.	mm.•
2·6356 2·6360	(66·944) (66·954)	To suit + ·0200 bore	2·6381 2·6385	(67·008) (67·018)
2·6361 2·6365	(66·957) (66·967)	To suit + ·0205 bore	2·6386 2·6390	(67·021) (67·031)
2·6366 2·6370	(66·970) (66·980)	To suit + ·0210 bore	2·6391 2·6395	(67·033) (67·043)
2·6371 2·6375	(66·982) (66·992)	To suit + ·0215 bore	2·6396 2·6400	(67·046) (67·056)

Oversize Piston Sizes—.020-in. range

Piston Size (across thrust faces below oil ring)		Piston Marking	Suitable for Bore Size	
in.	mm.		in.	mm.
2·6556 2·6560	(67·453) (67·463)	To suit + ·0400 bore	2·6581 2·6585	(67·516) (67·526)
2·6561 2·6565	(67·465) (67·475)	To suit + ·0405 bore	2·6586 2·6590	(67·529) (67·539)
2·6566 2·6570	(67·478) (67·488)	To suit + ·0410 bore	2·6591 2·6595	(67·541) (67·551)
2·6571 2·6575	(67·490) (67·500)	To suit + ·0415 bore	2·6596 2·6600	(67·554) (67·564)

Oversize Piston Sizes—.040-in. range

All tables refer to 1250 *c.c. engines (nominal capacity).*

THE LUBRICATION SYSTEM

The lubrication system is just about identical with the preceding engines as far as earlier TD types are concerned, with the exception that the running pressure is slightly lower, i.e., about 40 lb. per sq. in. The pump-relief valve is housed in the cover of the pump, and it should be noted that the cover is a machined-face fit on to the pump body, no washer being used. The usual paper washer is, of course, fitted between the pump body and the crankcase.

Later TD models have an important modification involving the discontinuation of the " throw-away " type of filter, with its external connecting pipe, and its substitution by a combined pump body and filter mounting. This improvement, commencing at engine no. XPAG/TD2/14224, eliminates the nuisance of making pipe connections when changing the element, and the possibility of fractured pipes. The element, which is fitted by a simple screwed attachment into the filter mounting, is of two types, either Tecalemit FG2381 or Puralator, M.G. part no. 162429.

The latest pumps having this type of filter, are also fitted with a priming plug immediately above the relief valve on the cover. This

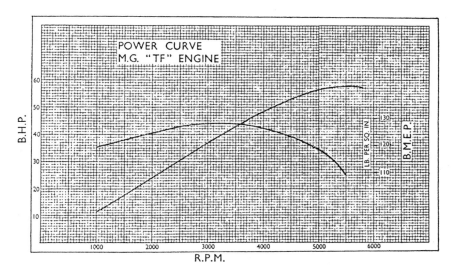

plug is hexagon-headed, and facilitates obtaining full oil pressure immediately on starting up after the circulating system has been completely drained for any reason.

At the same time as the incorporation of the combined pump body and filter-mounting unit, the oil-pump intake was moved from the side of the sump to a more central position. This is illustrated on page 173. From engine no. XPAG/TD2/14948, a sump having a capacity of 10.5 pints instead of the previous 9 pints was fitted.

HEAD AND BLOCK MODIFICATIONS

Improved water circulation is a feature of all TD cylinder blocks subsequent to engine no. XPAG/TD2/17968. It is necessary to ensure that the correct gasket is used with these blocks, though this gasket is suitable for all engines previous to the above number, and is supplied as standard for them. Starting at engine no. XPAG/TD2/22735, the cylinder head water passages also were modified, necessitating a further change in the gasket. With these heads, earlier-type gaskets are not suitable, the correct part no. being 168423.

While trouble with water-pump gland leakage, or other faults in this component are best dealt with by fitting a service replacement, it might be mentioned that an improved type of gland was fitted commencing at engine no. XPAG/TD/6482. This has the gland seating against the impeller boss instead of the pump body, but otherwise the pump construction is virtually unchanged.

Unlike earlier models, with the cooling water at atmospheric pressure, the TF type has a pressurized cooling system, the under-bonnet filler cap incorporating a spring-loaded valve which has to open before any pressure can escape to the vent pipe. When the engine is hot, it is essential that the cap be removed very slowly, otherwise results may be unpleasant. The cap has a specially shaped cam action to enable a slow release to be obtained when disengaging. The water system holds 10.5 pints as against 12 pints of the atmospheric system on previous post-war engines.

CAMSHAFT AND VALVE-GEAR

A minor alteration to the push-rods, enabling longer adjusting screws, with more range of adjustment, to be fitted, was made to engines starting at no. XPAG/TD2/17298. The rods are naturally shorter than previous ones, and the point is easily checked when ordering replacements by taking along one of the existing rods.

With engine no. XPAG/TD2/24116, an important modification was made to the valve timing, resulting in much quieter valve operation by enabling the rocker clearance to be reduced to .012 in. (hot), instead

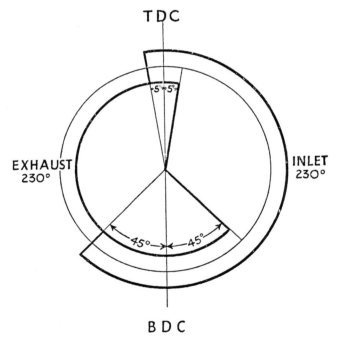

*Valve timing diagram, TD engines with modified camshaft,
and TF engines*

of the previous .019 in. This camshaft can, of course, be fitted to previous engines, the dimensions, apart from the cam contours, being identical, as is the valve lift.

This camshaft gives the following timing:—
Inlet opens 5 degs. before t.d.c.
Inlet closes 45 degs. after b.d.c.
Exhaust opens 45 degs. before b.d.c.
Exhaust closes 5 degs. after t.d.c.
Overlap 10 degs.

All TD engines as standard, even those fitted with the modified camshaft, have valve-spring strength and valve dimensions identical with the TC unit. TF engines, however, in addition to the camshaft giving the aforementioned timing, are provided with larger valves and stronger valve springs. The details are as follows:—

	Inlet	*Exhaust*
Head diameter of valve	36 mm.	34 mm.
Stem diameter	8 mm.	8 mm.
Face angle	30 degs.	30 degs.

	Inner spring	*Outer spring*
Free length of spring	2.565 in.	2.927 in.
Fitted length of spring	1.438 in.	1.532 in.
At load of	55 lb.	95 lb.

It will be noted that these valve and spring dimensions correspond to the ones quoted in Chapter 30 in connection with modifications for extra power on engines of type T.B to TD.

CHAPTER 26

The TD/TF Gearbox and Chassis

THE CLUTCH. CLUTCH CONTROL. THE GEARBOX.
CHASSIS AND SUSPENSION. THE FRONT SPRINGING.
HYDRAULIC DAMPERS. TESTING THE DAMPERS.

The Clutch

The TD/TF clutch is of similar construction to that of the TC, being of the normal Borg and Beck pattern. Fitted originally with a 7.25-in. plate, as on the TC, the diameter was increased to 8 in. at TD engine number 9408. This alteration was responsible for the change in engine nomenclature from XPAG/TD to XPAG/TD2, and it is necessary to emphasize that engines and gearboxes cannot be interchanged (one item with the other), as between the two nomenclatures. The reason for this is that the fitting of the 8-in. plate necessitated a change both in the engine flywheel housing and the gearbox housing, in order correctly to position the thrust race. The type of gearbox can be identified by the diameter of the clutch withdrawal fork shaft, which is .625 in. on XPAG/TD boxes, and .75 in. on XPAG/TD2 ditto.

Clutch Control

The clutch operation on TD up to chassis number TD22251 is by a flexible cable from the pedal to a link, mounted on the side of the sump on a bracket bolted thereto. A push-rod transmits the motion from the link to the clutch-shaft lever, and adjustment is made at the point where the cable is anchored to the end of the link. The free movement at the pedal pad (before the thrust block contacts the thrust pad on the internal withdrawal levers) must be not less than .75 in. This corresponds to about $\frac{1}{16}$ in. at the carbon thrust block face.

It is advisable always to keep the cable end heavily covered in graphite grease to prevent rust. Even with this precaution, fraying of the cable is by no means unknown, and it should receive regular inspection, as breakage can be a real nuisance.

Commencing at the chassis number quoted above, a rod replaced the cable, providing a more reliable connection. This has no effect on the amount of clearance necessary, which is unaltered from that mentioned.

The Gearbox

The gearbox is similar in construction to that of the TC. The ratios, however, are somewhat wider, being as follows:—TD type

The rear end of a TD engine unit prior to removal.

A TD engine ready for removal.

[Reproduced by courtesy of the Nuffield Organization]
(Left) *A jig for holding the gearbox when dismantling, threaded into the drain plug hole*
(Right) *Withdrawing the TD mainshaft assembly through the top of the box.*

Improved appearance of the engine and a decided reduction in valve gear noise. An alloy rocker-box design by the author. Note quick filler and H.T. cable conduit.

(axle ratio 5.125:1), 5.125, 7.098, 10.609, 17.938; TF type (axle ratio 4.875:1), 4.875, 6.752, 10.09, 17.06.

For specially tuned cars, an alternative crown wheel and pinion is available giving the following:—Axle ratio 4.55:1, 4.55, 6.309, 9.429, 15.942.

It should be emphasized that very high ratios are quite unsuitable for normal use, and it is difficult to beat the standard ratios for the two types of car with engines in standard trim. With progressive tuning as detailed in chapter 30, it is feasible to use the TF ratios on the TD, but anything higher calls for a much lighter body and a lot of extra urge in the power unit.

The crown-wheel/pinion teeth combinations corresponding to the above are respectively 8/41, 8/39, and 9/41.

If it is desired for any reason to dismantle the gearbox, the job should start from the rear end, a drawer being used to remove the driving flange from the output shaft, after which removal of the rear cover can be tackled. When removing the selector shafts, be careful not to lose the locking balls. The layshaft spindle can be taken out by using a copper drift on its forward end. Likewise, the drive gear complete with its bearing is removed by tapping the mainshaft towards the front of the box, again using a copper drift. After extracting the journal bearing from its housing, the whole mainshaft assembly can be withdrawn through the top of the box. Further dismantling follows the normal procedure with synchromesh boxes. However, it is recommended that any serious gearbox trouble be dealt with by an M.G. specialist, particularly if this occurs in the synchromesh mechanism.

CHASSIS AND SUSPENSION

The chassis of TD and TF models differs considerably from preceding T types. It is of very rigid construction, and has the rear semi-elliptic springs mounted so that the axle passes under the side-members, which are arched to give considerable axle movement. Independent front suspension by coil springs is also a feature.

The rear springs have flexible rubber bushes all round, so that no lubrication is necessary. Further, the leaves of the springs are separated by rubber interleaving. Lubrication of the spring leaves is " officially " discouraged, but the writer has found no ill-effect, and in fact a definite improvement, as a result of wrapping the springs with " Drevo " wrapping tape (obtainable at accessory shops), just as he has done on all his previous T types.

Apart from checking periodically to make sure that all bolts are tight, little maintenance is called for. The rubber shackle bushes are readily renewed when worn, as they are a push fit, and only compress when tightened. It is essential, however, before tightening up, that the normal load is applied to the springs, i.e., the car is not jacked under the chassis. This precaution ensures that the rubber is in its " neutral " position, and flexes equally under working conditions, instead of being overstressed one way. Care should also be taken to ensure that the two bushes are inserted for an equal distance from either side so that everything is central.

THE FRONT SPRINGING

If it is desired to carry out a measurement check of the front suspension, the following particulars will be useful:—

Camber (static position) : TD—Nil
TF—1 deg. positive } Tolerance ± 1 deg.
Castor angle : 2 deg. ± 0.5 deg. with side-members parallel to road.
Toe-in. : Nil.
King-pin inclination : 9 to 10.5 deg. full bump.
Track : 47.5 in. front.   50 in. rear.

The wishbone bearings are of the rubber-bushed type, similar to those used for the rear springs. When clamping up, the bottom wishbones should be parallel to the ground, to ensure equal stressing of the rubber.

HYDRAULIC DAMPERS

Hydraulic dampers form an integral part of the i.f.s. system, and are of the double-acting type of Armstrong or Girling manufacture.

No adjustment is provided or required, periodical checking of the fluid level, and the attachments to the chassis and suspension, being all that is required in the way of maintenance routine. Replenishment should not be necessary at intervals of less than 12,000 miles, the fluid being topped up to the bottom of the filler plug hole; it is, of course, essential that only the right kind of fluid be used, and that no dirt is allowed to enter.

If it is suspected that the dampers are not functioning properly, a simple test can be carried out, after removing the damper. The car should be jacked up under the lower wishbone pan until the tyre is clear of the ground. The road wheel is next removed, also the top pivot bolt for the swivel pin. This will enable the hub assembly to be swung clear of the damper-arm-cum-top wishbone; the hub should be supported, to prevent the brake hose from getting damaged by stretching. The damper can now be slipped clear after taking out the four setscrews securing its housing to the chassis.

TESTING THE DAMPERS

A steel plate about $\frac{3}{16}$-in. thick should be made into a jig for clamping in the vice, four holes being drilled in it to receive nuts and bolts for attaching the damper body thereto. (If the body is clamped between the vice jaws it may be distorted.) The damper, on the plate, should then be clamped, in its normal upright position, and the lever moved up and down, steadily, throughout its full stroke. The resistance to movement should be steady and constant. If there is erratic or free movement at any part of the stroke, shortage of fluid may be the cause. The damper must therefore be replenished, the arm being worked through its stroke while fluid is added, so as to expel the air which is causing the trouble. (Regular fluid check will, of course, prevent this happening.)

If no improvement is effected, it will be necessary to replace the damper by a service fitting. No attempt must be made to dismantle the internal mechanism. The rear dampers can, of course, be checked in the same manner. The rubber bushes fitted to the rear damper links are, however, only replaceable by the use of special tools comprising a punch, guide pin, and guide funnel, and although these are easily made up, it is probably best in the long run to change the dampers complete when an excessive amount of wear has taken place in the bushes. All dampers have a movement of 35 deg. either side of the centre line. If by any chance a damper arm has been removed from its spindle splines, it is essential that it is replaced to give this movement, as if the relative position of the lever is wrong, the internal mechanism of the damper will be damaged.

PART III

CHAPTER 27

Cylinder Bore Renovation

BORE MEASUREMENT. RINGS AND PISTONS. FITTING NEW RINGS.
OVERSIZE BORES OR LINERS.

The cylinders and pistons comprise possibly the most important components in the engine, and too much stress cannot be laid on the necessity of bringing their condition to the highest pitch of accuracy. The requirements do not differ materially for all types of M.G. engines, and the details given herewith should prove of assistance in assessing just what attention is required to any particular power unit.

The internal dimensions of the bores can be measured by means of an internal micrometer, or a cylinder bore gauge for preference. The point regarding wear is to remember that the bore at the bottom end will be very near its original diameter, since very little wear takes place at this point. This diameter should be checked against the diameter just below the top of the ring travel, that is, just below the ridge which will be present right at the top of the bore.

If the difference between the two diameters does not exceed .007 in., it is not essential to rebore on account of wear only, but, of course, should damage be apparent, in the way of scoring, or if hot-spots caused by local overheating have resulted in patches of discoloration, a degree of renovation will be called for. Slight surface scratches can be lapped out, and this process will be described later. For the moment it will be assumed that the surfaces are found in order after a most careful scrutiny with an electric light, and that wear does not exceed the .007 in. already mentioned. Providing oil consumption was not previously excessive, the original rings may be used again, but having gone so far, the owner will no doubt prefer to fit new rings, and this is certainly to be recommended.

RINGS AND PISTONS

The existing rings should be removed from the pistons, and if any carbon is present on the ends of the ring at the gap, it should be scraped off. The ring is then inserted in the cylinder bore at the very top, that is, above the wear ridge, and the gap measured with a feeler gauge. This should not exceed .008 in. If it does, it indicates that the ring itself has worn. In any case, however, the gap will obviously be too large when the ring is operating in the worn part of the bore, and in addition, some of the ring tension will have gone, so that this test is mainly a matter of interest.

Having removed all the rings, the pistons must be thoroughly cleaned inside and out. The ring grooves can be cleared with a piece of broken ring held in a file handle, but great care must be taken not to score the aluminium when using this weapon. The piston crown and interior can be scoured in a mild way with a wire brush, but this must be kept clear of the ring lands and skirt. The former are particularly important, as on the perfection of the lands depends the gas-tightness of the rings. So be careful to avoid scratching. The drain holes, if any, in and below the oil-control ring groove, can be cleaned with a twist-drill of the right size held in the hand. When all the pistons have been duly cleaned, examine them for faults. The crown and skirt are hardly likely to be cracked, though such things can happen, so everything must be suspect. The ring grooves are more likely sources of trouble, as they are often damaged by unskilled handling in fitting and removing of rings. Slight scratches can be removed by very careful work with superfine emery cloth and very smooth files, but this work must be done with skill, otherwise the last state will be worse than the first. The edges of the ring grooves may be given the merest trace of a chamfer with a file so as to reduce any tendency to sticking on the part of the new rings.

Fitting New Rings

The new rings will require very careful fitting both as regards the side clearance in the groove and the gap. The former should be between .001 in. to .002 in. If less than this, the ring can be rubbed down on a sheet of emery cloth on a perfectly flat plate. (A sheet of plate glass is ideal for this.) One side only of the ring should be rubbed down, and this side should subsequently be fitted facing the top, so that the untouched side maintains the seal against the lower face of the groove. The ring gap should be adjusted with a fine file, taking care to keep the gap edges parallel to one another. Some juggling will be needed to arrive at a good average gap for a worn bore. The best way to do this is to check the gap at the lowest part of the ring travel, and adjust this to .006 in. It will probably be rather wide at the point of maximum bore wear near the top, but too wide a gap is less harmful than too little, and very little gas is clever enough to get through. With " new " bores or liners, the gap should be not less than .006 in. and is not too big at .010 in.

When new rings have been fitted without reboring the cylinders, it will be necessary to remove the ridge at the top of each bore, this being the unworn part of the bore which has been subjected to ring travel. It will be appreciated that whilst the old rings wear in unison with the ridge, the new ones would strike it, with unpleasant results for them and the piston. The ridge can be removed by careful scraping, but this method requires a good deal of skill, and if the reader has any doubts about his capabilities in this direction, it is better to entrust the work to an expert. Well-equipped workshops have a cutter or boring machine which is a more effective way than scraping. It is desirable that the renovated surface is made to merge with the part of the bore subjected to the ring travel in as precise a manner as possible, but at the same time the cutter should not encroach on the travel area of the rings any further than necessary.

The technique of ring fitting has already been described, but it might be worth while emphasizing that the new rings should be selected from a reputable maker's recommendations; if full details are given regarding the amount of wear which was found in the bore, it will be possible to obtain an absolutely correct oversize for the job. Haphazard purchasing is to be avoided. The fit of scraper or oil-control rings is not so vital as is the case with compression rings, but it is as well to replace these at the same time. Some forms of scraper ring, which present a relatively small contact area of high pressure against the bore in the interests of effective oil-control, tend to wear rapidly in consequence.

Attention to the cylinder bores (other than reboring) is limited to the removal of minor scores or scratches which, unless something has been very much amiss, should be of negligible depth, but can be caused by broken rings or grit. The operation for removing such scratches entails the use of a " lap " ; this can be made of an old piston of the same size as those fitted to the engine. The piston should be provided with a full set of rings, and a hammer handle fitted to the gudgeon pin to enable it to be pushed up and down the bore. Metal polish of Brasso consistency is used as the lapping medium. The lap, liberally anointed with polish, should be pushed up and down the bore, but not twisted or rotated. After every dozen or so strokes it should be withdrawn, given another supply of polish, and re-entered. This treatment will be found to remove all discoloration and scratching, and leave the bores with a mirror finish.

OVERSIZE BORES OR LINERS

So much for attention to the existing bores and pistons. If the amount of wear is such that reboring is essential, the matter resolves itself into the question of giving the job to a competent specialist. There is, however, a point to be considered, that is, whether to have the bores finished oversize, or whether to have them sleeved, retaining the original dimensions. As regards the former, the normal rebore has the effect of increasing the swept volume of the engine, and the amount so gained is by no means to be sneezed at. For example, a rebore of .040 in. on the cylinder diameter of an 847-c.c. engine results in an increase to 878 c.c. With this, also, one obtains a higher compression ratio, since the head volume is unaltered. In this connection, however, it might be mentioned that it is impracticable to rebore the P-type engine of 57-mm. bore, to the PB size of 60 mm., as the removal of this large amount of metal would leave the walls far too thin.

The advantage of fitting cylinder liners, apart from the fact that it keeps the engine " standard," is that the liners can be made of special wear-resisting material which is likely to have a longer life than the original bore. Naturally, when fitting liners the bores are opened out to a much greater extent than is used for a normal rebore, and in view of the necessity of ensuring the correct interference fit of the liner in the bore, and subsequent accuracy in finishing-off the bore of the liner, this method of renovation is more expensive than an ordinary "oversize" rebore. On balance, the writer would say that if the exchequer will stand it, liners are the answer.

The standard pistons fitted to most M.G. engines are of Aerolite manufacture. There are also other types of piston which are extremely effective for high-speed work. There is no need to mention the names of makers who will be readily identifiable, and so long as their recommendations are followed all will be well. But never in any circumstances attempt to economize by fitting "any old" pistons. If the job is discussed intelligently with the specialist who is doing the work, he will see that pistons and clearances are correct for the purposes to which the car will be put. There are still one or two so-called reborers whose stock phrase is "I've left her a bit tight, sir," imagining this to be a sign of superlative fitting. Needless to say, they should be avoided. On the other hand, there is no need for excessive clearance which will only lead to slap and too rapid wear. Free running is essential, and naturally takes precedence over extreme silence in operation; the answer to this is to get the clearances correct.

CHAPTER 28

Overhaul and Tuning of S.U. Carburetters

COMMON FAULTS. ENSURING FREE PISTON MOVEMENT.
POSITIONING THE NEEDLE. ASSEMBLY OF THE JET BLOCK.
THE FLOAT CHAMBER ASSEMBLY. SYNCHRONISM OF TWIN
CARBURETTERS. TUNING TECHNIQUE. ORAL CHECK.

The importance of the correct functioning of the twin-carburetter system fitted to most M.G. cars, cannot be over-estimated. Properly adjusted and tuned, the system is wellnigh perfect. Mal-adjustment or incorrect operation can completely mar the engine's performance.

The S.U. carburetter is of extremely straightforward design and construction. So much so, that it sometimes suffers through being pulled apart far too frequently by unskilled hands. In tackling a thorough overhaul of the instruments, therefore, the first thing to do is to examine each carburetter carefully, when it will be easy to decide whether abuse has been carried to such a pitch that a reconditioned carburetter is the best policy.

This should only be necessary in most extreme cases, as fortunately the parts most liable to derangement are easily replaced. Readers will be familiar with the working principle of the S.U., which, in brief, is that the fuel flow is controlled by a specially tapered needle moving in the jet under the influence of a piston operated by induction vacuum. The piston has an air-control barrel attached to it so that the intake of air is controlled in correct ratio to fuel delivery.

The most common fault in the carburetter is concerned with this arrangement of mixture control; lack of lubrication, or the presence of dirt can cause sticking of the piston in its dashpot, and badly neglected carburetters are prone to this trouble. Apart from the question of neglect, however, it is possible for such sticking to take place due to other causes, particularly on M.G. engines where the dashpots are slightly out of the vertical (the carburetters being of the semi-downdraught pattern).

ENSURING FREE PISTON MOVEMENT

It will be appreciated that the clearances inside the dashpot, particularly between the rim of the piston and the dashpot wall, are machined to very close limits. Slight wear in the centre guide, or a very small amount of distortion of the dashpot, can easily cause the piston to touch the dashpot. Such contact, however slight, cannot be allowed; the piston must fall absolutely freely by gravity when lifted. Having dismantled and cleaned thoroughly both dashpot and piston, paying special attention to the annular grooves in the latter, all should be well. If, with everything clean, it is not possible to slide the piston throughout its travel, at the same time spinning it on its central guide so that its periphery describes a spiral up and down the dashpot, without actual contact taking place, the fouling point must be found. If the movement is carried out slowly, with the dashpot horizontal and the air-piston held between finger and thumb, it should be possible to feel the spot. In extreme cases, lamp-black on the surfaces may be necessary, but invariably the " touch " test is sufficient.

This contact indicates minute distortion of the dashpot, usually caused by uneven tightening down or possibly dropping the component on a hard floor! The remedy is judicious use of emery cloth on the offending spot, in conjunction with metal polish. It will be found that very little metal need be removed to give clearance, and it will be obvious that no more clearance must be provided than is absolutely necessary, since air leakage past the piston will be caused if the gap is excessive. This use of abrasives on aluminium surfaces may be frowned on by the purists. The answer to this is that far more damage can be caused by ham-fisted use of scrapers, which only the most skilled of fitters ever learn to use properly, and that providing discretion is used, emery cloth and similar aids do the job extremely well.

Slight wear in the centre guide, otherwise of little consequence, may cause piston-dashpot contact due to the angularity of the carburetter, therefore test for freedom with the parts held at their working angle. In this case, it will probably be found that the area of fouling is rather larger than that caused by a high-spot or distortion, but the degree of contact is very slight. Still, it must be remedied. Patience and a " little at a time," will ensure a perfect fit. Finally, a polish all over, inside and out, with metal polish, and a thorough wash in petrol will finish the job.

Incidentally, the correct lubricant for the centre guide is thin cycle oil, and not much of it. It is worth while screwing small cycle-type spring-lid oil cups into the caps at the tops of the dashpots, to allow the correct amount of lubricant to be inserted. This is a much more practical idea than attempting to insert oil through the microscopic hole in the cap, whilst frequent removal of the cap itself is undesirable. (This does not apply to hydraulically damped carburetters.)

POSITIONING THE NEEDLE

There is only one position for the needle in the air-piston, that is, with its shoulder flush with the face of the hole. No attempt should be made to get any kind of adjustment by moving the needle in the air-piston away from this position, and it must be locked securely by the screw, which will stand tightening good and hard.

The jet is movable under the influence of the mixture control, the jet being drawn down to enrich the mixture. Special washers are provided to maintain a fuel seal and at the same time allow the jet to slide freely. Naturally the jet must be central, otherwise it will be fouled by the needle. Thus, if the needle has been passed as perfectly straight, and the piston is sliding freely, any restriction of movement must be caused by fouling of the jet by the needle, and steps must be taken to centralize the jet.

It will be obvious that when the needle is well home in the jet, there is very little clearance. Any contact, apart from causing undesirable sluggishness in operation, will cause rapid wear of jet and

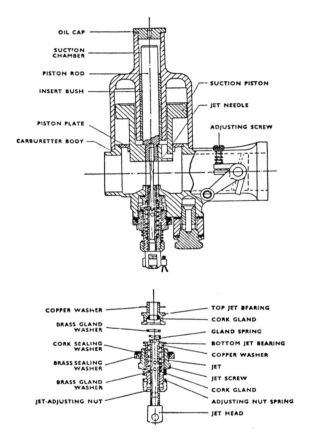

OIL CAP
SUCTION CHAMBER
PISTON ROD
INSERT BUSH
PISTON PLATE
CARBURETTER BODY
SUCTION PISTON
JET NEEDLE
ADJUSTING SCREW

COPPER WASHER
BRASS GLAND WASHER
CORK SEALING WASHER
BRASS SEALING WASHER
BRASS GLAND WASHER
JET-ADJUSTING NUT
TOP JET BEARING
CORK GLAND
GLAND SPRING
BOTTOM JET BEARING
COPPER WASHER
JET
JET SCREW
CORK GLAND
ADJUSTING NUT SPRING
JET HEAD

*S.U. carburetter: dashpot components
and jet assembly*

needle. There is no particular difficulty about attending to the well-being of the jet assembly, though naturally the carburetter makers do not recommend haphazard dismantling. The essential items are a supply of the necessary sealing washers and reasonable care. The jet block can readily be unscrewed from the carburetter body after first removing the jet control lever. The jet can then be withdrawn, when it should be examined to ascertain whether constant use of the mixture control has caused any ridging on the outside of the jet barrel.

If this is present to any marked degree, a new jet should be used; if slight, a polish with carborundum cloth will do the trick. It must be realized that the fuel-tightness of the assembly depends on the fit of the outside of the jet against the cork washers, and that the seal has to be maintained even when the jet is pulled down by the mixture control. So many S.U. carburetters are to be seen with a minute " drip " at the base of the jet, that it is considered advisable to stress this point.

Assembling the Jet Block

When refitting the new sealing washers it is easy to go wrong with the various bits and pieces which comprise the jet-block assembly. The appended sectional view will make all clear. The only requirement for ensuring that the jet is absolutely central is to get the two gland washers which actually bear against the outside of the jet, correctly in position; a smear of oil on the jet will help it to slide easily, and will discourage the washers from tilting. See that the gland spring and its brass washers at each end thereof are free on the jet, introduce everything carefully into position in the carburetter body, and tighten up the block against its large washers. If the job has been done correctly, the jet should slide without undue force, but in judging this, make allowances for the fact that new washers are in. If the jet is still not central, or if in doubt about any other point, dismantle and try again. As stated earlier, the job is not difficult, but there are quite a lot of bits. However, reference to the diagram with the unit on the bench, should make all clear.

The Float Chamber Assembly

The float chamber assembly is quite straightforward, the filter and needle valve being housed in the lid. If the filter is damaged or missing, fit a new one. Likewise, the needle valve and seating are readily detachable; the needle is prone to shoulder after about 25,000 miles, and although the fault only shows up when idling (enriching of the mixture due to flooding being apparent) it should not be tolerated, and a new needle plus seating is indicated. This needle valve will " hold " indefinitely against the fuel pressure from the standard S.U. pressure pump, and if the pump clicks when the engine is stationary, and there are no pipe leaks, suspect the needle valve, and remedy matters. The float locates on a central guide rod which is screwed into the base of the chamber. Make sure this rod is tight in its tapped hole. The fuel level is adjusted by judicious bending of the toggle actuating the needle valve, but, of course, this operation will be carried out during the final tuning under running conditions.

Some types of S.U. carburetter have a hydraulic damper embodied in the piston guide. This comprises a plunger which is carried on a rod attached to the top brass cap of the dashpot. Sliding in the bore formed for the purpose in the centre of the piston guide, the plunger gives a retarding action to the piston, producing a momentarily rich mixture when the throttle is opened suddenly, with, in some cases, improvement in acceleration. If it is desired to experiment in this direction, it is possible to obtain the necessary parts from the S.U. people to convert non-damped instruments to the damped type.

The correct grade of oil for use in the damper is Castrolite, or Essolube 20.

This completes work on the carburetters; the only final word is that when reassembling, remember that the instruments are made largely of

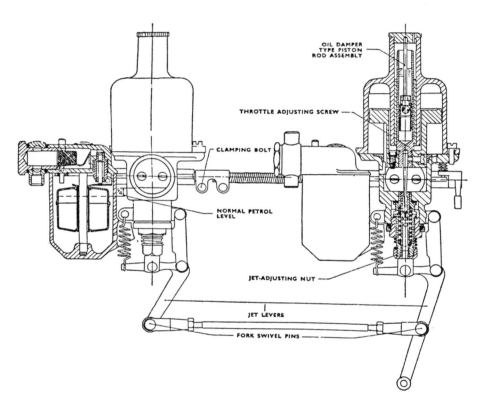

Lay-out diagram of twin S.U. carburetters

alloy, and easily distorted, and that threads can be stripped by too hearty tightening. In particular, watch these points when refitting the two dashpot screws; see that the dashpot is seating properly on its register, and tighten the screws equally and moderately. After refitting the carburetters on the induction pipe, examine the action of the two throttles and their interconnecting spring coupling. See that there is a throttle-stop screw on each instrument, and that both are operating with their respective throttles in the same position. Then adjust the coupling accordingly.

SYNCHRONISM OF TWIN CARBURETTERS

At some stage during the running-in period it is necessary to synchronize the carburetters (if these are of the twin type). Engines with single carburetters need somewhat less complicated attention but the mixture strength is still adjusted by movement of the jet in the same manner as for dual instruments.

Once set, the carburetters will remain in correct adjustment indefinitely. Even if minor adjustment to mixture strength is dictated by outside conditions at a later stage, this will not affect the synchronism, as the degree of adjustment will be substantially the same for both instruments.

Assuming therefore that the carburetters have been overhauled in accordance with previous information, and that the engine has completed its preliminary road-work in good style, the first step is to test the fuel level. Switch on the engine (and thus the fuel pump) without starting-up.

Then lift up the air-piston in each carburetter in turn, using a cycle spoke or the like, and observe if any petrol is issuing from the jet. Unless the pump clicks, there should be no leakage at the jet, but should the pump operate, watch for this. The petrol will be seen piling up against the throttle valve. Assuming the needle valve and seating have been correctly attended to as previously described, it must be assumed that the fuel level is too high, and this can be corrected by carefully bending the toggle operating the float needle. Very little bending is necessary, and when correct, the fuel level should be just below the top of the jet—about $\frac{1}{16}$ in. is right.

TUNING TECHNIQUE

Screw up the jet adjusting hexagons to their topmost position, but not tight, as we want them easily movable. Start the engine; it will be necessary to pull down the jets by the mixture control to do this, and a degree of throttle opening will also be necessary. With the engine started, set the throttles by the slow-running screws to a steady 1,000 r.p.m. Gradually move the jet control to the topmost position of the jets as the engine warms up. Next, with the cycle spoke aforementioned, very carefully lift the air-piston on the first carburetter about $\frac{1}{16}$ in., taking care not to obstruct the air intake while doing so. It will be found by this action that the two cylinders served by the carburetter will misfire, and the engine will tend to stall. Do likewise with the other carburetter, and the same result will be noted.

Now go back to the first carburetter again, and screw the hexagon down, that is, clockwise, half a turn. Try the action with the spoke again. This time it may be found that the engine does not misfire, which is what we are aiming at. Apply the same treatment to the second carburetter, moving the jet hexagon the same amount on each instrument. Test between each movement, until a position is arrived at where no effect is shown in the running of the engine when the air-piston is lifted (taking care not to lift it more than the fraction mentioned).

It will probably be found that the engine speed is tending to drop, and so the idling screws should be reset to give 1,000 r.p.m. as before. Next, move each hexagon one " flat," or 1/6 of a turn clockwise. We should now find that lifting the air slide causes the engine speed to increase slightly, showing that the mixture is very slightly on the rich side when idling; this is the object, and it may be found that a very slight difference in the positions of the two hexagons may be needed to obtain the same speed increase on each carburetter. The difference, however, should not amount to more than one " flat."

ORAL CHECK

As a final check, listen to the hiss from each intake, which should be equal in intensity. Also listen to the exhaust note. A splashy beat indicates weak mixture, and a heavy thumpy note shows over-richness, this latter being accompanied by black smoke. However, if the tuning sequence has been properly carried out, all should be well, and at 900 to 1,000 r.p.m. the engine should idle perfectly regularly. As the engine loosens up, and especially in very hot weather, it may be possible to weaken the mixture to the extent of one " flat " or so on each jet. Always be careful to move both jets in turn, and never have more than one " flat " difference; if one jet is moved drastically without the other, the original settings will be hopelessly lost.

CHAPTER 29

Supercharger Installations

"BLOWING" THE STANDARD ENGINE. THE SHORROCK
SUPERCHARGER. INSTALLATION OF THE SHORROCK BLOWER.
MAINTENANCE OF THE SHORROCK BLOWER. THE WADE
SUPERCHARGER. INSTALLATION OF THE WADE BLOWER.
MAINTENANCE OF THE WADE BLOWER.

The makers of M.G. cars were right in the forefront in the application of forced induction to racing cars. It was natural therefore that they should be one of the first (if not the first) manufacturers to offer a car (the P-type Midget) for sale to the ordinary motoring enthusiast, which was designed for use, if desired, with an "added" supercharger exactly as standard, with the proviso that a certain maximum blower pressure should not be exceeded.

In the hey-day of the P types, there were several proprietary makes of blower available, and names like Zoller, Marshall, and Centric, come readily to mind. These blowers were used with outstanding success by M.G. trials drivers of the 1934-1939 era, and there must be very many of them still in use.

With the post-war advent of the TC engine, the M.G. people have again given their "O.K." as regards supercharging, and details concerning the extra performance obtainable by this means will be found in a later chapter dealing with special tuning. In the case of such engines as the TA and pre-P types, supercharging is, of course, feasible, but because of the different construction of essential parts of these engines compared with P- and TC-types blower pressure must be kept on the low side, and some restraint has to be used in driving, there being a greater element of risk than in the case of the other types mentioned. In this connection it will be appreciated that reference to the TC will automatically include also the TD and TF engines.

These notes regarding the installation and operation of two typical makes of proprietary blower will indicate what is involved in supercharging the standard TC engine. Readers concerned with other models are advised to seek the advice of both the M.G. works and the supercharger makers before taking any action.

The first point to be noted is that the blower pressure is in the region of 6 lb. sq. in. With this as maximum, the engine below the head remains as standard, i.e., no special parts such as pistons or crankshaft are required, and the lubrication and cooling system can readily cope with the extra loading. As it is possible to obtain over 95 b.h.p. with 6 lb. pressure, it can be considered that anything higher is really getting to the racing-car stage, demanding somewhat special treatment of the whole car, and is thus outside the scope of this book.

THE SHORROCK SUPERCHARGER

The makers of the Shorrock blower have had a great many years of experience in the design of high-efficiency compressors. Their latest machine, which is supplied complete for fitting by the average competent M.G. owner, absorbs relatively little power, and is quiet in operation, and very reliable.

The Shorrock compressor is of the positive displacement eccentric-drum type. The vanes are mounted radially to the compressor casing, each being carried by two ball-bearings on a shaft concentric with the outer casing. The vanes are carried round by their contact with the eccentric rotor drum, which is driven from the engine. Specially designed trunnions are fitted where the vanes pass through the drum, these allowing for the angular movement of the vanes relative to the periphery of the rotor. It will be appreciated that this feature allows the vanes to maintain a very close clearance from the casing, as they always remain at the same radial distance from it. This is one of the features making for high volumetric efficiency.

The rotor itself is carried on ball and roller bearings, the latter being fitted at the driving end. The lubricating oil supply is obtained from the engine pressure system, and is fed by special metering arrangements to ensure that an excess of oil does not enter the blower casing. This is, of course, an essential feature, as all oil fed to the blower is passed into the engine cylinders.

As supplied for TC and similar M.G. engines, the Shorrock blower specified is size S 75, having a swept volume of 0.72 litre per revolution of the blower shaft. Driven at the specified step-up ratio of 1.16 to 1 on the engine speed, this gives the following pressures above atmospheric:—

r.p.m.	Boost lb. per sq. in.
1,000	1.5
2,000	2.5
3,000	3.8
4,000	5.5
5,000	6.0

INSTALLATION OF THE SHORROCK BLOWER

The Shorrock blower is arranged for mounting on the inlet manifold side of the engine, and for driving from the nose of the crankshaft by means of a double vee-rope drive. The supercharger casing has its own inlet manifold, which is clamped to the engine by the standard manifold clamps. A further support takes the form of a plate which is bolted to two of the bolts holding the water elbow to the front of the head, the plate being attached to a lug on the blower drive housing. Another point of attachment is to a special cylinder-

Exploded view of a Wade blower.

The Wade supercharger installation fitted to a type TC engine.

The Shorrock installation on a TD engine.

View showing internal arrangement of Shorrock supercharger.

head nut which is fitted to the stud just behind the rearmost inlet port, and holds a stay-plate projecting from the back of the blower casing.

The existing belt pulley is removed from the crankshaft, and the 3-groove pulley fitted in its place. Two of the grooves look after the supercharger drive, the third one taking the existing dynamo and fan belt. The blower shaft pulley comes rather close to the radiator header tank web, and it may be necessary to cut away a small portion of the web to allow the belts to be passed over the pulley.

A suitable horizontal carburetter is supplied for use with the blower, and this is complete with all accessories to enable it to be connected to the existing controls and fuel pipe. The oil supply to the blower casing is obtained by replacing the cylinder-head oil-pipe union with the special tee-piece, which enables the oil supply to the head to be tapped. A flexible line connected to the tee-piece delivers oil under pressure to the blower oil inlet. As regards the blower drive housing, this is independently lubricated, and has a plug at the top through which it is filled with engine oil of S.A.E. 30 viscosity. The correct oil level is governed by the plug on the underside of the housing.

Ignition and carburetter settings have to be obtained by road test. It is, however, essential to bear in mind that the blower needs running-in and should be driven gently for at least 200 miles. It should be unnecessary to mention that absolute cleanliness of the engine oil is necessary, but it is worthy of note that graphited oil is not recommended as it is liable to clog the lubricating passages of the blower.

Maintenance of the Shorrock Blower

As supplied, the blower is fitted with a No. 9 metering pin in the lubricator which is connected to the engine oil supply. This size of pin is recommended for running-in the blower, as it passes an adequate oil feed for this critical period. It is quite likely that the pin will be correct even after the running-in period, but this can be gauged by the colour of the exhaust. When starting-up from cold, there will be a slight amount of smoke, but this should clear after a few minutes running. If the smoke persists, or is excessive, a metering pin size No. 10 should be fitted in place of the No. 9.

It will be appreciated that the metering pin is an extremely important part of the oiling system; if it becomes clogged, serious damage will be caused. It must therefore be removed every 1,000 miles and cleaned with a soft cloth. (Abrasives must not be used.) The pin is quite easy to remove, as it has a backing-spring which pushes it out of its housing when the union or plug is unscrewed. Apart from cleaning this item, the oil level in the drive housing should also be checked at the same time, and the oil changed every 5,000 miles.

The Wade Supercharger

The makers of the Wade blower have adopted the Roots (geared-rotor) type of construction which is, of course, in common use throughout the engineering industry, as well as being extremely popular in the specialized field of Grand Prix car racing. The blower consists basically of a casing with ports on either side, containing two contra-rotating rotors which are kept in phase by external gearing. The mixture is carried round by the lobes of the rotors after entering the inlet port, and is expelled through the delivery port.

In this type of construction, there are no sliding parts inside the blower casing, and although the rotors run in very close proximity to each other, there is no actual rubbing contact. Thus, no oil is required in the pumping chamber. The combination of four-lobed rotors and skewed inlet and outlet ports give a pulsation-free delivery, and the minimum of noise. The coupling gears for the rotors are steel-to-bronze, providing long life and silence in operation.

The supercharger is arranged for driving by twin vee-ropes which have a jockey pulley for tensioning. The blower pulley is mounted on an outrigger bracket, with couplings between the blower shaft and the pulley. Thus, the blower bearings do not take any of the belt pull. The special inlet manifold incorporates a blow-off safety valve.

In standard form, a maximum pressure of 4.75 lb. per sq. in. above atmospheric is delivered at 5,000 r.p.m. The blower is type R 010, and runs at 1.1 times engine speed.

INSTALLATION OF THE WADE BLOWER

The Wade blower is arranged for mounting on the inlet manifold side of the engine, and for driving from the nose of the crankshaft by means of a double vee-rope drive. The supercharger casing has its own inlet manifold, which is clamped to the engine by the standard manifold clamps.

The outrigger bearing assembly is supported by a plate which is held under the two bolts on one side of the water elbow on the front of the head. Stay-rods are also fitted between the blower casing and the outrigger bearing, and a leather disc coupling is incorporated in the drive shaft between the pulley and the blower shaft. It is possible to line-up the pulleys perfectly accurately, due to the flexibility of the mountings, but these are perfectly rigid when everything has been tightened up. The jockey pulley is hung from the same mounting that carries the outrigger bearing assembly.

The existing pulley is removed from the crankshaft and the 3-groove pulley fitted in its place. The fan and fan pulley are next removed, and the replacement 3-groove pulley fitted in place of the existing item, the fan being then replaced.

The original belt passes round the dynamo pulley and rides in one of the grooves in the crankshaft and fan pulleys. The two new belts ride in the remaining two grooves in crankshaft and fan pulleys and, of course, also locate in the blower pulley and the tensioning jockey. One of the existing " atmospheric " carburetters is used with the Wade blower, a special instrument not being necessary. All linkages are supplied to enable the controls to be connected up.

The oil supply to the blower is taken from the pressure engine supply via a control valve, which latter is mounted in an accessible position on the instrument panel. Operation of the control valve push-button every 100 miles or so ensures adequate replenishment of the oil chambers. Initially, these are filled by removing the front and rear brass plugs on the top of the supercharger housing, and filling with engine oil.

MAINTENANCE OF THE WADE BLOWER

Three spare carburetter needles are included with the equipment, and it is advisable to try the richest (DR) first. If after prolonged experiment with the carburetter adjustment as detailed in the chapter devoted to carburetter tuning, it is decided that the mixture is excessively rich, the other needles can be tried, DQ being medium and DP the leanest. Very erratic running with the pronounced " flat spots " is an indication of excessively weak mixture, but before blaming the carburation, test for air leaks at the manifold joints.

The ignition setting will, of course, also have to be obtained by road-test.

The outrigger bearing and jockey pulley will require grease lubrication about every 500 miles. Particular care must be taken regarding the tension of the blower driving belts. These have to transmit a lot of power and require to be appreciably tighter than the belt driving the dynamo.

CHAPTER 30

Super-tuning the T-Type Engine

STANDARD ENGINE DATA. STAGE 1 TUNING. STAGE 2 TUNING.
STAGE 3 TUNING. STAGE 4 TUNING. STAGE 5 TUNING.
GENERAL OBSERVATIONS. ALLOY HEAD.

All M.G. engines, as delivered, have of necessity to be supplied to suit the "average" driver. Consequently, such items as compression ratios, for example, are chosen on the assumption that normal fuel will be used. Furthermore, each engine is inbuilt with a margin of safety to allow for a degree of inefficient driving. It follows, therefore, that providing the owner is prepared to really handle his car as a high-efficiency machine should be driven, and to seek ways and means of obtaining fuel of a higher octane rating than usually available, an appreciable increase of power is at his disposal if he is willing and competent enough to get to work on engine modifications. It cannot be emphasized too strongly that the performance obtainable from the standard engine, when in perfect tune, is more than sufficient for most people's requirements. Unless everything is working just as it should, in standard trim, any form of modification for extra power is a waster of time.

As far as reliability is concerned, it must be appreciated that any considerable increase in power output must lead to a reduction in the reliability factor. This does not mean that a modified engine automatically becomes hopelessly unreliable. In fact, it will, if properly handled, be as reliable as a standard engine in the hands of a less thoughtful driver.

As far as P-, PB- and TA-type engines are concerned, details have been given of suggested increases in compression ratio to give enhanced performance. Much can also be done, again as already indicated, by matching-up manifolding, polishing gas passages and combustion chambers and so on. In the case of the TB and later 1,250-c.c. engines, however, the M.G. Company has really " done their owners proud " in marketing special components with which to carry out more far-reaching modifications. With these components, super-tuning can be carried out in stages varying from a modest increase in power resulting from a slightly higher compression ratio, to a really wholesale jump in b.h.p. using special valves and supercharger, with a methanol fuel.

STANDARD ENGINE DATA

It will be useful before giving details of the modifications involved at each stage of super-tuning, to tabulate the standard engine data so as to have a basis for comparison. The usual specification details such as bore and stroke, etc., have been given earlier in the book. Further useful figures are as follows: —

Valve lift, inlet and exhaust: 8 mm.

Fuel requirements: Knock-free, 74 octane; Maximum power, 82 octane.

Carburetter bore: $1\frac{1}{4}$ in.

Carburetter jet: .090 in.

Carburetter needles: Standard, ES; Richer, DK; Weaker, E.F.

Brake M.E.P.: 125 lb. sq. in. at 2,600 r.p.m.

B.H.P.: See chart, page 151.

Safe maximum r.p.m.: 5,700.

Valve crash r.p.m.: 6,000.

Capacity of combustion space: 45.5 c.c.

Cylinder-head depth, top to bottom faces: 76.75 mm.

Cylinder-head gasket thickness: .045 in.

" Capacity " of cylinder-head gasket: (Approx.) 4.5 c.c. (in position).

STAGE 1 TUNING

This stage of power increase involves largely the treatment of the combustion chambers, ports and manifold flanges as detailed in Chapter 19. In addition, the comp. r. is raised to 8.6 : 1 by machining 3/32 in. from the face of the head. The head thickness after machining (top to bottom faces) will then be 74.37 mm. The standard gasket is retained, care being taken that its edge is clear of the combustion chamber. This should be watched at the point where the plug aperture meets the face, as it will probably be necessary to file back a sharp edge at this point. The edge should be not less than 1/32-in. thick, and should be radiused nicely into the shape of the combustion chamber. Although there should be plenty of machined face for the protection of the gasket after this operation, there is no point in filing back too far.

The reduced depth of head will necessitate the use of packing pieces under the rocker standards, and these should be $\frac{1}{16}$-in. thick, of mild steel, holes being drilled as necessary to match the bases of the standards. 3/32-in. thick washers will also be required on the cylinder head studs under the holding-down nuts.

When polishing the inlet ports, do not alter the shape internally. The separating boss between the siamesed ports may be filed and streamlined in the direction of gas flow, so that oblong ports are obtained with a height of 1 3/16 in. and a width of 11/16 in. The boss must on no account be removed altogether, as it has an important effect on the distribution of mixture between the ports.

For reduction of valve gear friction (and thus an increase in mechanical efficiency), the spacing springs on the rocker shaft should be replaced by tubing. The tubing should preferably be phosphor-bronze, but mild-steel will serve. The end-float on the rockers must not exceed .003 in.

The 8.6:1 comp. r. is very suitable for use with premium brand fuels, and for fast touring the author has found the standard Champion L 10S plugs perfectly adequate. However, for sustained high speeds, it may be necessary to use a slightly hotter plug such as Champion LA 11 or Lodge R 49.

The power output for Stage 1 is approximately 58 b.h.p. at 5,000 r.p.m., and 60 at 5,500 to 6,000 r.p.m.

Performance curves for all stages of tuning are shown on page 151.

STAGE 2 TUNING

This stage involves another increase in compression ratio, plus the fitting of larger valves and stronger valve springs, with ports modified to take the valves. The replacement springs allow of 6,000 r.p.m. without valve-crash.

The compression ratio is raised to 9.3:1 by machining $\frac{1}{8}$ in. from the head face, the depth from top to bottom faces after machining then being 73.575 mm. This is the absolute maximum that may be removed, any further comp. r. increase being obtained by the use of special pistons.

The effect (of machining the head) on the spark plug recess will be even more marked than in the case of Stage 1, and this must be watched. To fit the larger inlet valves, which have 36-mm. heads, part of the combustion chamber wall must be cut away to clear the head. This can be done with a 38-mm. diameter side-and-face cutter, using the valve guide as a pilot. The cutter corner should have a 1-mm. radius. Alternatively to the use of a cutter, the combustion chamber can be ground carefully, until the valve head has 1 mm. working clearance. The valve port below the valve is similarly increased to 33-mm. diameter, and the seat recut to 34.9-mm. top diameter, with an angle of 30 deg. Any ridges left by these operations should be smoothed off.

The exhaust valve ports require similar treatment to allow the 34-mm. headed valves to be installed. In this case, the cutter is 36-mm. diameter, the valve port below valve 29-mm. diameter, and the valve seat 32.8 mm. with 30-deg. angle.

The stronger valve springs are interchangeable with the standard springs, but have staggered pitch, the closed coils going next to the cylinder head. The loading is 150 lb. open, and valve-crash occurs at about 6,500 r.p.m. The rocker-shaft standards require packing up as for Stage 1. $\frac{1}{8}$-in. thick washers are necessary on the head studs. Using plugs, carburetter, rocker and ignition settings as for Stage 1, with fuel 75 per cent. benzol and 25 per cent. petrol, the following output should be available:—

$$
\begin{array}{lll}
61 \text{ b.h.p. at} & 5,000 & \text{r.p.m.} \\
65 & 5,500 & \text{,,} \\
63 & 6,000 & \text{,,}
\end{array}
$$

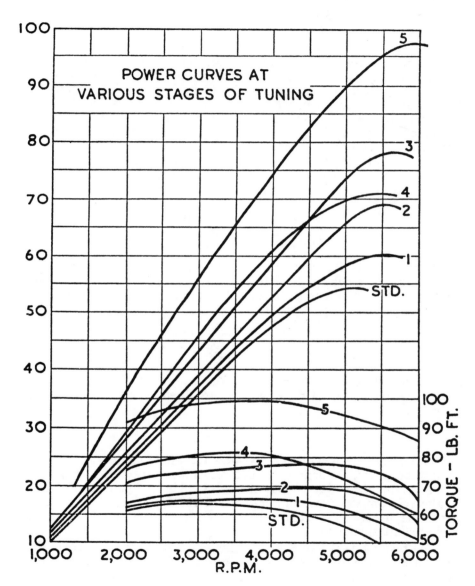

Power curves of Type TB, TC, and TD engines, with various stages of tuning

With carburetter needles RO in jets .090 in., and using fuel of 50 per cent. methanol, 20 per cent. petrol and 30 per cent. benzol, power should be as follows:—

62.5 b.h.p. at 5,000 r.p.m.
66.5   ,,   5,500 ,,
64   ,,   6,000 ,,

Where a methanol fuel is used, 1 per cent. (approximately) castor oil should be added. Carburetter needles alternative to those specified are—richer, RLS, or weaker, No. 5. Quite a lot of fuel is required to flow at times, and twin S.U. pumps are desirable, using a fuel line from each of the pumps to a carburetter, with an interconnecting pipe between the two carburetters. This will need a double-feed banjo union to be fitted on each float-chamber.

In place of the standard carburetters, 1½-in. instruments can be fitted, with needles EL in jets .090 in. Using fuel comprising 75 per cent. benzol and 25 per cent. petrol, the following output should be obtained:—

63 b.h.p. at 5,000 r.p.m.
68   ,,   5,500 ,,
66   ,,   6,000 ,,

Alternative carburetter needles are—richer, AA, or weaker, EO. With carburetter needles RLS in jets .090 in., and with fuel of 50 per cent. methanol, 20 per cent. petrol and 30 per cent. benzol, the following should be the output:—

66 b.h.p. at 5,000 r.p.m.
70   ,,   5,500 ,,
68   ,,   6,000 ,,

Alternative carburetter needles for the above fuel are—richer, CS2, or weaker, RO. If richer needles are fitted, change to the .100 in. jet range.

STAGE 3 TUNING

This stage of super-tuning provides the highest output obtainable with atmospheric induction. A compression ratio of 12 to 1 is used, this involving the fitting of special pistons. The cylinder head remains unaltered from standard, with a depth of 76.75 mm., and the standard gasket is used. No packing pieces are therefore required on the rocker-shaft standards.

The pistons have flame grooves therein, and must be fitted so that these are on the spark plug side. For this high compression ratio, very particular attention has to be given to the fuel, which is as follows: 80 per cent. dry blending methanol, with specific gravity of .796 at 60 deg. F.; 10 per cent. benzol (90), specific gravity .8758 at 60 deg. F.; 10 per cent. petrol, 70 or 80 octane; 1 per cent. castor oil.

The standard carburetters can be used, with jets .100 in. and needles GK. Richer needles are RC, and weaker, RV. The float-chamber needles and seatings must be S.U. type T.3, to suit the increased fuel flow. Champion plugs LA 14 or Lodge R 49 will be suitable, and the ignition setting should be altered to 4 deg. after t.d.c., for initial try-out. Duplicate fuel pumps will be necessary, arranged as detailed for Stage 2.

The rockers should be set at .022 in. clearance.

With the above alterations, the output available should be:

69 b.h.p.	at	5,000	r.p.m.
73	,,	5,500	,,
74	,,	5,800	,,
73	,,	6,000	,,

If larger valves and stronger springs are fitted, as for Stage 2, the maximum power will be increased to 76 b.h.p. at 5,800 r.p.m.

A further increase is obtainable by fitting the $1\frac{1}{2}$-in. carburetters, to which reference was made in dealing with Stage 2. When mounting these, the manifold entrance ports should be enlarged to $1\frac{1}{2}$ in. to match the carburetter outlets. The increased diameter of $1\frac{1}{2}$ in. cannot be taken right through, but must be tapered off to $1\frac{3}{8}$ in. in a length of about $\frac{3}{4}$ in. of pipe. This minimum of $1\frac{3}{8}$ in., representing an area of 1.5 sq. in., should be maintained right through.

The carburetters should have .125-in. jets with VE needles. Richer needle is VG, weaker, VA. The return springs above the light aluminium carburetter pistons can be removed if maximum power is required, but for acceleration and general efficient running, they are better left in position.

Assuming the use of the large valves, fuel, etc., as already detailed for Stage 2, the maximum power will be 80 b.h.p. at 6,000 r.p.m. If a fuel mixture of 100 per cent. methanol is used, with VJ needles in the .125-in. jets (richer VL, weaker V1) 83 b.h.p. will be developed at the same revolutions.

STAGE 4 TUNING

This stage covers the use of a supercharger of the type described in Chapter 24, fitted to the standard engine. Taking the Shorrock equipment as typical, with a maximum boost of 6 lb. per sq. in. at 5,000 r.p.m., this is fitted with $1\frac{3}{8}$-in. carburetter with jet .090 in. and needle RLS. Fuel is petrol of 70 octane rating. Spark plugs should be Champion L 11S or Lodge HNP, and the rocker clearance is set at .022 in. The following output should be obtained:—

45 b.h.p.	at	3,000	r.p.m.
58	,,	4,000	,,
69	,,	5,000	,,
69	,,	5,500	,,

If 90 octane fuel can be obtained another 1 b.h.p. will be added to the above figures at the upper end of the r.p.m. scale.

With a fuel mixture comprising 50 per cent. methanol, 20 per cent. petrol, and 30 per cent. benzol, the carburetter will need modifications comprising .125-in. jet and VE needle (richer, VG, weaker, VA), T3 float needle and seating in the float chamber, and twin pumps. Plugs should be Champion L 11S or Lodge HNP. If harder plugs are found necessary, try Champion LA 11 or Lodge R 49. With these modifications, the following power should be developed:—

52	b.h.p. at	3,000	r.p.m.
68.5	„	4,000	„
75	„	5,000	„
75.5	„	5,500	„
75	„	6,000	„

STAGE 5 TUNING

This, the final stage, incorporates many of the Stage 2 alterations, plus the use of a blower as Stage 4. The compression ratio is raised to 9.3 to 1, and large inlet and exhaust valves are installed, plus stronger springs, all as detailed for Stage 2. The carburetter is fitted with VG needle in the .125-in. jet, the richer needle being V1, and weaker VE. All these needles have $\frac{1}{8}$-in. shanks.

Twin fuel pumps will, of course, be required, and suitable plugs are Champion LA 11 or LA 14, or Lodge R 49 or R 51. Using a fuel mixture comprising 50 per cent. methanol, 20 per cent. petrol, and 30 per cent. benzol, plus 1 per cent. castor oil, the following performance should be obtained:—

55.5	b.h.p. at	3,000	r.p.m.
73.5	„	4,000	„
85.5	„	5,000	„
88	„	5,500	„
88	„	6,000	„

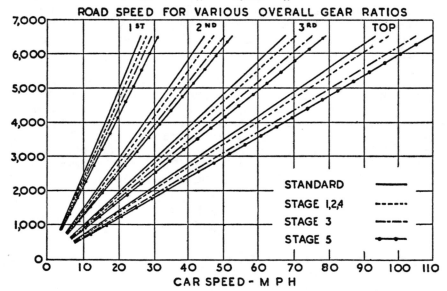

Road speeds at various stages of tuning the TD-type M.G., with gear ratios as follows: Standard 5.125:1, 14.42 m.p.h. per 1,000 r.p.m.; Stages 1, 2 and 4, 4.875:1, 15.195 m.p.h. per 1,000 r.p.m.; Stage 3, 4.55:1, 16.25 m.p.h. per 1,000 r.p.m.; Stage 5, 4.55:1, 17 m.p.h. per 1,000 r.p.m. (6-in. tyres)

A further increase can be obtained by fitting a carburetter of 1¾-in. diameter, this being S.U. type H 6, Spec. No. 538. This must be fitted to a special elbow to match up with the blower inlet, the inside diameter of the pipe being 1¼ in. The jet diameter is .1875 in., with needle RM 7 (richer RM 8, weaker RM 6).

With a fuel of 80 per cent. methanol, 10 per cent. petrol, and 10 per cent. benzol, the following figures should be available:—

74.5	b.h.p. at	4,000	r.p.m.
82	„	4,500	„
89	„	5,000	„
94.25	„	5,500	„
97.5	„	6,000	„

GENERAL OBSERVATIONS

It is a good idea to add a small percentage of castor oil whenever methanol is used in the fuel. An additional 1 b.h.p. is also available at maximum revs if the fan blades are removed, this representing the power absorbed by this component. Cooling without the fan is adequate providing the speed can be kept above about 40 m.p.h.

The increase in rocker clearance to .022 in. will lead to quite a lot of extra noise from the valve gear. If this is objected to, the standard clearance of .019 in. can be retained, but a loss of about 1 b.h.p. must be accepted.

A considerable reduction in valve-gear noise, even with the larger clearance, can be effected by fitting an aluminium alloy rocker-cover, a type designed by the author being illustrated facing page 129. Such a fitting also enables an absolutely oil-tight joint to be obtained, a matter of some difficulty on the standard fitting.

If carburetter vibration is experienced with the carburetter fitted to the blower, this may affect the mixture strength. It can be cured by using a Neoprene washer, about ⅛-in. thick, between the carburetter flange and the blower intake. The nuts should then be tightened only sufficiently to make an air-tight joint, after which they will require lock-nutting or wiring to prevent them from slackening off. Longer studs will, of course, be required.

The following schedule of material is given for easy reference, the parts being obtainable from the M.G. Car Company Ltd., or as detailed.

Item.	Part No.
Rocker shaft packing pieces, 1/16-in. thick ...	MG 862/459
36-mm. inlet valve	MG 862/460
34-mm. exhaust valve	MG 862/461
Piston, 12:1 comp. r. with rings and pin ...	MG 862/458
Valve spring, outer, 150 lb.	MG 862/462
Valve spring, inner, 150 lb.	MG 862/463
S.U. carburetter, two off, 1.5-in. dia., Spec. 532	Refer to makers
.100 jets, S.U., No. 1394-112/L	„ „
.125 jets, S.U., No. 4185	„ „
.1875 jets, fixed type	„ „

Jet needles, as S.U. list, obtainable from makers.
Float chamber seat and needle assemblies, S.U., No. T 3 (these are identifiable by three grooves machined around body).
1.75-in. carburetter for use with blower, S.U., Spec. 538.

Plugs—Champion

    L   11S Super sports.
    LA 11   Racing 1st step.
    LA 14   Racing 2nd step.
    LA 15   Racing 3rd step.

Plugs—Lodge

    HNP   Super sports.
    R 49   Racing 1st step.
    R 51   Racing 2nd step.
    R 53   Racing 3rd step.

Lucas high-performance coil, type BR 12, for r.p.m. up to 8,000.
Standard coil is satisfactory up to 6,000 r.p.m.
Lucas 4 VRA vertical magneto. Lucas Part No. ENM 2002.

    This has a suitable advance curve for the M.G. engine. To fit, it is necessary to indent push-rod cover plate and move breather pipe elbow.

ALLOY HEAD

Reference should also be made to the Laystall alloy cylinder head (illustrated facing page 113). This is normally made to Stage 2 tuning requirements, complete with large valves, etc., and is suitable for all models from TB to TF inclusive, and for Wolseley 4/44 engines.

PART IV

WIRING DIAGRAMS
LUBRICATION CHARTS
AND
SECTIONAL DRAWINGS

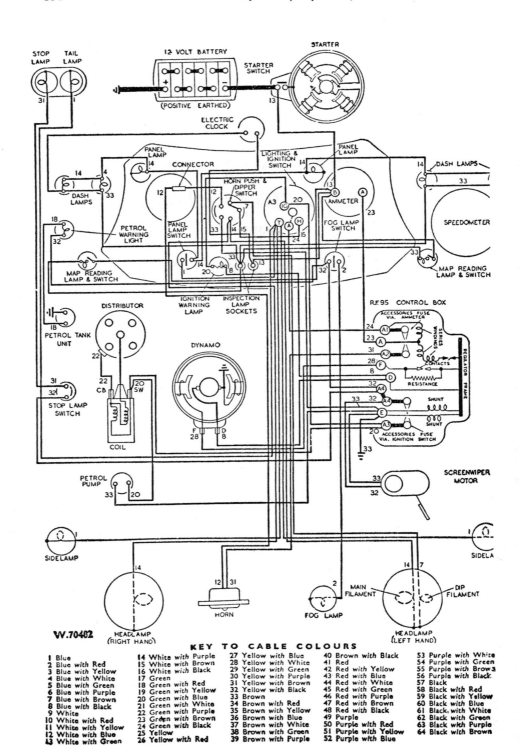

W.70402

KEY TO CABLE COLOURS

1 Blue	14 White with Purple	27 Yellow with Blue	40 Brown with Black	53 Purple with White
2 Blue with Red	15 White with Brown	28 Yellow with White	41 Red	54 Purple with Green
3 Blue with Yellow	16 White with Black	29 Yellow with Green	42 Red with Yellow	55 Purple with Brown
4 Blue with White	17 Green	30 Yellow with Purple	43 Red with Blue	56 Purple with Black
5 Blue with Green	18 Green with Red	31 Yellow with Brown	44 Red with White	57 Black
6 Blue with Purple	19 Green with Yellow	32 Yellow with Black	45 Red with Green	58 Black with Red
7 Blue with Brown	20 Green with Blue	33 Brown	46 Red with Purple	59 Black with Yellow
8 Blue with Black	21 Green with White	34 Brown with Red	47 Red with Brown	60 Black with Blue
9 White	22 Green with Purple	35 Brown with Yellow	48 Red with Black	61 Black with White
10 White with Red	23 Green with Brown	36 Brown with Blue	49 Purple	62 Black with Green
11 White with Yellow	24 Green with Black	37 Brown with White	50 Purple with Red	63 Black with Purple
12 White with Blue	25 Yellow	38 Brown with Green	51 Purple with Yellow	64 Black with Brown
13 White with Green	26 Yellow with Red	39 Brown with Purple	52 Purple with Blue	

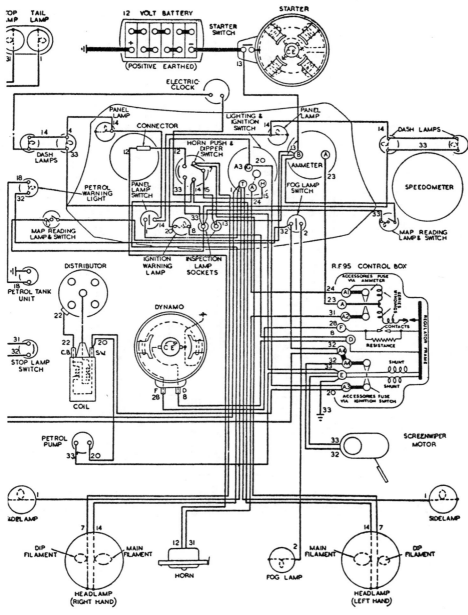

W.71081

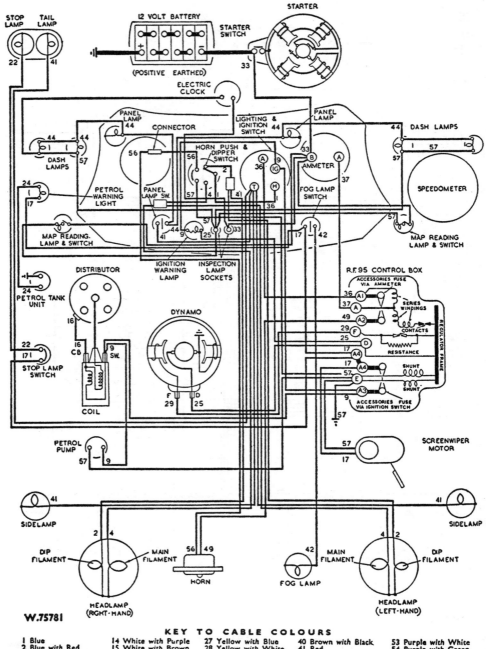

W.75781

KEY TO CABLE COLOURS

1 Blue	14 White with Purple	27 Yellow with Blue	40 Brown with Black	53 Purple with White
2 Blue with Red	15 White with Brown	28 Yellow with White	41 Red	54 Purple with Green
3 Blue with Yellow	16 White with Black	29 Yellow with Green	42 Red with Yellow	55 Purple with Brown
4 Blue with White	17 Green	30 Yellow with Purple	43 Red with Blue	56 Purple with Black
5 Blue with Green	18 Green with Red	31 Yellow with Brown	44 Red with White	57 Black
6 Blue with Purple	19 Green with Yellow	32 Yellow with Black	45 Red with Green	58 Black with Red
7 Blue with Brown	20 Green with Blue	33 Brown	46 Red with Purple	59 Black with Yellow
8 Blue with Black	21 Green with White	34 Brown with Red	47 Red with Brown	60 Black with Blue
9 White	22 Green with Purple	35 Brown with Yellow	48 Red with Black	61 Black with White
10 White with Red	23 Green with Brown	36 Brown with Blue	49 Purple	62 Black with Green
11 White with Yellow	24 Green with Black	37 Brown with White	50 Purple with Red	63 Black with Purple
12 White with Blue	25 Yellow	38 Brown with Green	51 Purple with Yellow	64 Black with Brown
13 White with Green	26 Yellow with Red	39 Brown with Purple	52 Purple with Blue	

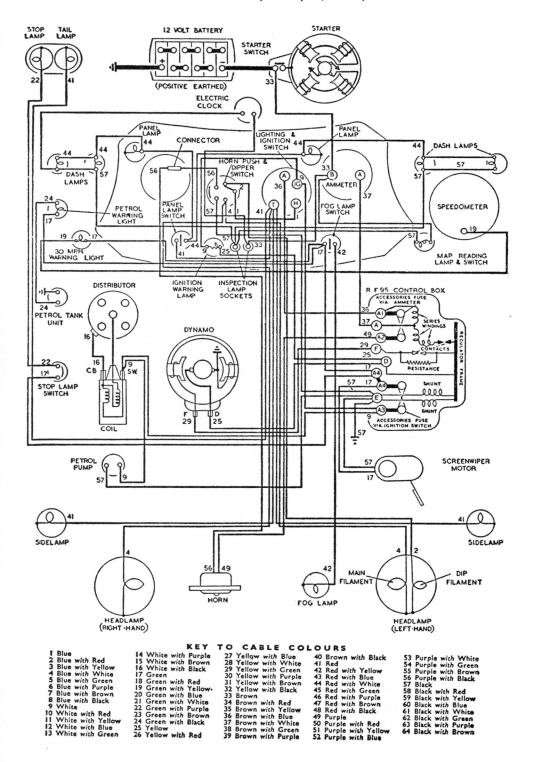

KEY TO CABLE COLOURS

1 Blue	14 White with Purple	27 Yellow with Blue	40 Brown with Black	53 Purple with White
2 Blue with Red	15 White with Brown	28 Yellow with White	41 Red	54 Purple with Green
3 Blue with Yellow	16 White with Black	29 Yellow with Green	42 Red with Yellow	55 Purple with Brown
4 Blue with White	17 Green	30 Yellow with Purple	43 Red with Blue	56 Purple with Black
5 Blue with Green	18 Green with Red	31 Yellow with Brown	44 Red with White	57 Black
6 Blue with Purple	19 Green with Yellow	32 Yellow with Black	45 Red with Green	58 Black with Red
7 Blue with Brown	20 Green with Blue	33 Brown	46 Red with Purple	59 Black with Yellow
8 Blue with Black	21 Green with White	34 Brown with Red	47 Red with Brown	60 Black with Blue
9 White	22 Green with Purple	35 Brown with Yellow	48 Red with Black	61 Black with White
10 White with Red	23 Green with Brown	36 Brown with Blue	49 Purple	62 Black with Green
11 White with Yellow	24 Green with Black	37 Brown with White	50 Purple with Red	63 Black with Purple
12 White with Blue	25 Yellow	38 Brown with Green	51 Purple with Yellow	64 Black with Brown
13 White with Green	26 Yellow with Red	39 Brown with Purple	52 Purple with Blue	

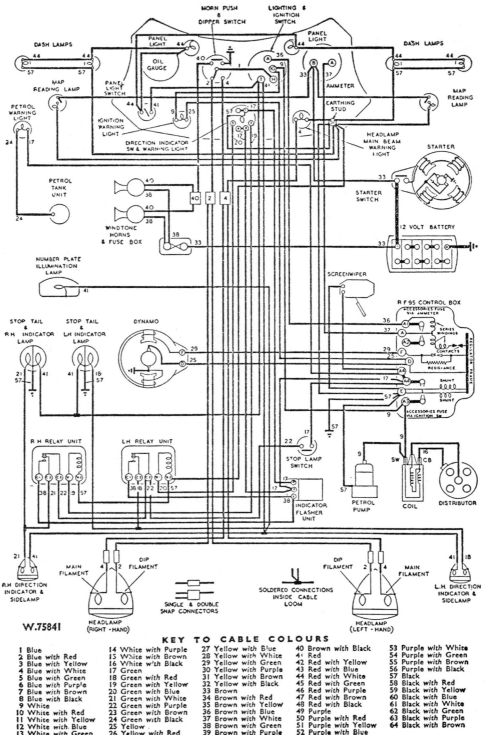

W.75841

KEY TO CABLE COLOURS

1 Blue	14 White with Purple	27 Yellow with Blue	40 Brown with Black	53 Purple with White
2 Blue with Red	15 White with Brown	28 Yellow with White	41 Red	54 Purple with Green
3 Blue with Yellow	16 White with Black	29 Yellow with Green	42 Red with Yellow	55 Purple with Brown
4 Blue with White	17 Green	30 Yellow with Purple	43 Red with Blue	56 Purple with Black
5 Blue with Green	18 Green with Red	31 Yellow with Brown	44 Red with White	57 Black
6 Blue with Purple	19 Green with Yellow	32 Yellow with Black	45 Red with Green	58 Black with Red
7 Blue with Brown	20 Green with Blue	33 Brown	46 Red with Purple	59 Black with Yellow
8 Blue with Black	21 Green with White	34 Brown with Red	47 Red with Brown	60 Black with Blue
9 White	22 Green with Purple	35 Brown with Yellow	48 Red with Black	61 Black with White
10 White with Red	23 Green with Brown	36 Brown with Blue	49 Purple	62 Black with Green
11 White with Yellow	24 Green with Black	37 Brown with White	50 Purple with Red	63 Black with Purple
12 White with Blue	25 Yellow	38 Brown with Green	51 Purple with Yellow	64 Black with Brown
13 White with Green	26 Yellow with Red	39 Brown with Purple	52 Purple with Blue	

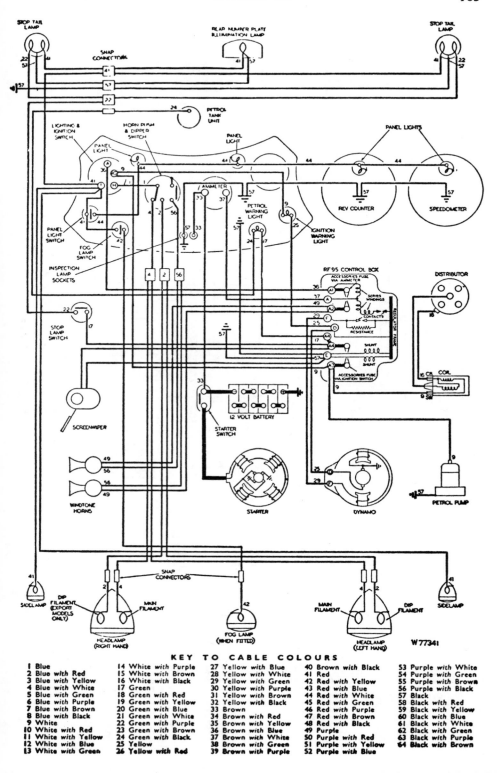

KEY TO CABLE COLOURS

1 Blue	14 White with Purple	27 Yellow with Blue	40 Brown with Black	53 Purple with White
2 Blue with Red	15 White with Brown	28 Yellow with White	41 Red	54 Purple with Green
3 Blue with Yellow	16 White with Black	29 Yellow with Green	42 Red with Yellow	55 Purple with Brown
4 Blue with White	17 Green	30 Yellow with Purple	43 Red with Blue	56 Purple with Black
5 Blue with Green	18 Green with Red	31 Yellow with Brown	44 Red with White	57 Black
6 Blue with Purple	19 Green with Yellow	32 Yellow with Black	45 Red with Green	58 Black with Red
7 Blue with Brown	20 Green with Blue	33 Brown	46 Red with Purple	59 Black with Yellow
8 Blue with Black	21 Green with White	34 Brown with Red	47 Red with Brown	60 Black with Blue
9 White	22 Green with Purple	35 Brown with Yellow	48 Red with Black	61 Black with White
10 White with Red	23 Green with Brown	36 Brown with Blue	49 Purple	62 Black with Green
11 White with Yellow	24 Green with Black	37 Brown with White	50 Purple with Red	63 Black with Purple
12 White with Blue	25 Yellow	38 Brown with Green	51 Purple with Yellow	64 Black with Brown
13 White with Green	26 Yellow with Red	39 Brown with Purple	52 Purple with Blue	

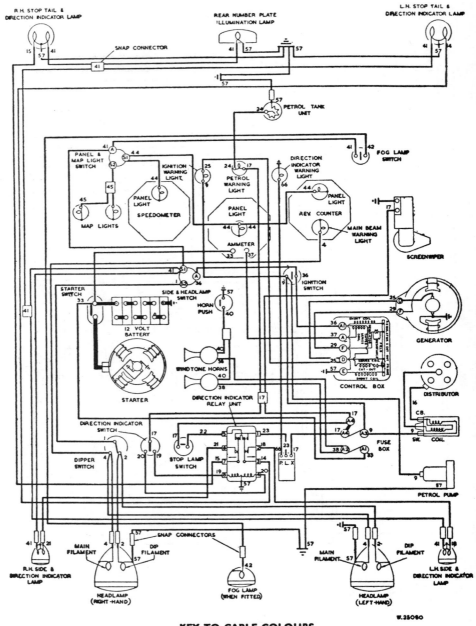

KEY TO CABLE COLOURS

1 Blue	15 White with Brown	28 Yellow with White	41 Red	54 Purple with Green
2 Blue with Red	16 White with Black	29 Yellow with Green	42 Red with Yellow	55 Purple with Brown
3 Blue with Yellow	17 Green	30 Yellow with Purple	43 Red with Blue	56 Purple with Black
4 Blue with White	18 Green with Red	31 Yellow with Brown	44 Red with White	57 Black
5 Blue with Green	19 Green with Yellow	32 Yellow with Black	45 Red with Green	58 Black with Red
6 Blue with Purple	20 Green with Blue	33 Brown	46 Red with Purple	59 Black with Yellow
7 Blue with Brown	21 Green with White	34 Brown with Red	47 Red with Brown	60 Black with Blue
8 Blue with Black	22 Green with Purple	35 Brown with Yellow	48 Red with Black	61 Black with White
9 White	23 Green with Brown	36 Brown with Blue	49 Purple	62 Black with Green
10 White with Red	24 Green with Black	37 Brown with White	50 Purple with Red	63 Black with Purple
11 White with Yellow	25 Yellow	38 Brown with Green	51 Purple with Yellow	64 Black with Brown
12 White with Blue	26 Yellow with Red	39 Brown with Purple	52 Purple with Blue	65 Dark Green
13 White with Green	27 Yellow with Blue	40 Brown with Black	53 Purple with White	66 Light Green
14 White with Purple				

W.25060

KEY TO RECOMMENDED LUBRICANTS Series 1C

Component / Climatic Conditions	A — Engine and Air Cleaner			B — Gearbox, Steering Gearbox and Rear Axle		C — Wheel Hubs and Bearings	D — Chassis Greasing Nipples etc.	E — Cables and Control joints	F — Oilcan and Carburetter
	Tropical and temperate down to 32° F. (0° C.)	Cold and extreme cold down to 0° F. (−18° C.)	Arctic below 0° F. (−18° C.)	Tropical and temperate down to 10° F. (−12° C.)	Extreme cold below 10° F. (1−2° C.)	All conditions	All conditions	All conditions	All conditions
"DUCKHAM'S" Alexander Duckham & Co. Ltd.	Duckham's N.O.L. "Thirty"	Duckham's N.O.L. "Twenty"	Duckham's N.O.L. "Ten"	Duckham's N.O.L. "E.P." Transmission 140	Duckham's N.O.L. "E.P." Transmission 80	Duckham's H.B.B. Grease	Duckham's H.P.G. Grease	Duckham's "Keenol" K.G. 16 Grease	Duckham's N.O.L. "Twenty"
"CASTROL" (C. C. Wakefield & Co. Ltd.)	"Castrol" X.L.	"Castrolite"	"Castrol" Z	"Castrol" Hi-Press	"Castrol" Hypoy 80	"Castrolease" Heavy	"Castrolease" Medium	"Castrolease" Brake Cable Grease	"Castrolite"
"ESSOLUBE" (Anglo-American Oil Co. Ltd.)	"Essolube" 30	"Essolube" 20	"Essolube" 10	"Esso" Expee Compound 140	"Esso" Expee Compound 80	Esso-Grease	"Esso" Pressure Gun Grease	"Esso" Pressure Gun Grease	"Essolube" 20
"MOBILOIL" (Vacuum Oil Co. Ltd.)	Mobiloil "A"	Mobiloil "Arctic"	Mobiloil "Arctic" Special	Mobilube "G.X." 140	Mobilube "G.X." 80	Mobil Hub Grease	Mobilgrease No. 2 or 4	Mobilgrease No. 2 or 4	Mobiloil "Arctic"
"ENERGOL" (Price's Lubricants Ltd.)	"Energol" S.A.E. 30	"Energol" S.A.E. 20	"Energol" S.A.E. 10	"Energol" "E.P." S.A.E. 140	"Energol" "E.P." S.A.E. 80	"Belmoline" C	"Belmoline" D	"Belmoline" D	"Energol" S.A.E. 20
"SHELL" (Shell Mex & B.P. Ltd.)	Double "Shell"	Single "Shell"	Silver "Shell"	"Shell" Spirax 140 E.P.	"Shell" Spirax 80 E.P.	"Shell" Retinax R.B.	"Shell" Retinax C	"Shell" Retinax C	Single "Shell"
"FILTRATE" (Edward Joy & Sons Ltd.)	Medium "Filtrate"	Zero "Filtrate"	Sub-Zero "Filtrate"	E.P. "Filtrate"	E.P. "Filtrate" 80	"Filtrate" R.B. Grease	H.P. Solidified "Filtrate"	"Filtrate" A.F. Grease	Zero "Filtrate"
"STERNOL" (Sternol Ltd.)	"Sternol" W.W. 30	"Sternol" W.W. 20	"Sternol" W.W. 10	"Sternol" Liquid Ambroleum E.P. 140	"Sternol" Liquid Ambroleum E.P. 80	"Ambroline" R.B. Grease	"Ambroline" M.M. Grease	"Ambroline" A.F. Grease	"Sternol" W.W. 20

166

C		D		D		B
6,000 MILES or 10,000 KM.		6,000 MILES or 10,000 KM.		500 MILES or 800 KM.		2,000 MILES
REMOVE HUB CAP AND APPLY GREASE AT NIPPLE INSIDE HUB		LUBRICATE PROPELLER SHAFT JOINTS AT NIPPLE FROM BELOW		TO LUBRICATE PROPELLER SHAFT SPLINE AT FRONT END ROTATE SHAFT UNTIL NIPPLE IS OPPOSITE HOLE IN TUNNEL		FILL TO MARK O

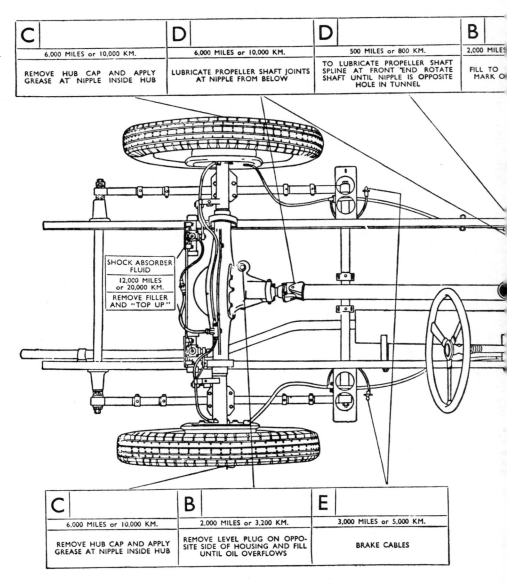

SHOCK ABSORBER FLUID

12,000 MILES or 20,000 KM.

REMOVE FILLER AND "TOP UP"

C		B		E	
6,000 MILES or 10,000 KM.		2,000 MILES or 3,200 KM.		3,000 MILES or 5,000 KM.	
REMOVE HUB CAP AND APPLY GREASE AT NIPPLE INSIDE HUB		REMOVE LEVEL PLUG ON OPPOSITE SIDE OF HOUSING AND FILL UNTIL OIL OVERFLOWS		BRAKE CABLES	

NOTE :—FOR KEY TO LETTER REFERENCES SEE LIST ON PAGE 165

LUBRICATION CHART

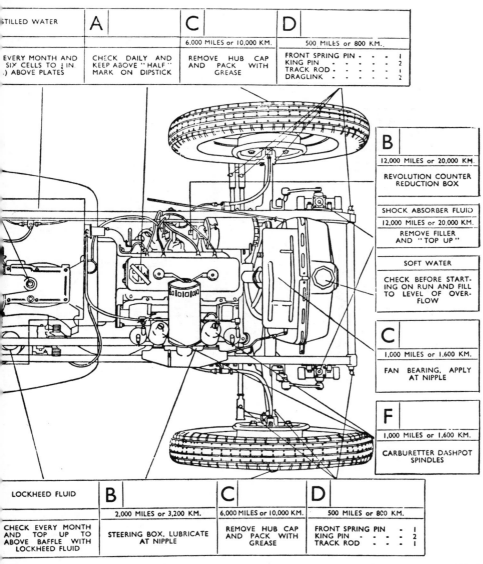

...STILLED WATER	A	C	D
		6,000 MILES or 10,000 KM.	500 MILES or 800 KM.
EVERY MONTH AND SIX CELLS TO ⅛ IN. ...) ABOVE PLATES	CHECK DAILY AND KEEP ABOVE "HALF" MARK ON DIPSTICK	REMOVE HUB CAP AND PACK WITH GREASE	FRONT SPRING PIN - - - 1 KING PIN - - - - - 2 TRACK ROD - - - - - 1 DRAGLINK - - - - - 2

B 12,000 MILES or 20,000 KM.
REVOLUTION COUNTER REDUCTION BOX

SHOCK ABSORBER FLUID 12,000 MILES or 20,000 KM.
REMOVE FILLER AND "TOP UP"

SOFT WATER
CHECK BEFORE STARTING ON RUN AND FILL TO LEVEL OF OVERFLOW

C 1,000 MILES or 1,600 KM.
FAN BEARING, APPLY AT NIPPLE

F 1,000 MILES or 1,600 KM.
CARBURETTER DASHPOT SPINDLES

LOCKHEED FLUID	B	C	D
	2,000 MILES or 3,200 KM.	6,000 MILES or 10,000 KM.	500 MILES or 800 KM.
CHECK EVERY MONTH AND TOP UP TO ABOVE BAFFLE WITH LOCKHEED FLUID	STEERING BOX, LUBRICATE AT NIPPLE	REMOVE HUB CAP AND PACK WITH GREASE	FRONT SPRING PIN - - 1 KING PIN - - - - 2 TRACK ROD - - - - 1

...HANGING OIL : Drain Engine and refill with New Oil every 3,000 miles or 5,000 KM
Drain Gearbox and refill with New Oil every 6,000 miles or 10,000 KM
Drain Rear Axle and refill with New Oil every 6,000 miles or 10,000 KM

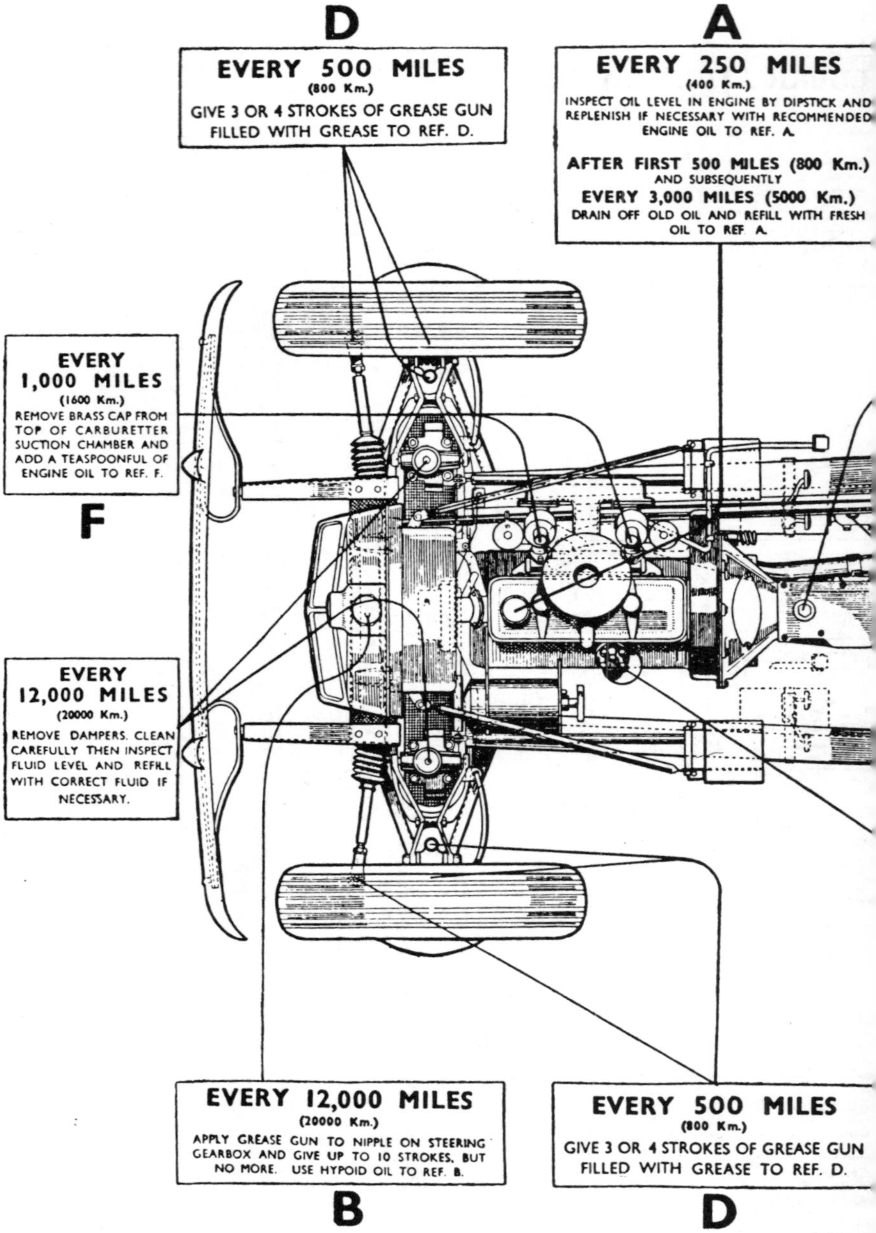
D
EVERY 500 MILES
(800 Km.)
GIVE 3 OR 4 STROKES OF GREASE GUN FILLED WITH GREASE TO REF. D.
A
EVERY 250 MILES
(400 Km.)
INSPECT OIL LEVEL IN ENGINE BY DIPSTICK AND REPLENISH IF NECESSARY WITH RECOMMENDED ENGINE OIL TO REF. A.
AFTER FIRST 500 MILES (800 Km.)
AND SUBSEQUENTLY
EVERY 3,000 MILES (5000 Km.)
DRAIN OFF OLD OIL AND REFILL WITH FRESH OIL TO REF A.
EVERY 1,000 MILES
(1600 Km.)
REMOVE BRASS CAP FROM TOP OF CARBURETTER SUCTION CHAMBER AND ADD A TEASPOONFUL OF ENGINE OIL TO REF. F.
F
EVERY 12,000 MILES
(20000 Km.)
REMOVE DAMPERS. CLEAN CAREFULLY THEN INSPECT FLUID LEVEL AND REFILL WITH CORRECT FLUID IF NECESSARY.
EVERY 12,000 MILES
(20000 Km.)
APPLY GREASE GUN TO NIPPLE ON STEERING GEARBOX AND GIVE UP TO 10 STROKES, BUT NO MORE. USE HYPOID OIL TO REF. B.
B
EVERY 500 MILES
(800 Km.)
GIVE 3 OR 4 STROKES OF GREASE GUN FILLED WITH GREASE TO REF. D.
D

EVERY 1,000 MILES (1,600 KM.). Use Oilcan on all Contro Joints, Door Locks, Hinges to Ref. F.

EVERY 6,000 MILES (10,000 KM.). Remove Front Wheel Hub Disc from Hub. Apply Grease Gun filled with Grease to Ref. C. and give one stroke.

EVERY 1,000 MILES (1,600 KM.). Apply Grease Gun filled with Grease to Ref. D to Propeller Shaft Sliding Joint Greaser and give two or three strokes.

B

EVERY 1,000 MILES
(1600 Km.)

OIL LEVEL IN GEARBOX BY DIPSTICK
PLENISH IF NECESSARY WITH RECOM-
NDED HYPOID OIL TO REF. B.

FIRST 500 MILES (800 Km.)
AND SUBSEQUENTLY
6,000 MILES (10000 Km.)
FF OLD OIL AND REFILL WITH FRESH
OIL TO REF. B.

B

EVERY 1,000 MILES
(1600 Km.)

INSPECT OIL LEVEL IN AXLE THROUGH FILLER
AND REPLENISH IF NECESSARY WITH RECOM-
MENDED HYPOID OIL TO REF. B.

AFTER FIRST 500 MILES (800 Km.)
AND SUBSEQUENTLY
EVERY 6,000 MILES (10000 Km.)
DRAIN OFF OLD OIL AND REFILL WITH FRESH
OIL TO REF. B.

EVERY 12,000 MILES
(20000 Km.)

REMOVE REAR HYDRAULIC DAMPERS. CAREFULLY
CLEAN EXTERIOR AND THEN INSPECT FLUID LEVEL.
REPLENISH WITH CORRECT FLUID IF NECESSARY.

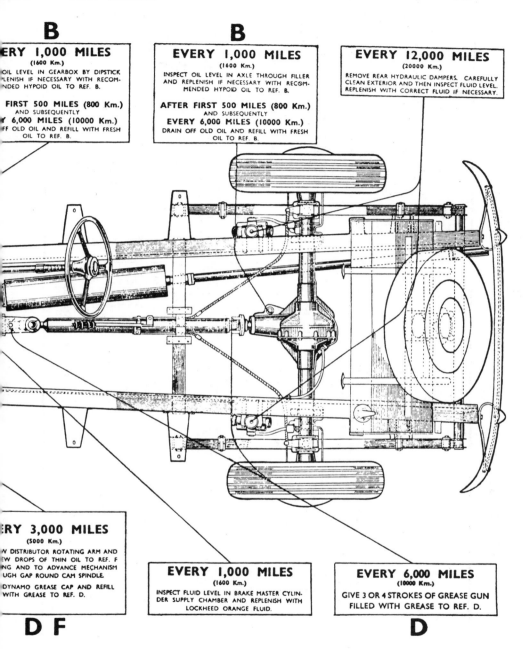

ERY 3,000 MILES
(5000 Km.)

W DISTRIBUTOR ROTATING ARM AND
EW DROPS OF THIN OIL TO REF. F
NG AND TO ADVANCE MECHANISM
UGH GAP ROUND CAM SPINDLE.

DYNAMO GREASE CAP AND REFILL
WITH GREASE TO REF. D.

D F

EVERY 1,000 MILES
(1600 Km.)

INSPECT FLUID LEVEL IN BRAKE MASTER CYLIN-
DER SUPPLY CHAMBER AND REPLENISH WITH
LOCKHEED ORANGE FLUID.

EVERY 6,000 MILES
(10000 Km.)

GIVE 3 OR 4 STROKES OF GREASE GUN
FILLED WITH GREASE TO REF. D.

D

EVERY 3,000 MILES (5,000 KM.).   Clean and Re-Oil Air Intake Cleaner.

EVERY 1,000 MILES (1,600 KM.).   Apply Grease Gun filled with Grease
to Ref. C. to Fan Bearing Lubricator and give two strokes.

EVERY 12,000 MILES (20,000 KM.).   Apply Grease Gun filled with Grease
to Ref. D to Revolution Indicator Gearbox and give two strokes.

SPECIAL NOTE.   Only Hypoid Oils must be used in the rear axle.

NOTE:—FOR KEY TO LETTER REFERENCES SEE LIST
ON PAGE 170

KEY TO RECOMMENDED LUBRICANTS Series TD/TF

Component	A — Engine and Air Cleaner			B — Gearbox, Steering Gearbox and Rear Axle (Hypoid Gears)		C — Wheel Hubs and Fan Bearings	D — Steering Connections, King-Pins, Propeller Shaft, Clevis Pins and Lever Fulcrums	E — Cables and Vital Control Joints	F — Utility Lubricant, S.U. Carburetter Dashpot, Oilcan Points, etc.
Climatic Conditions	Tropical and temperate down to 32° F. (0° C.)	Cold and extreme cold down to 0° F. (−18° C.)	Arctic below 0° F. (−18° C.)	Tropical and temperate down to 10° F. (−12° C.)	Extreme cold below 10° F. (−12° C.)	All conditions	All conditions	All conditions	All conditions
"DUCKHAM'S" (Alexander Duckham & Co. Ltd.)	Duckham's N.O.L. "Thirty"	Duckham's N.O.L. "Twenty"	Duckham's N.O.L. "Ten"	Duckham's Hypoid 90	Duckham's Hypoid 80	Duckham's H.B.B. Grease	Duckham's H.P.G. Grease	Duckham's "Keenol" K.G. 16 Grease	Duckham's N.O.L. "Twenty"
"CASTROL" (C. C. Wakefield & Co. Ltd.)	"Castrol" X.L.	"Castrolite"	"Castrol" Z	"Castrol" Hypoy	"Castrol" Hypoy 80	"Castrolease" Heavy	"Castrolease" Medium	"Castrolease" Brake Cable Grease	"Castrolite"
"ESSOLUBE" (Anglo-American Oil Co. Ltd.)	"Essolube" 30	"Essolube" 20	"Essolube" 10	"Esso" Expee Compound 90	"Esso" Expee Compound 80	Esso-grease	"Esso" Pressure Gun Grease	"Esso" Pressure Gun Grease	"Essolube" 20
"MOBILOIL" (Vacuum Oil Co. Ltd.)	Mobiloil "A"	Mobiloil "Arctic"	Mobiloil "Arctic" Special	Mobilube "G.X." 90	Mobilube "G.X." 80	Mobil Hub Grease	Mobilgrease No. 2 or 4	Mobilgrease No. 2 or 4	Mobiloil "Arctic"
"ENERGOL" (Price's Lubricants Ltd.)	"Energol" S.A.E. 30	"Energol" S.A.E. 20	"Energol" S.A.E. 10	"Energol" "E.P." S.A.E. 90	"Energol" "E.P." S.A.E. 80	"Belmoline" C	"Belmoline" D	"Belmoline" D	"Energol" S.A.E. 20
"SHELL" (Shell Mex & B.P. Ltd.)	Double "Shell"	Single "Shell"	Silver "Shell"	"Shell" Spirax 90 E.P.	"Shell" Spirax 80 E.P.	"Shell" Retinax R.B.	"Shell" Retinax C	"Shell" Retinax C	Single "Shell"
"FILTRATE" (Edward Joy & Sons Ltd.)	Medium "Filtrate"	Zero "Filtrate"	Sub-Zero "Filtrate"	Hypoid "Filtrate" 90	Hypoid "Filtrate" 80	"Filtrate" R.B. Grease	H.P. Solidified "Filtrate"	"Filtrate" A.F. Grease	Zero "Filtrate"
"STERNOL" (Sternol Ltd.)	"Sternol" W.W. 30	"Sternol" W.W. 20	"Sternol" W.W. 10	"Sternol" Liquid Ambroleum Hypoid 90	"Sternol" Liquid Ambroleum Hypoid 80	"Ambroline" R.B. Grease	"Ambroline" M.M. Grease	"Ambroline" A.F. Grease	"Sternol" W.W. 20

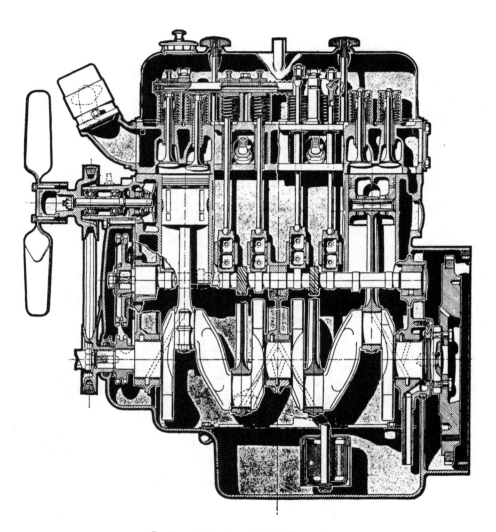

Sectional drawing of the TD engine

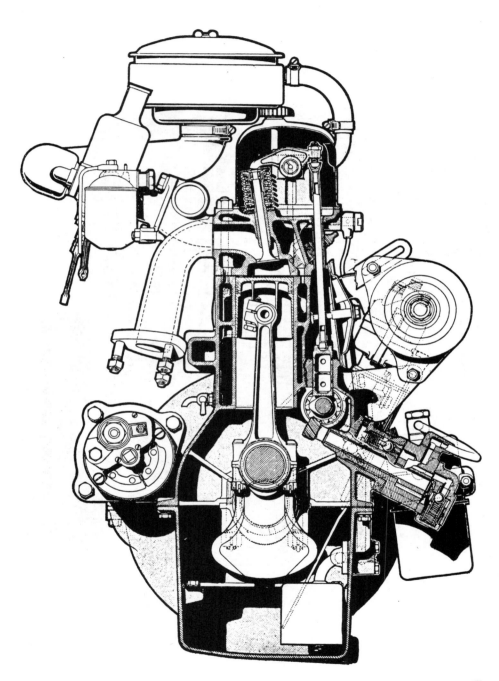

Transverse sectional drawing of the TD engine
Prior to engine No. 14224

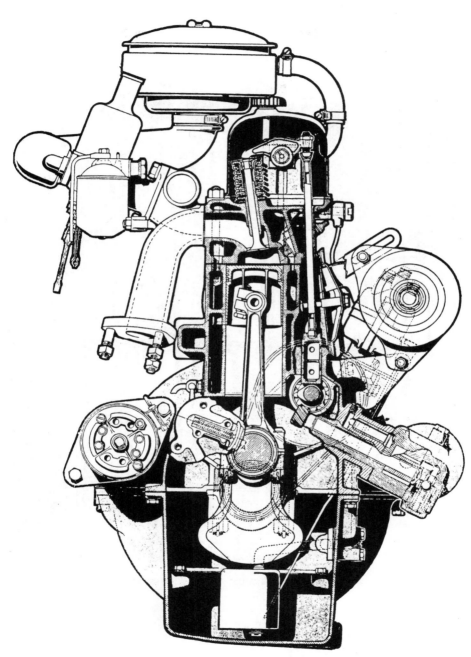

Transverse sectional drawing of the TD engine
Series No. 14224 onwards

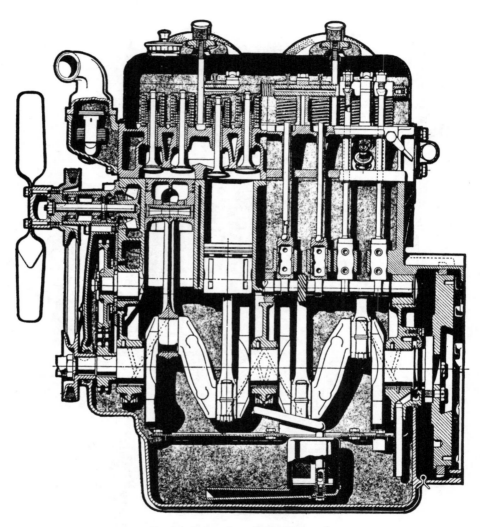

Sectional drawing of the TF engine

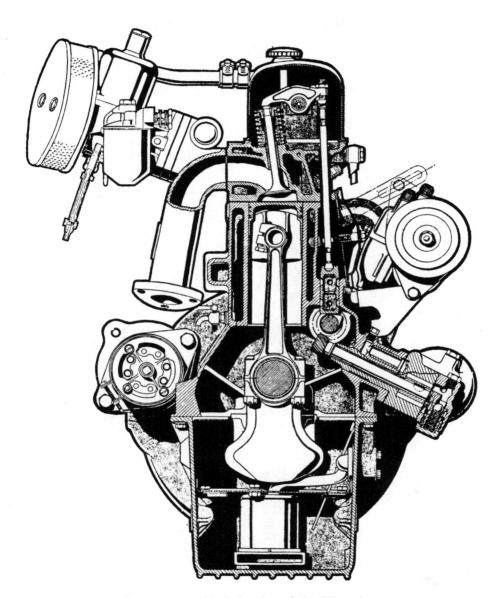

Transverse sectional drawing of the TF engine

176

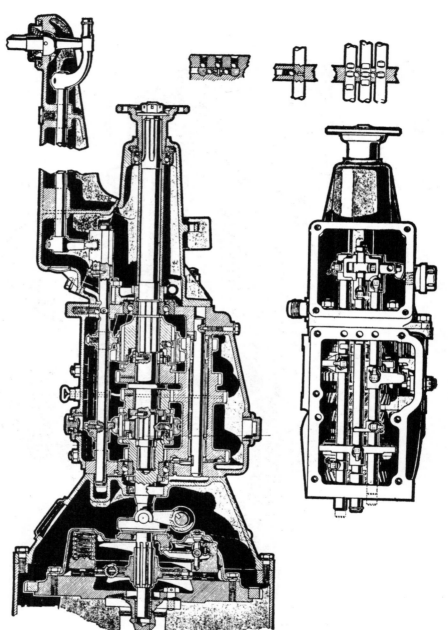

Sectional drawing of the Gearbox and Clutch, TD/TF

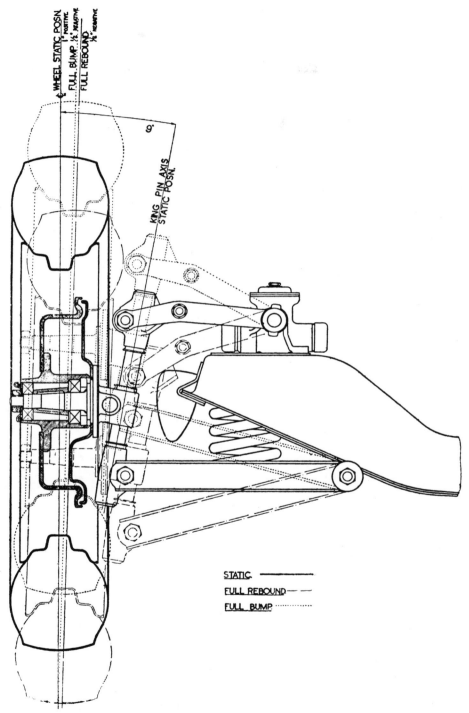

WHEEL STATIC POSN.
FULL BUMP. 1½° POSITIVE
FULL REBOUND. ½° NEGATIVE
½° NEGATIVE

9°

KING PIN AXIS
STATIC POSN.

STATIC ———————
FULL REBOUND — — —
FULL BUMP ....

Sectional drawing of the Front Suspension TD/TF

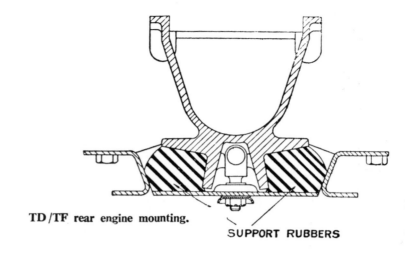

TD/TF rear engine mounting.

SUPPORT RUBBERS

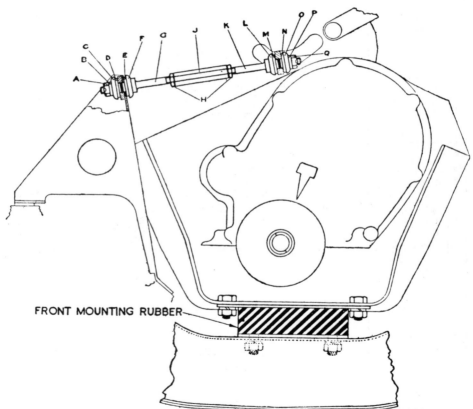

FRONT MOUNTING RUBBER

TD/TF front engine mounting and control link.

A. Slotted nut.	B. Washer.	C. Cup.	D. Rubber.
E. Rubber.	F. Cup.	G. Link rod.	H. Locknuts.
J. Adjuster.	K. Link rod.	L. Cup.	M. Rubber.
N. Rubber.	O. Cup.	P. Washer.	Q. Slotted nut.

Index

Advance mechanism, 36, 81, 109
Aerolite pistons, 135
Air intake, 141, 142
Angularity of rockers, 23, 75, 106
Armature, dynamo, 28, 82
Armature, starter, 82, 109

Bearing, clutch-shaft spigot, 15, 16, 64, 68, 91, 116
Bearing, clutch withdrawal, 48, 49, 91, 117
Bearings, big-end, 15, 18, 67, 71, 98, 101,
Bearings, camshaft, 26, 76, 107   [128
Bearings, distributor, 37, 81
Bearings, dynamo, 28
Bearings, main, 15, 18, 67, 71, 99, 101,
Bearings, water pump, 82, 109   [123
B.h.p. curve, PA/PB type (illus.), 36
B.h.p. curve, TA type (illus.), 95
B.h.p. curve, TC type (illus.), 120
B.h.p. curve, TF type, 125
B.h.p. curves, tuned engines, 151
B.h.p. of supertuned engines, 149–154
Blower installation, 143/6, 154/5
Boost pressure, Shorrock blower, 144
Brakes, 56, 57, 121

Cable, clutch operating, 128
Cam, contact-breaker, accuracy, 36, 81
Cam follower adjustment (illus.), 23
Camshaft end-float, 26, 76, 77, 107
Carburetters, assembly (illus.), 138, 140
Carburetters, specially large, 152, 153, 154, 156
Carburetters, synchronizing, 141
Carburetters twin layout (illus.), 140
Centric supercharger, 143
Chain, clutch actuating, 116
Chain, timing, wear measurement, 107
Chassis, general, 55, 120, 121, 129
Clutch adjustment, 48, 49, 94, 117, 128
Clutch housing joint, TA, 91
Clutch plate dimensions, 114, 128
Combustion chamber, modifications to, 150
Compression ratio modifications, 21, 22, 73, 149, 150, 152
Contact-breaker adjustment, 36, 81
Crankshaft end-float, 19, 84, 101, 123
Cylinder head nuts, order of attack, PA/PB type (illus.), 12
Cylinder head nuts, order of attack, TA type (illus.), 66, 89
Cylinder head nuts, order of attack, TC type (illus.), 98, 115
Cylinder head nuts, tightening down, 44, 89, 115
Dampers, hydraulic, 121, 130, 131
Dimensional data, bearings, 101, 107,
Distributor drive, meshing, 41, 90   [123

Dog, starting handle, positioning, 113
Dynamo coupling, correct lie (illus.), 28

Eccentric bushes, rocker shaft, 24, 25
Eccentric-drum supercharger, 144
Endplates, crankcase, TA, 68
Endplay, camshaft, 26, 76, 77, 107
Endplay, crankshaft, 19, 84, 101
Excessive ignition advance, symptoms, 53, 96, 118

Filter, oil, correct assembly (illus.), 32
Floating oil intake, TA, 67, 79
Flywheel flange, taper fitting, 16, 39
Fuel, Ethyl and Discol, 22
Fuel, methanol-benzol, 152–155
Fuming, excessive, from breather, 19

Gasket replacement, 43, 44, 89, 114
Gearbox dismantling, 55, 56, 96, 97, 129
Gear lever rattle, 58
Gear ratios, alternative, 96, 119, 129
Grinding flywheel taper, 39
Grinding-in tool for valves, 105

Hartford shock absorbers, 56
High-compression pistons, 152, 156
High-tension wiring, 37, 81, 82
Hydraulic dampers, 121, 131–132

Ignition control, characteristics, 109
Ignition control, hand-operated, 53, 119
Ignition timing, 48, 93, 116
Impeller, water, 14, 82, 109
Induction pipe, modifying, 142
Inlet ports, modifying, 21, 73, 103, 149,
Inlet valves, oversize, 150, 156   [150
Inspection of cylinder bores, 132

Lapping cylinder bores, 134
Large carburetters, 152, 153, 155
Large valves, 150, 156
Lining, clutch-plate, 88, 114
Lining-up the clutch, 43, 91, 114
Link-chain, clutch, TC, 116
Link, engine control, 122
Links, timing-chain, bright, 87, 112
Lockheed brakes, 121
Lubricant, upper cylinder, 50, 94, 117
Lubrication, carburetter piston, 137

Machining cylinder head, 21, 22, 73, 139, 149, 150
Manifold alignment, 21, 73, 103, 104
Marshall supercharger, 143
Meshing of oil-pump gears, 30, 31, 78, 108
Meshing of o.h.c. gears, 26, 27, 28, 29
Methanol fuel, 152/155
Misfiring, test for mixture strength, 131
Mixture correction, 141

Mixture distribution, 103
Morris basis of engines, 9, 60
M.p.h./r.p.m. curve, PA type (illus.), 46
M.p.h./r.p.m. curve, PB type (illus.), 47
M.p.h./r.p.m. curve, early TA type (illus.), 92
M.p.h./r.p.m. curve, later TA type (illus.), 93
M.p.h./r.p.m. curve, TC type (illus.), 118

Oil feed to o.h.c. gear, 45
Oil feed to supercharger, 146/7
Oil filter, correct assembly (illus.), 32
Oil intake strainer, 14, 33, 79, 108, 125
Oil pressures, 50, 51, 52, 94, 117, 124
Oil pump gears, clearance of, 30, 31, 78, 108
Oil restrictor pin, dimensions (illus.), 45
Order of attack, cylinder head nuts, PA/PB type (illus.), 12
Order of attack, cylinder head nuts, TA type (illus.), 66, 89
Order of attack, cylinder head nuts, TC type (illus.), 98, 115

Packings for rocker-standards, 76, 106, 149, 150
Petrol level in jets, 141
Petrol pumps, duplicated, 152
Pinking, excessive advance, 53, 96, 118
Piston rings, fitting, 133
Pistons, oversize data, 102, 123/4
Pressure plate, clutch, 16, 43, 68, 89, 114, 128

Quantity of oil in sump, 52, 94, 117, 125

Racing, tuning for, 149/156
Raising compression ratio, 21, 22, 73, 149, 151, 152
Rear axle, alternative ratios, 96, 119, 129
Restrictor pin, o.h.c. oil supply (illus.), 45
Road speed for gear ratios (illus.), 154
Rod, clutch operating, 128
R.p.m./m.p.h. curve, PA type (illus.), 46
R.p.m./m.p.h. curve, PB type (illus.), 47
R.p.m./m.p.h. curve, early TA type (illus.), 92
R.p.m./m.p.h. curve, later TA type (illus.), 93
R.p.m./m.p.h. curve, TC type (illus.), 118
Rocker ends, renovation of, 75, 105, 106
Rocker-shaft bushes, positioning (illus), 23
Roller chain for clutch operation, TC, 116
Rolling test for rocker-shaft, 75, 105
Roots-type supercharger, 144/5
Roughness, excessive advance symptoms, 53, 96
Running-in, r.p.m. limits, 52, 94, 95, 117, 118

Sealing washers on valve stems, 74, 75, 105
Self-oiling bushes on clutch-operating shaft, TC, 119
Shake in rocker bushes, 25, 75, 106
Shock absorbers, 56, 121, 130, 131
Shorrock supercharger, 144/5
Silencing springs, rocker-shaft, 75, 106
Small-end bushes, removing, 18, 19
Smoke from exhaust, 135
Spring link, timing chain, 77, 113
Springs, road, special wrapping tape, 121, 129
Springs, valve, special, 23, 74, 150, 152, 156
Starting-up after overhaul, 50, 94, 117
Steering gearbox, taking up play, 58, 121
Strainer, oil intake, 14, 33, 79, 108, 125
Sump flange joint, 42, 87, 114
Super-tuning, parts for, 156
Suspension and springs, 56, 120, 121, 129, 130

Table of o.h.c. types, 10
Table of push-rod-engined types, 61
Tensioner, timing chain, TC, 107
Timing chain, testing for wear, 107
Timing diagram, P/PB type (illus.), 31
Timing diagram, TA type (illus.), 86
Timing diagram, TC type (illus.), 112
Trials gear ratios, TA type, 96
Triple valve springs, TA type, 74
Trunnion spring mountings, 56, 120

Uncoupling the o.h.c. drive, 13
Universal joints, propeller shaft, 55

Valve clearances, P type, 51
  „   „   TA, 96
  „   „   TC, 117, 118
  „   „   TD/TF, 126
Valve ports, enlarging, 150
Valve springs, special strong, 150, 152, 156
Valve timing diagram, PA/PB type (illus.), 31
Valve timing diagram, TA type (illus.), 86
Valve timing diagram, TC type (illus.), 112
Valve timing diagram, TD/TF (illus.), 126
Vane-type supercharger, 144/145
Variation in contact-breaker gap, 36, 81
Vernier ignition setting, 53, 96, 119
Vertical drive on o.h.c., correct lie (illus.), 28

Wade supercharger, 135, 136
Water pump, 14, 82, 109
Withdrawing crankshaft, 15, 16, 69, 99

Zoller supercharger, 143